Changing Channels

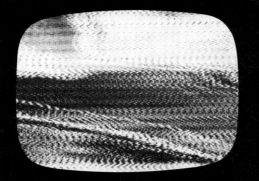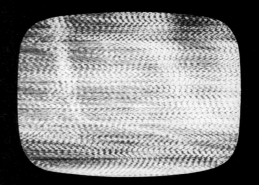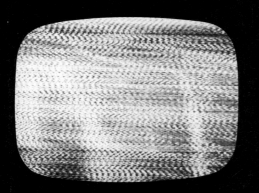

Addison-Wesley
Publishing Company

Reading, Massachusetts
Menlo Park, California
London
Amsterdam
Don Mills, Ontario
Sydney

Changing Channels
Living (Sensibly) with Television

KOREN

Peggy Charren and Martin W. Sandler

ISBN 0-201-07253-X

ISBN 0-201-07254-8 (pbk.)

ABCDEFGHIJ-HA-89876543

Cover illustration © 1983 by Ed Koren

Book design by Thomas Sumida, WGBH Design, with special assistance by Sylvia Steiner

Library of Congress Cataloging in Publication Data

Charren, Peggy.
  Changing channels.

  Bibliography: p. 259
  Includes index.
    1. Television broadcasting--United States.
    2. Television viewers--Psychology. 3. Television broadcasting--Social aspects--United States. 4. Television industry--United States.

I. Sandler, Martin W.
II. Title.
PN1992.3.U5C4   1982   384.55′4′0973   82-16243
ISBN 0-201-07253-X
ISBN 0-201-07254-8 (pbk.)

Acknowledgments

A book of this scope could never be completed without the expert help and encouragement of a number of people. We want to thank especially Bridget Harron, whose major contribution made this book possible and is part of every page. We also want to acknowledge the invaluable assistance of ACT staffers Kim Hays, Cynthia Alperowicz, Judith Rubenstein, and particularly Paula Rohrlick, who gave her time unstintingly. For special help with visual materials, we are indebted to Jill Yager of ABC, Elise Katz of WGBH, Dan Jones, and Photoworks. For research assistance, we are grateful to Sam Tyler of WGBH, Jim Poteat and Leslie Slocum of the Television Information Office, Nancy Dietz, and Mary Hurley. We wish also to acknowledge the help of Elinor Neville, Elaine Moretti, and Rosemary MacKenzie, with special thanks to Tom Sumida of WGBH Design, whose creativity and patience have made this a better book. Finally, we are pleased that Doe Coover is not only our editor, but our friend.

Contents

Foreword

There has been a lot of criticism—I'm responsible for some of it—about television's overwhelming influence on all of us. From poor role models to excessive violence to gratuitous sex; from the way TV refracts instead of reflects; from the hazy line between news and entertainment—television's the target everybody loves to hit. Nobody admits to actually watching, but everyone has an opinion.

We can't expect television to improve, however, unless we take responsibility for it. The problem is ours: we who are content to let television be an easy baby-sitter for our children, for the lonely and alone. We owe it to ourselves to take control of television. I don't mean boycotting what we don't like, but rather working *to change* it. And not just complaining about what's bad, but encouraging and nurturing what's good. It's our responsibility as viewers to watch television as creatively and critically as it watches us.

This book is intended to help us do just that—to learn to live more sensibly with television, coping with its problems and enjoying its benefits. TV is one of our most prominent national resources; with *Changing Channels* we can help make it a national treasure.

Norman Lear

America's Favorite Pastime

I

In Defense of Television

In March 1939 a New York *Times* reporter, assigned to the World's Fair, at which television was introduced, offered a prediction about the new invention. "The problem with television," he wrote, "is that the people must sit and keep their eyes glued to a screen: the average American family hasn't time for it. Therefore . . . for this reason, if no other, television will never be a serious competitor of broadcasting."

The reporter was one of the first of a long line of people who predicted that, as the novelty of television wore off, TV-watching would decline. They could not have been more wrong. Since 1948, when television first became widely available to the American public, TV-viewing has risen so steadily that today Americans spend more time watching television than doing

TV Households in America

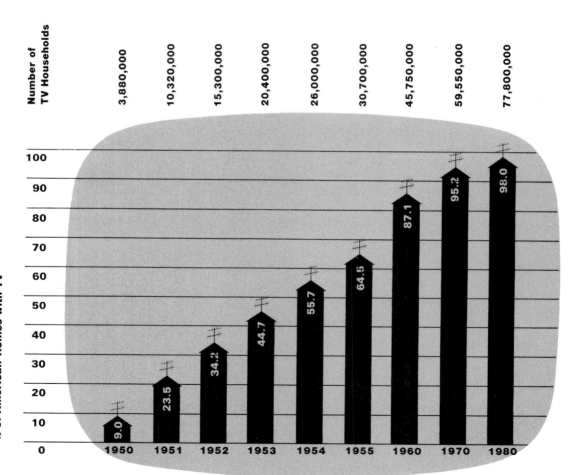

	1950	1951	1952	1953	1954	1955	1960	1970	1980
Number of TV Households	3,880,000	10,320,000	15,300,000	20,400,000	26,000,000	30,700,000	45,750,000	59,550,000	77,800,000
% of American Homes with TV	9.0	23.5	34.2	44.7	55.7	64.5	87.1	95.2	98.0

anything else except sleeping. Television has become such an important part of our lives that by the age of sixty-five the average American will have spent nine full years watching TV.

Television is this nation's common denominator, its shared experience. Millions watch the same programs every night, laughing at the same jokes, absorbing the same information, being subjected to the same points of view. And chances are that the next day at school or the office or the factory much of the talk will center around the characters and stories of television dramas and situation comedies, the antics of Howard Cosell or Johnny Carson, or one of the many "specials" that appear throughout the year. Wherever we go in the nation we take this experience with us. If we begin watching a week-long miniseries in Chicago one night and we need to make a business trip, we turn on our set in Boston or Los Angeles or New Orleans the next night and tune in Part Two. For millions of people, not to watch television is to be out of the flow of American life. More than one set of parents in this country, after years of forbidding certain TV programs in their home, have relaxed their rules, concluding that they could not continue to keep their children out of touch with what their classmates talked about.

◄ More than 98 percent of American households have at least one working TV set; nearly half have two sets or more, and more than half have color sets. Even in families with annual incomes of less than $5,000, one out of three has a color set. In fact, more homes in America have television sets than have telephones or indoor plumbing. *TV Facts,* 1980.

Television's unique strengths lie in the way it is able to present people with interesting topics of conversation and in its ability to transmit pictures of events to all parts of the world at the moment they are happening. Someone once said that the best thing on television is golf—because no one can write a script for the ball. Television thus far has been most effective when it has gone outside the studio. The highest

"Once I thought the most important political statement we could make about television was to turn it off. But television can instruct, inform, and inspire, as well as distract, distort, and demean. And turning it off rejects the good with the bad. My family wants its voice added to the summons for quality, and I urge you to speak up, too, in every way possible. This marvelous medium, with all its potential for laughter and light, is worth fighting for." Bill Moyers

ratings throughout television history have not gone to situation comedies, soap operas, miniseries, or even lavishly promoted network spectaculars. They have gone to what Israeli sociologist Elihu Katz calls the "live broadcasting of history" or "the high holidays of mass communication." Time and again in the last two decades the activities of the entire nation have come practically to a halt as we have shared a common collective experience by watching a live televised event.

Some of these events have been awe-inspiring—the moon landings, the manned space shuttle flights, the victory of the underdog United States hockey team at the 1980 Olympics. Televised events of this type take on the quality of holidays. In an era when a sense of community seems to be slipping steadily, these occasions have given us the opportunity to share together, rejoice together, and exult in our accomplishments as a nation and as human beings.

UPI

America's first space shuttle launch, John F. Kennedy's funeral, the United States' stunning Olympic hockey victory, the first American to orbit the earth—for millions of people around the world what they will remember about these events is what they saw on TV. That millions of people can share in watching a live televised event is one of the medium's finest attributes.

NASA

Steve Fenn/ABC

Wide World Photo

This shared experience is one of the most important aspects of the televised event. Just as television has allowed us to share our joy and pride, witnessing triumphs and discoveries, so have we found collective solace in viewing together the tragedies of the nation. Somehow—by sharing the experience of the Kennedy and Sadat funerals, the plight of the Iranian hostages, the assassination attempts on our Presidents—we have been able to comfort ourselves, renew our commitment to democracy, and carry on.

UPI

UPI

"There are times, and today was one of those times, when television approaches the truly magical, when it becomes the sort of instrument that, 50 or 60 years ago, would have been regarded as supernatural. . . . This has been, without question, one of the more memorable days in our nation's history; and television, much maligned television, which frequently does numb the brain and dull the senses, today produced a technological miracle. Never has any generation of Americans had greater reason to claim they were eyewitness to history."
Ted Koppel, "Nightline," January 20, 1980

If television binds us in joy and sorrow, it also unites us as creatures dependent on an electronic box for many human needs. In less than four decades, television has become educator, comforter, entertainer, baby-sitter, titillator, salesman, patriot, investigator, *paterfamilias* to the nation, and psychiatrist to the individual. We watch television when we are bored and when we are anxious, alone and together, to laugh and to cry, to learn and to avoid learning. Even so, watching television is like sex in Victorian England. Almost everybody does it, but few brag about it. As one critic has said, "Disparagement of television is second only to watching television as a national pastime."

Television, like comic books and the movies before it, has been blamed for all the ills of society—from the quality of our candidates to crime in the streets. This is not a particularly happy time in history. Populations are growing so quickly, resources are being used up so rapidly, and poverty is such a significant problem that the very survival of the human race is in

> "Television is a medium of expression which permits millions of people to listen to the same joke at the same time, and yet remain lonesome." T.S. Eliot

question. Yet, terrorism and crime are probably no more commonplace and pervasive than in certain other times in history. The difference is that with TV, the world now has a messenger that brings the actual sights and sounds of these disruptions into living rooms night after night. Our tendency is to place the blame for these disruptions not on their complex causes but instead on the messenger.

If television is not entirely to blame, neither is it the innocent messenger. The truth is that television both reflects and affects behavior, and it does neither perfectly. TV does not cause poverty, but it does affect our attitudes toward the poor and their condition. It does not cause crime, but it affects our attitudes toward the role of violence in our society. To say that television didn't invent the most serious problems and isn't responsible for most of them is not to say, however, that this infant medium has not presented us with a myriad of significant problems of its own.

Much of this book is dedicated to helping you understand these problems and to presenting practical ways in which you can deal with them. In an age when, as a nation, we have come to regard TV as one of the essentials of life, it is vital for us to learn how to make the most of it. Television is here to stay. And today more than at any other time in its history, it is growing and expanding. When we speak of television, we no longer mean simply the programs that are sent out to us over the air by the networks and the independent stations. The term *television* today applies to everything that comes and will come through that electronic box that occupies so prominent a place in our homes and our lives. This includes cable, cassette, videodisc, direct broadcast satellite, low power TV, interactive video, videotext, and who knows how many other telecasting developments that at the moment we can't even imagine. And so this book is also dedicated to celebrating the fruits of this new technology and helping you enjoy them to the fullest.

TV technology has come a long way from the early days of primitive equipment and limited locations. Today there is no place too remote for TV's cameras. The whole world has become television's stage.

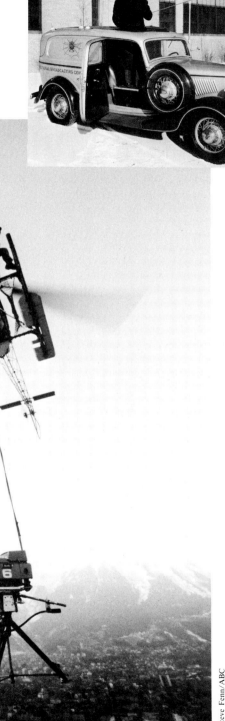

Will the "new" television make our life better? Will the increased entertainment, information, and services it brings compensate for the problems that are bound to accompany it? For almost every wonderful facet of the TV experience there is a corresponding negative effect. For example, through television we are able to see worlds of fact and fantasy that we would not otherwise see. But do we pay for this with a dulling of our own imaginations? With television, unlike radio, others supply the images that accompany the sound. It is someone else's image, not our own, that defines our vision of violence or beauty or despair or ecstasy. Through television children come into contact with worlds that extend far beyond their own immediate experience. But at the same time these young viewers are presented with thousands of images that they are simply too young or too inexperienced to deal with. How do we balance our joy at TV's teachings about animals or African plains with our horror at TV's examples of violence on urban streets?

All of us, thanks to TV, are continually given the opportunity to see close up, warts and all, the people who shape our world. When a President trips getting off a plane, or trips up on a press conference question, we are there. On the other hand, television deprives us of the chance to create heroes out of people who have not been given access to the TV airwaves because of lack of power or charisma or funds.

In less than fifty years, television has changed how we see ourselves. Shut-ins, the elderly, people who live in remote areas— all are aware of worlds that, in earlier times, even the most privileged and most adventurous never knew. And it won't be long before millions of us use our TV sets to manage our lives as well: to shop, receive our mail, carry on our banking, and conduct almost every type of personal and public transaction imaginable. But at what price? Will we lose the opportunity and ability to communicate with other human beings? How can you compare hours in a video game arcade to a board game played between friends?

"Oh, I'm just killing time till the TV is repaired."

The new technologies may make a difference. But for the most part television is a potential that has gone unfulfilled. We have spent the better part of the first four decades watching drivel far more than substance. The most serious problem regarding television has been its lack of diversity—diversity of programs,

> **"Why should people go out and pay money to see bad films when they can stay at home and see bad television for nothing?"** Samuel Goldwyn

diversity of control, diversity of access. TV is an infant medium. Yet from its beginning there was the opportunity for more diversity. The potential existed for the creation of a system that would provide for all kinds of programs —programs that would meet the needs and interests of a great variety of Americans. Unfortunately, as we shall detail later in this book, the chance was squandered. Through expediency, short-sightedness, and errors of judgment, American television was set up so that a relatively few companies gained control of the medium. The opportunity for individuals or ideas to gain access to air time was severely restricted. From the outset, a system was established in which the majority of programming was created simply as a vehicle to sell commercial products to the largest number of consumers. The quality and diversity of programs have, for the most part, been secondary to finding the lowest common denominator for the mass market.

Today, the limited diversity of TV is further threatened by censorship. We've come a long way from the 1939 debut of *Gone with the Wind,* when much of the nation was shocked and the Hollywood censors were scandalized by Rhett Butler's exclamation, "Frankly, my dear, I don't give a damn." But censorship is not only still with us—it poses a more serious threat to our freedom than ever before. There are certainly things on television today that many of us find objectionable. And the proliferation of cable, pay-TV, and other new technologies will increase the number of programs we find offensive and don't want our children to watch. Yet censoring speech is even more objectionable. Learning to contend with what some consider outrageous is the price we pay for free speech. Learning to control our own viewing is preferable to ceding control to others.

Would You Believe?

When TV began there were many who feared it. In 1949, the International Catholic Association for Radio and TV proposed a minimum age for viewing.

Handling the vagaries of television is made even more difficult by the advent of the television of abundance. We are now in the midst of a telecommunications revolution so far-reaching that everything that has taken place thus far can be appropriately termed the predawn of television history. The multitude of new video technologies that have burst upon us present a genuine opportunity to fulfill the fondest hopes of those who, from the beginning, saw in TV a medium that would not only instruct and entertain but would meet the needs and wishes of

The Top of the Charts

The all-time top 50 TV shows are based on the average percentage of possible viewers, an equitable system of tallying winners from several decades, since TV ownership has increased so dramatically and comparing sheer numbers of viewers would eliminate most shows produced before 1970.

General drama and sit coms compete for America's favorite type of programming. By far the most impressive showing is the "Beverly Hillbillies" series, which appears in the top 50 nine times. Six of those shows appeared consecutively in January and February 1964 (in the weeks following JFK's assassination). Of the four movies to make it, there are three love stories (*Gone With the Wind, Love Story, Cinderella*) and one disaster film (*Airport*).

Certain individual programs couldn't miss: The Beatles visit to Ed Sullivan (2/9/64), the last episode of the "Fugitive" series (8/29/67), and the "Who Shot JR?" segment of "Dallas" (which tops the list with a reported 83 million people tuned in). Other individual shows that made the historical list: "All in the Family" (1972), the 1961 Miss America Pageant, Bob Hope's Christmas Show in 1970 and 1971, and the Academy Awards in 1967 and 1970.

NTI Top 50 Programs Average Audience Estimates (%)

Rank	Program Name	Telecast Date	Avg. Audience (%)
1	Dallas	Nov. 21, 1980	53.3
2	Roots	Jan. 30, 1977	51.1
3	Super Bowl XVI Game	Jan. 24, 1982	49.1
4	Gone with the Wind-Pt. 1 (Big Event Pt. 1)	Nov. 7, 1976	47.7
5	Gone with the Wind-Pt. 2 (NBC Mon. Mov.)	Nov. 8, 1976	47.4
6	Super Bowl XII Game	Jan. 15, 1978	47.2
7	Super Bowl XIII Game	Jan. 21, 1979	47.1
8	Bob Hope Christmas Show	Jan. 15, 1970	46.6
9	Super Bowl XIV Game	Jan. 20, 1980	46.3
10	Roots	Jan. 28, 1977	45.9
10	The Fugitive	Aug. 29, 1967	45.9
12	Roots	Jan. 27, 1977	45.7
13	Ed Sullivan	Feb. 9, 1964	45.3
14	Bob Hope Christmas Show	Jan. 14, 1971	45.0
15	Roots	Jan. 25, 1977	44.8
16	Super Bowl XI	Jan. 9, 1977	44.4
16	Super Bowl XV	Jan. 25, 1981	44.4
18	Super Bowl VI	Jan. 16, 1972	44.2

19	Roots	Jan. 24, 1977	44.1
20	Beverly Hillbillies	Jan. 8, 1964	44.0
21	Roots	Jan. 26, 1977	43.8
21	Ed Sullivan	Feb. 16, 1964	43.8
23	Academy Awards	Apr. 7, 1970	43.4
24	CBS NFC Championship Game	Jan. 10, 1982	42.9
25	Beverly Hillbillies	Jan. 15, 1964	42.8
26	Super Bowl VII	Jan. 14, 1973	42.7
27	Super Bowl IX	Jan. 12, 1975	42.4
27	Beverly Hillbillies	Feb. 26, 1964	42.4
29	Super Bowl X	Jan. 18, 1976	42.3
29	Airport (Movie Special)	Nov. 11, 1973	42.3
29	Love Story (Sun. Night Mov.)	Oct. 1, 1972	42.3
29	Cinderella	Feb. 22, 1965	42.3
29	Roots	Jan. 29, 1977	42.3
34	Beverly Hillbillies	Mar. 25, 1964	42.2
35	Beverly Hillbillies	Feb. 5, 1964	42.0
36	Beverly Hillbillies	Jan. 29, 1964	41.9
37	Miss America Pageant	Sep. 9, 1961	41.8
37	Beverly Hillbillies	Jan. 1, 1964	41.8
39	Super Bowl VIII	Jan. 13, 1974	41.6
39	Bonanza	Mar. 8, 1964	41.6
41	Beverly Hillbillies	Jan. 22, 1964	41.5
42	Bonanza	Feb. 16, 1964	41.4
43	Academy Awards	Apr. 10, 1967	41.2
44	Bonanza	Feb. 9, 1964	41.0
45	Gunsmoke	Jan. 28, 1961	40.9
46	Bonanza	Mar. 28, 1965	40.8
47	Bonanza	Mar. 7, 1965	40.7
47	All in the Family	Jan. 8, 1972	40.7
49	Roots	Jan. 23, 1977	40.5
49	Bonanza	Feb. 2, 1964	40.5
49	Beverly Hillbillies	May 1, 1963	40.5
49	Gunsmoke	Feb. 25, 1961	40.5

Nielsen, April 1982

even the smallest audiences. These new technologies have the potential of allowing viewers to become their own programmers, opening the door to shows that speak to the needs of every segment of the population. Ordinary citizens can create and air their own programs and even become part of the broadcasting establishment. But these new forms of TV, like any new tech-

nologies, carry with them a set of their own problems and challenges. They introduce the potential for serious invasion of privacy and the creation of a telecommunications system in which only the well-to-do can afford to participate.

The Growth of Cable

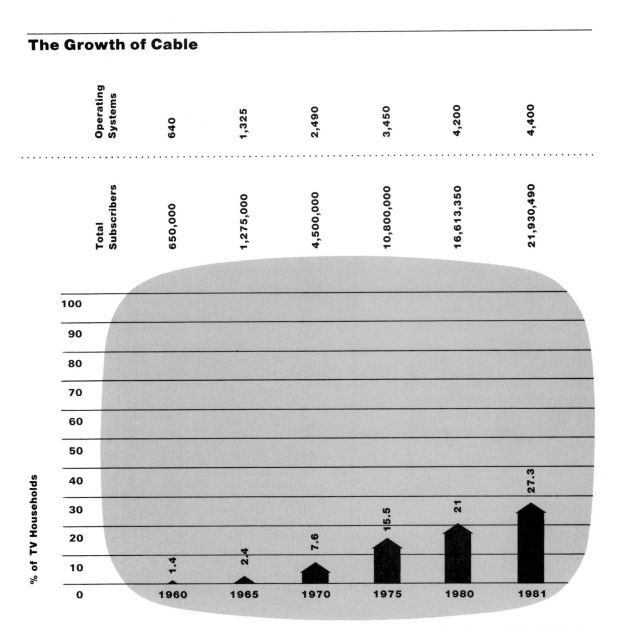

	1960	1965	1970	1975	1980	1981
Operating Systems	640	1,325	2,490	3,450	4,200	4,400
Total Subscribers	650,000	1,275,000	4,500,000	10,800,000	16,613,350	21,930,490
% of TV Households	1.4	2.4	7.6	15.5	21	27.3

Broadcasting Cable Yearbook

Today the American public has a second chance, a second chance not to repeat the mistakes of the past, a second chance to be served by a television system that takes us out of the "vast wasteland" of Newton Minow's experience to a system in which TV, as predicted by E. B. White, becomes "our Lyceum, our Chautauqua, our Minsky's, and our Camelot."

"You must provide a wider range of choices, more diversity, more alternatives. It is not enough to cater to the nation's whims—you must also serve the nation's needs."
FCC Chairman Newton Minow, 1961

There are practical, effective things that we as individuals, parents, and members of a community can do in order to make television the diverse and rewarding experience it ought to be. That is what this book is about.

We can begin to make changes— changes in the way our families watch TV, changes in the TV experience in our communities. *We, the public, own the airwaves.* That the broadcasters exist to serve us is a fact supported by law. As cable TV becomes a more vital part of the television experience, we must get involved, either in the franchising process in our community or in the way that cable already operates in our city or town.

In an ideal situation the responsibility for seeing to it that television serves the needs of all the people would be shared by three groups— the broadcasters, the government, and the American people. But the way the system has operated to date gives us little reason to expect anything different from broadcasters. Acting in the traditions of the American entrepreneurial system, broadcasters have focused their attention on gaining the highest possible ratings that will bring them the highest rates for their advertising minutes. Because of the way the broadcasting system was established, it is simply not good business for commercial broadcasters to operate any other way. It is probable that the federal government will not be much help to us either; the policy of Washington regulators is one of deferring to the broadcasters and removing almost every major control on TV that has existed.

If the new technologies are indeed to present a second chance to the American public, then each of us will have to get involved. If we are to have diversity, both in the new technologies and in over-the-air television, if we are to begin dealing with our own TV-watching habits and those of our children, then we all have to take an active role. The opportunity exists for us to take advantage of what we have learned thus far about the impact television has had on us. This book presents a variety of information and suggestions on ways that you can take action. It also outlines practical ways in which individuals and groups are already beginning to effect change, so that the second chance represented by the new technologies results in a TV system that does justice to the enormous potential of this marvel of our age.

"We have lived through a communications revolution in the last few decades. We may now be in for the counter-revolution that can help revive a sense of the local, of the neighborhood. . . . I look forward to growing numbers of young journalists covering their neighborhoods with highly local news programs, using the leased facilities of common carrier channels. I can see the day when the young journalist will look forward to owning a community cable telecast just as my generation dreamed of owning a country paper." Walter Cronkite

1 Resources

Books

Barnouw, Erik. *Tube of Plenty: The Evolution of American Television*. New York: Oxford University Press, 1975. A definitive, illustrated social history of television, condensed from Barnouw's three-part series, *A Tower in Babel, The Golden Web,* and *The Image Empire.*

Bergreen, Laurence. *Look Now, Pay Later: The Rise of Network Broadcasting.* New York: Doubleday, 1980. A perceptive history of the radio and TV national networks, how they grew, and how they were (sometimes) regulated.

Brown, Les. *The New York Times Encyclopedia of Television.* New York: Times Books, 1977. An alphabetical listing of facts and short articles on a wide variety of television topics—programs, people, organizations, legal cases, technical terms, and issues—illustrated with photographs.

Cole, Barry, ed. *Television Today: A Close-Up View.* New York: Oxford University Press, 1981. Sixty-five articles from *TV Guide* that cover programming, the audience, censorship and control, public television, and the future.

Frank, Ronald E., and Greenberg, Marshall G. *The Public's Use of Television: Who Watches and Why.* Beverly Hills, Calif.: Sage Publications, 1980. Profiles different types of TV viewers, based on a national survey of over 2,400 people.

Greenfield, Jeff. *Television: The First Fifty Years.* New York: Abrams, 1977. Lavishly illustrated with hundreds of color photographs, this is an enjoyable popular history of television and its effects on American society.

Nielsen Report on Television. Published annually. Available free of charge by writing A.C. Nielsen Company, Nielsen Plaza, Northbrook, Ill. 60062. Gives statistical information on the viewing public: the number of households with TV sets; average household usage; viewing activity by age, sex, and time of day; and top programs.

Steinberg, Cobbett S. *TV Facts.* New York: Facts on File, Inc., 1980. A useful collection of facts and figures on programs, viewers, ratings, advertisers, awards, polls and surveys, and the networks and stations.

Sterling, Christopher H., and Kittross, John M. *Stay Tuned: A Concise History of American Broadcasting.* Belmont, Calif.: Wadsworth Publishing Co., 1978. An attractively illustrated text, organized chronologically, that includes many handy statistics.

Wilk, Max. *The Golden Age of Television.* New York: Dell Publishing Co., Inc., 1976. An entertaining account of the years from 1948 until the invention of videotape.

Periodical

TV Guide. Box 900, Radnor, Penn. 19088.
Weekly. Often overlooked as a source of
information, *TV Guide* features articles on
many issues in broadcasting as well as giving TV program listings.

Films and Tapes

Television: The Enchanted Mirror. A 16-mm
film or ¾" video cassette. Color, 30 minutes. 1981. A look at the role of TV in
everyday life, featuring interviews with TV
directors, writers, an ABC executive, a
brain behavior scientist, an advertiser, and
members of the viewing public. Available
from George Csicsery and Julene Blair,
P.O. Box 2833, Oakland, Calif. 94618;
415-821-7324 or 415-848-7337.

The Electronic Rainbow: Television. A 16-mm
color film, 23 minutes. 1977. Leonard
Nimoy conducts a tour through the world
of television, giving a brief history of the
development of TV, showing in animation
the basic physical principles of broadcasting and receiving, and explaining the special uses of the different kinds of TV systems (broadcast, microwave, cable, closed
circuit, cassette, etc.) with TV sequences.
Available from Pyramid Films, Box 1048,
Santa Monica, Calif. 90406, 213-828-7577.

Television's Impact

It has been said that trying to gauge the impact of television on American society is like trying to understand the nature of a tidal wave while standing in the middle of it. Television affects us at every stage of our lives. Children watch it before they learn to speak. The elderly rely upon it for companionship. Television connects the country, setting a standard of knowledge, promoting fads, homogenizing our tastes. And it is everywhere. Living rooms, bedrooms, hotel rooms, offices, children's classrooms—all have one piece of furniture in common: the TV set.

Cobbett Steinberg, author of *TV Facts*, has pointed out the incredible speed with which television has come to dominate our lives. In 1950 only 9 percent of American homes had TV sets. By 1954 the figure had risen to 55 percent. Only six years later there were more than forty-five million TV households in this country. According to Steinberg, it took radio thirty-two years to reach those figures, and it wasn't until eighty-seven years after it was invented that the telephone entered that many American homes.

Television has had an impact upon almost everything Americans do. The time we spend reading, traveling, going to the movies, socializing, and performing household tasks have all been reduced in favor of time spent in front of the set. Surveys now show that as a nation we sleep less because of TV. And when is the last time any of us walked through a neighborhood and visited with the folks sitting on their front porches or stoops? We can't, because they're not there anymore. Everyone's inside watching television.

TV in the skies. The increased use of television to entertain passengers in flight has not only presented a new way to keep travelers amused but has opened up an important new market for those who produce TV programs.

American Airlines Photo by Bob Takis

Would You Believe?

What started in the coffee shop of a southern California Ramada Inn has become a familiar sight in fast food spots, coffee shops, pizza parlors, and bus stations across the nation: coin-operated TV sets.

These sets, anchored to restaurant tables or waiting room armrests, are descendants of the mini juke boxes fastened to the wall of red-cushioned booths at local diners. A quarter buys fifteen minutes of TV viewing. What next? Portable TVs you can strap to your belt while you jog or roller skate to "The Today Show" or "All My Children"?

The Numbers

Big numbers in other media are
dwarfed by the size of television
audiences

**Daily TV Viewers
89,740,000**

**TV Show
("Dallas": Who Shot JR?
11/21/80)
83,000,000**

**Daily Movie Attendance
3,104,109**

**Cultural Exhibit
(King Tut in America)
8,000,000**

**Bestselling Novel
(Jacqueline Suzanne's
Valley of the Dolls)
22,042,000**

**Rock Concert
(Watkins Glen, NY) 7/29/73
600,000**

**Daily Newspaper Circulation
62,200,000**

Millions of Americans are now more familiar with Hawkeye Pierce or Jane Pauley than they are with the corner druggist or the people in the house or apartment next door. Television voices fill the empty spaces in many homes. In the words of one observer, "Television is the grandmother I never had."

There are very few aspects of our life that have been unaffected by television. TV influences the way we speak, the words we use, the expressions that creep into our vocabulary. News anchors, in their desire to appeal to the broadest audience possible, speak what can only be described as a new national language, one stripped clean of local or regional dialects, intonations, or idioms.

Even the concept of time has been affected by TV. Author Tony Schwartz has pointed out that the NBC "Today" show has a one-handed clock that indicates minutes past the hour. The program is aired simultaneously in different time zones and the audience is simply told, "It's ten minutes past the hour."

Television has revolutionized the way people get information. When George Washington was elected President it took approximately six months for the news to spread to the corners of the newly formed country; by the time Lincoln was assassinated we could transmit information across the continent in three months; when Ronald Reagan was shot in March of 1981 the news was on television screens around the world in minutes.

In little more than three decades television has also become the overwhelmingly dominant information medium in the United States. Various polls now indicate that Americans, by a margin of more than twenty points over newspapers, its closest rival, pick television as their chief source of news. And, according to a 1981 Roper Poll, 40 percent of the American people now get *all* of their news information from televison alone. By a wide margin, Americans find television to be their most believable news source. Asked in the same poll which they would believe if they were given conflicting news stories, 51 percent of the respondents chose television, 22 percent selected newspapers, 9 percent picked magazines, and 8 percent chose radio. And it is not only in America that TV has become the dominant information medium. In an overseas poll, also released in 1981, 48 percent of all West Europeans questioned named television as their most trustworthy source of information, 32 percent chose newspapers, and the rest picked radio.

The influence of television exists well beyond our own borders. In the major countries of the world, television's impact equals that of our own. Russian children, for example, now choose Soviet television as their favorite leisure activity. And the Japanese spend even more hours a day watching TV than Americans do.

The fact that so many American-produced television programs are now being exported has also raised serious issues both in this country and overseas. For example, concern has been expressed abroad that since it is much less expensive for less developed nations to purchase American programs than to produce their own, the needs of the viewers of these nations will not be addressed.

The most serious concern is that because so many viewers in foreign countries tend to judge Americans by the representations they see on our television programs, a damaging image of this country and its people is being created. On the other hand, this country sees relatively little foreign product. There is drama from England in public broadcasting but little else. There is almost no children's programming from other countries. As cable and direct satellite grow in importance and as new markets for foreign programs are created, this situation may change, but for now television remains a one-way cultural exchange.

Television has not only outdistanced other media—both here and abroad—but it has brought about wide-ranging changes in them as well. In order to exist in the age of television, magazines have narrowed their scope, appealing to readers with specific tastes such as boating or automobile racing or gourmet dining. The movie industry, too, has been changed by television. As they have seen their once dominant position in family entertainment fade away, movie-makers have responded by producing the kinds of films that commercial television has not dared to show. In seeking the teenage and young adult audience that films need in order to survive, Hollywood has turned to increasingly violent and sexually explicit films. The distinctions between the television and movie industries have blurred, as many Hollywood producers and directors are now employed making "made-for-television"

movies, and commercial movies rely on the income from TV sales to recoup production costs.

Book publishing, too, has been affected by television. For while TV-watching has in general cut into the sale of fiction, publishers have found that TV can be used to create best-sellers. Books based on highly promoted commercial network miniseries have been phenomenal successes, as have been those based on public broadcasting series such as "Ascent of Man" and "Free to Choose." Publishers have also found that the best source of publicity for any

Foreign Favorites

American-produced shows consistently top the list of audience favorites in countries around the world. According to *Variety*, the following shows

were at the top of the charts in England, France, Japan, Australia, and West Germany. *Variety*, 1981

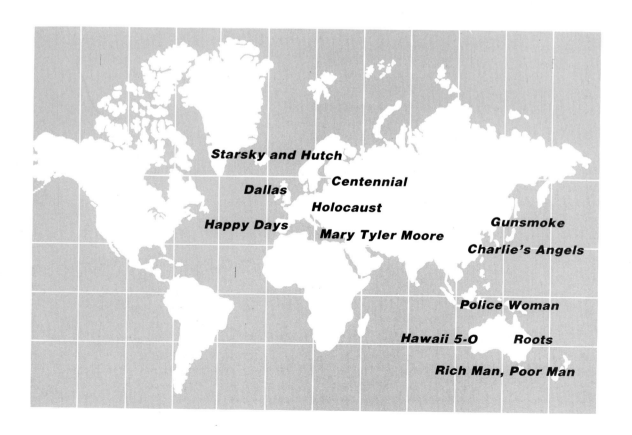

TV Sets Around the World

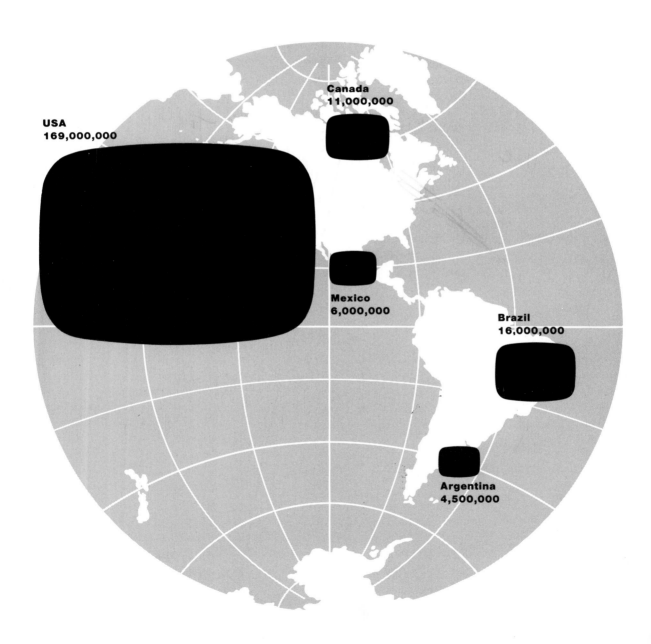

Although the number of TV sets in Europe has doubled in the last ten years, the United States still accounts for 40 percent of the world's 406.1 million sets. *Encyclopedia Britannica,* 1980

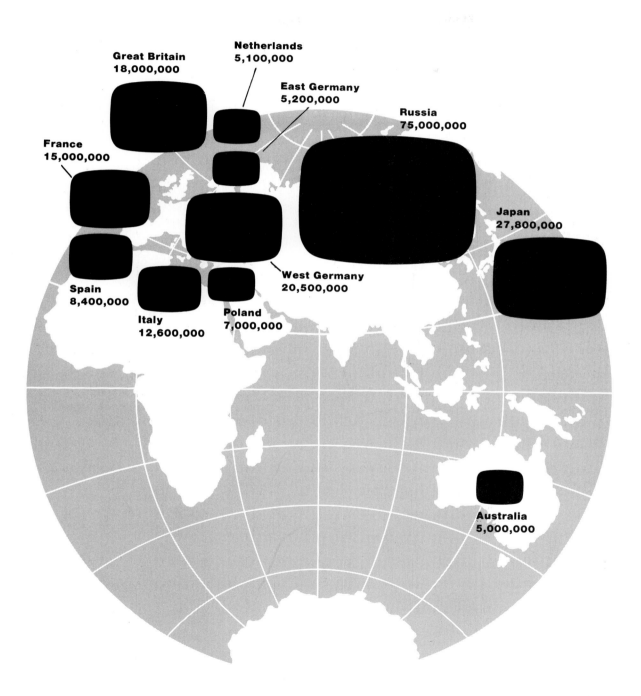

Great Britain
18,000,000

Netherlands
5,100,000

East Germany
5,200,000

Russia
75,000,000

France
15,000,000

Japan
27,800,000

Spain
8,400,000

West Germany
20,500,000

Italy
12,600,000

Poland
7,000,000

Australia
5,000,000

"It's the book of the television series."

Publishers have found that authors' appearances on programs like "The Phil Donahue Show" can be a valuable shot in the arm for book sales.

book is an appearance by the author on a national talk show. Today the potential for this kind of exposure is often the criterion by which a book is accepted for publication. Just as the need to compete with TV has brought about the age of the movie spectacular, so too has it brought about the blockbuster book.

Newspapers have felt the effects of television, although to a lesser extent than other media. Because newspapers can provide more in-depth coverage in their stories, and because they offer much lower advertising rates to local merchants, morning newspapers, at least, are relatively unscathed. But the evening TV news and its fifty-million-plus audience are probably to blame for the demise of dozens of major city evening newspapers. It will be interesting to see how this changes even more in the not-too-distant future, as all-news cable channels become common and home TV sets become capable of providing viewers with actual printed pages describing the day's events.

The strongest evidence of TV's ubiquitous presence and pervasive influence are the simple statistics of how much television we watch. In 1981 the average American household viewed an estimated six hours and forty-four minutes of television a day. The average American now watches about twenty-three hundred hours of TV every year. And all of these figures will undoubtedly go up as cable, video recorders,

videodiscs, and other new telecasting methods become more accessible. It is estimated that by the end of the 1980s there will be cable hookups in at least half of all American homes. Those households that already have cable average ten hours a week more TV-viewing than those who have not as yet subscribed.

The size of the American television audience is indeed staggering. At any given moment in prime time, approximately thirty-eight million sets are turned on. It doesn't matter whether the shows are strong or weak; the size of the audience stays the same. Nor does the same person in a household necessarily watch through the whole evening. In fact, it isn't even the same thirty-eight million homes that make up the audience from one night to the next. The exact composition of the audience changes every half hour, night by night.

As with any statistics, the figures relating to television viewing can be misleading. We have sophisticated ways of determining how many television sets are turned on at any moment of the day. But these figures can't tell us whether viewers are concentrating on the program, or playing cards, or, in fact, whether anyone is actually in the room when the set is on. Unlike watching a film at the neighborhood movie house, TV-viewing is not continuous. Perhaps this is because, unlike movies or the

Magazine Circulation per Issue

	Circulation
TV GUIDE	18,870,730
NATIONAL GEOGRAPHIC	10,560,885
PLAYBOY	5,746,536
REDBOOK	4,463,315
TIME	4,451,816
Sports Illustrated	2,343,380
People	2,315,428
Popular Mechanics	1,695,733
BusinessWeek	816,366

Magazine Publishers Association, 1980

If you can't beat them, join them.
Outdistanced by TV as far as size of
audience is concerned, decision-mak-
ers in the other media have learned
that the best way to build up their own
markets is to plug their products
on TV.

Would You Believe?

In 1981, one out of every six people on earth watched Prince Charles and Lady Diana get married. The storybook wedding was viewed by 750 million people in 61 countries, using three satellites. In London, where 2,302,500 people got a chance to cheer the couple in person, box seats along the parade route were sold with color TVs.

UPI

theater, we do not have to pay for what we see on commercial or public TV (or don't think we are paying); there is little investment in "getting our money's worth" out of TV. People eat, talk, read, exercise, sew, play games, dress, and undress while "watching" TV. Most housework is done to the accompaniment of the flickering tube. People get up from in front of their sets and go into other rooms. Other members of the family come in, watch for a while, and leave. In fact, almost 20 percent of the time that a TV set is on in an average American household, it plays to an empty room.

Imprecise as they are, the statistics nevertheless give us a good picture of the American TV habit. Sunday evening, when the family is more likely to be together than at any other time of the week, attracts the largest number of viewers. Friday attracts more children than any other night of the week. The most popular month for viewing television is January, in many parts of the country the coldest time of the year and a time when many Americans like to stay home after the expensive and hectic Christmas holidays.

Women watch more television than men. In fact at 3:00 P.M., 25 percent of all the women in the United States between eighteen and forty-nine are watching television. When you consider that half of all American women are employed outside the home, this figure means that half of all women at home during the day have the television on in the afternoon. On weekends, men and women watch just about the same amount of TV.

American children spend more time watching television than they do in school or at play, with the average now at twenty-six viewing hours a week. Televison also plays a predominant role in the lives of Americans over sixty-five. As a group they watch more television than any other, and spend more time planning which shows they will watch. Such factors as income, education, or sex have litle bearing on how much time they spend with TV. Many of them live alone, and TV is their only companion. Because those who spend the most time at home are the heaviest TV-watchers, it is not surprising that children, the elderly, and women share the highest viewing time.

Educational background and level of income also affect how much television people watch. Until now, a household in which the chief wage earner has had less than one year of college consistently watched more TV than families headed by a college graduate. Lower

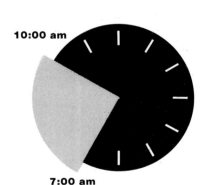

Monday to Friday: Only 7% of TV households are watching, with women and children comprising 73.9% of the total viewers

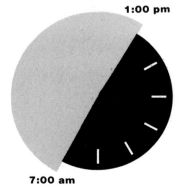

Saturdays: 64.8% of audience is children ages 2–17

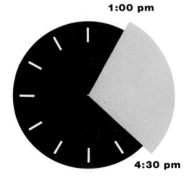

59.6% of audience is women, 17.4% is men

income families have always been heavier TV-watchers than their more affluent counterparts. However, as social scientist George Comstock has pointed out, "By the end of the 1970s, the socioeconomic differences appeared to be disappearing, as the time available for viewing began to be exhausted among the less educated and the more educated become less hostile toward the medium." With more programs serving their interests—PBS documentaries and arts productions, cultural cable channels, "Hill Street Blues," tennis and golf coverage—better educated people have joined the TV audience in large numbers.

"Hill Street Blues"

MTM Enterprises, Inc./Photo Courtesy of NBC

Does all this viewing really make a difference in how we live our lives, in how our world works? Let's look at two of America's favorite pastimes—politics and sports—and see how television has affected them.

By now it is a cliché to state that Abraham Lincoln, with his long nose, his dark beard, and his prominent mole, would have made a rather pathetic candidate in today's telegenic political arena. But like many other clichés, it is probably true. Today's candidates do not stand for election. They pose for it in front of TV cameras that bring their message, and, most important, their carefully manicured image, to millions of voters.

Because of TV, the days of stump speeches and smoke-filled caucus rooms are long gone. Almost all the political ground rules have been changed. The long-dominant roles of party leaders have been diminished and the primacy of the political party itself has been weakened. For, armed with enough money and adequate TV appeal, today's candidate can speak directly to the voter.

TV commercials, carefully orchestrated by media experts, allow the candidates to tell the voter what the pollsters have told them the majority of the public wants to hear. Everything is geared toward TV. Announcements, speeches, and personal appearances are all timed for coverage on the 6 P.M. and 11 P.M. news.

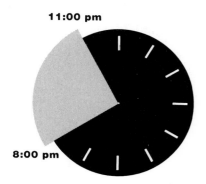

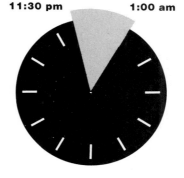

44% of American homes are tuned in, and 22.5% of total viewers are under 17

41% of audience is adult men, 47% is adult women

Events are staged with an eye toward the cameras. Is there any doubt that the turning point in the 1980 Republican presidential race took place when Ronald Reagan snatched the microphone in New Hampshire and with the determination and forcefulness of a real leader proclaimed, ''I'm paying for this debate''?

The cornerstone of all modern political campaigns—the nominating convention—has also been changed dramatically by television. Undecided delegates become instant celebrities; favorite sons and daughters are given their moments in the TV sun; anyone with anything of significance to say saves it until the camera arrives. By the time the nominating convention takes place there are usually only two viable candidates left in the field (and one of them is usually so far ahead as to ensure victory). This too is a result of the impact of television. For in the way it dramatizes the road to the convention, TV makes each state primary a life-or-death situation. By the time the national delegates gather together, the issue is all but settled. The role of the convention is to present the nominees to a huge TV audience during prime time. The lack of suspense in the outcome of the convention creates a problem for the TV networks, which spend millions of dollars every four years to cover the event. Floor reporters scour the hall, looking for statements that will stir up controversy. Anchorpersons conduct interviews, hoping to uncover something of substance, something to hold the audience's attention in the long hours ahead. Sometimes they succeed.

Today wherever politicans travel, TV cameras are sure to be there lending credence to their activities.

ABC News

At the 1980 Republican Convention the nominee was determined long before the delegates gathered in New York. For weeks Ronald Reagan had more than enough committed delegate votes to assure his victory. On the second night of the convention, Walter Cronkite interviewed ex-President Gerald Ford, asking him if he would accept the vice-presidential nomination. The answer was shocking. Perhaps, Mr. Ford hinted, he would. At that moment many of the delegates were doing just what millions of other Americans at home were doing—watching TV. Pandemonium broke out on the convention floor and in the meeting rooms, for the convention had its first real issue. For the next two days all the TV networks had a story with which to hold their audience.

Television's biggest political creation is undoubtedly the presidential debate. Here, too, the emphasis is on form, not substance. The stakes have become so high in these TV confrontations that the aim of most of the participants is not to win but simply to keep from making a major mistake. Their caution is well founded. Many political experts still believe that the close 1960 presidential election was decided by the fact that Richard Nixon had a poor makeup job in his confrontation with John F. Kennedy. And the polls were quick to ascertain that one mistake during his televised debate with Jimmy Carter did more to deny Gerald Ford re-election than any other single incident in the campaign.

Polls, too, have been changed by television. Not only do today's political polls indicate who is ahead in an election; they now tell us who has won—long before the voting booths are closed. The exit poll is the latest brainchild in the arsenal of the networks, eager to be first to proclaim the winner in a national election. Thanks to sophisticated computerized sampling, the winner of an election can now be projected by asking voters in selected precincts around the country how they voted as they exit from the voting booth. In California, some three hours before going to the polls, a voter is already told, within percentage points of the actual final outcome, who has won the election. Why should he bother to vote? And if, because the presidential race has already been decided, that voter and thousands of other people in the area do not cast a ballot, what effect does this have on candidates for other local offices on the ballot?

If TV has turned us into political voyeurs, it has also created a nation of sports fanatics and armchair coaches. Televised games have become so popular in this country that Congress was called upon to mandate when certain

Never was the impact of television on politics more apparent than in the first televised confrontation between John F. Kennedy and Richard Nixon. Today a TV presidential debate can virtually make or break a candidate.

ABC News

ABC News

Photos: ABC Sports

Television not only covers sports, it creates an ever-growing audience for them. Thanks to TV, figure skating, broncobusting, auto racing, gymnastics, and golf have become as familiar to millions of viewers as basketball and baseball.

events can be blacked out and when others must be televised. Several sports, including soccer, tennis, and women's basketball, owe their increased popularity to the exposure that TV has given them. And thanks to cable TV, other sports that have not previously attracted large national attention will undoubtedly become popular as more and more people get the opportunity to see them. Right now, for example, subscribers to cable sports networks such as ESPN get regular telecasts of lacrosse games, automobile races, and even polo matches.

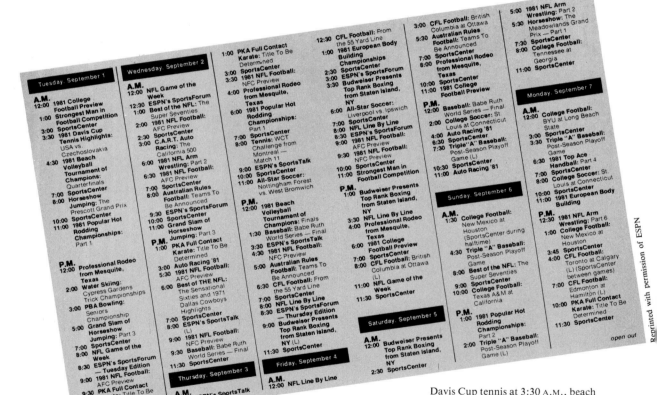

Reprinted with permission of ESPN

Davis Cup tennis at 3:30 A.M., beach volleyball at noon, all-star soccer at 6 P.M.—no wonder one TV executive calls 24-hour-a-day sports networks like ESPN "a service for sports addicts."

Many TV-inspired changes in sports have to do with money. Because televised athletic contests are so popular, because the networks can charge so much money for commercial time during the contests, and because games lend themselves to so many commercial breaks, they are among the most lucrative programs in all of television. And as any fan knows, if a particular sport doesn't have enough natural interruptions to suit the sponsors, then "TV timeouts" can easily be inserted. The amount of money garnered from televised sports will reach staggering dimensions as the number of cable subscribers increases.

The enormous revenues that have accompanied the rise of televised sports have changed almost every aspect of the professional games Americans watch. Leagues in every sport have been expanded (watered down, some critics would say) to take advantage of the increased interest TV has created. Players in every league have been able to demand salaries unthinkable only a short time ago. Terms such as *free agent, option year,* and *holdout* have become as familiar to sports fans as *double play, T formation,* or *body check.* Who could ever have imagined a summer in which there would be no major league baseball for almost two months? Yet it became a reality in 1981, thanks to the impasse

Would You Believe?

In 1980, Miami-Dade Community College offered a full-credit course entitled "Understanding Monday Night Football."

created by the astronomical sums available to owners and players through TV receipts.

Televised athletic contests have become so popular and profitable that the very structure of professional sports has been changed. In most sports, finishing first in the league at the end of the season no longer means victory. The assurance of additional TV revenue has brought about "the second season," the play-

offs that create new excitement and even larger gate receipts. To satisfy the public's seemingly insatiable appetite, new athletic events, geared especially to TV audiences, have been created. "Battle of the Network Celebrities," "Superstars," "Challenge of the Sexes"—all fit into the category of what critics now call "trash sports." As one wag has said, "We're really not that far away from contact yachting."

To keep spectator (and sponsor) interest at the highest possible peak, the networks and promoters have taken advantage of TV's unique ability to create instant celebrities. The news industry in general is people-crazy, and sports news is no exception. Players make the news regularly as we follow the machinations of salary negotiations, strikes, and injuries. Certain athletes catch the attention of the public and the press, either for their physical prowess or their personal idiosyncracies (who wouldn't love a pitcher who talks to the ball before he sends it flying over home plate?), and become that season's heroes. Sometimes this publicity build is planned. Certain boxers, for example, have been strategically hyped in order to build up interest in frequently held "fights of the century." Some athletes have attempted to make the leap from the playing field to the studio lot. With their vastly increased visibility, they have also found lucrative moonlighting jobs as hawkers of everything from men's cologne and underwear to cars, stereos, and political platforms.

Television has even affected the way we watch athletic contests. Most fans are now so accustomed to such TV inventions as instant replays and stop-action reruns that they prefer watching the games on their sets at home to going to the ball park. This is one of the reasons so many arenas and stadiums have huge television screens hanging in prominent locations. Many fans spend as much time looking at the screens as they do watching the live action in front of them.

Sports and the Stars. Tom Selleck, Jamie Farr, Gabe Kaplan, and Penny Marshall are but a few of the host of network celebrities who appear regularly in what has become a TV happening—doing battle for prizes . . . and ratings.

George Long/ABC

Jim Britt/ABC

George Long/ABC

George Long/ABC

Since sports heroes now rank among the most recognizable individuals in the world, it is not surprising that Bill Russell, Joe Namath, and Sugar Ray Leonard have become important pitchmen for a myriad of commercial products.

So popular have televised sports become that the phenomenon has created a new holiday in the United States. It is called Superbowl Sunday, and it is celebrated as passionately as any other holiday in the year. In 1981 the commissioner of the National Football League negotiated a television contract with the three commercial networks for $1 billion. And the TV rights to one football game alone, the Rose Bowl, are now worth almost $8 million.

The impact of television on sports of all kinds is becoming so pronounced that many observers, both inside and outside the TV industry, are openly predicting that we are fast approaching the time when all major sporting events become ''television-happenings'' rather than contests staged primarily for a live audience. Says Gustave Hauser, co-chairman of

Wherever a major sports event takes place the landscape is dominated by TV's presence. And no matter how crucial the moment the action stops until the television commentator gets the interview.

CBS Sports

TV Leads the League

1980 Total Attendance

Number of People Who Watched Superbowl XVI on TV 76,200,000

Warner Amex cable, "There is more demand to see more events in the home now, and that has created an entirely new marketplace. Ultimately it will disturb all the existing patterns involved in broadcasting sports. Whereas sports have been concentrated in the stadium, they will now become concentrated in the home."

Not all sports have benefited from TV's influence. Minor league baseball, for example, long an American institution, has suffered drastically. So, too, have high school sports. There simply aren't enough people willing to pay to see minor leaguers and amateurs in action when they can sit in their living rooms and watch the best athletes in the world free of charge on commercial television.

ABC Sports

**Professional Baseball
(American & National
Leagues combined)
43,014,136**

**Professional Football
(National Football League)
16,800,000**

**Professional Basketball
(National Basketball
Association)
9,449,340**

Watching television has affected how we play, how we vote, how we learn. And when it comes to learning, no group is more affected by TV than America's children. The average American child watches between twenty-five and thirty hours of television a week. Perhaps those of us reared in pretelevision days can get the full implication of this statistic by trying to imagine a childhood in which we spent more than four hours a day, week in and week out, at a movie theater. Even as children we would have laughed at such a suggestion.

Many children in this country are in nursery school by the time they are three or four. Certainly by the time they are five they are spending a good part of their day in school. They take time out for meals and spend up to twelve hours a night in bed. If we add up the number of hours a child spends sleeping, eating, and attending school, it leaves only about five or six hours a day for other activities. And if youngsters are spending four hours each day in front of the television set, they have almost no leisure time left for doing anything else but watching TV.

And what are they watching? They are watching programs designed for adults—80 percent of the time. Television marks the first time in recorded history that children have been exposed to a continual set of acted-out dramas from an early age. And as we all know, these dramas contain a great many violent acts. What

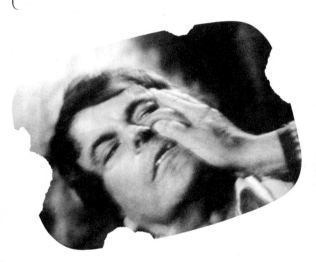

> **"The trouble is not that there is violence in television. There is violence in *Oedipus,* too, and *Lear* and *Hedda Gabler.* The trouble is that in television the violence is *only* violence. What speaks in the great tragedies speaks through the *Word,* speaks to the imagination, speaks for the understanding of human life—its misery—its wonder. But in television the Word is void and the violence is there as violence—like raw sewage in a river."**
> Archibald MacLeish

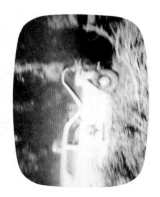

is the effect on children of watching so much verbal and physical aggression?

We know that children, more than adults, imitate what they see. Studies have shown that some children identify with the victims of television crimes rather than the aggressor. As a result these children tend to perceive the world as a more violent place than it really is. Since youngsters view so much violent action on TV, it seems reasonable to assume that the significance and impact of real-life conflicts will be diminished for them. In addition, they may well become desensitized to the fact that violence in the real world really hurts.

Physical aggression is only one form of violence that young viewers encounter. There are other forms which, because they are more subtle, may present even more problems for youngsters than the stabbings, muggings, or shootings. Television characters, whether in comedy or dramatic shows, continually abuse each other verbally. Wives demean husbands; brothers "put down" sisters; neighbors threaten neighbors; everyone, at one time or another, is insulted by someone else. Add to this the al-

most incalculable amount of lying, cheating, and deceit that takes place on television, and it is impossible not to be concerned about the effects of TV on children.

The fact that children watch so much television has had a profound impact on the classroom as well as the home. It has altered whom we learn from and how we teach. By the time today's youngsters graduate from high school they will have spent an average of eleven thousand hours in the classroom—but they will have watched fifteen thousand hours of television.

Reporter David Schoenburn was once offered a television job by Edward R. Murrow. Schoenburn told Murrow that he was thinking of going back to high school teaching. "Kid," said Murrow, "how would you like the biggest classroom in the world?" Television reaches and teaches hundreds of millions around the world. It does so seven days a week, year in and year out, without summer vacations or weekends off. In a world where 90 percent of American three-year-olds can identify Fred Flintstone, while only half of the world's adults can identify their national leaders, who can question the fact that TV, for good or bad, has had an unprecedented impact on the education of youngsters?

The educational process assumes that there is a sequence to learning. There are some things you must know before you can learn other things. This takes time and, very often, hard work and long hours of study. Things on television, however, are immediately accessible, though not in a logcial sequence. Because a youngster receives what the set has to offer instantly and without effort, teachers report that the attention span for schoolwork seems to be shrinking. And there is another issue. For four hours every day, the average youngster is entertained at home by the best performers in the world. He watches programs that are filmed at enormous expense at some of the world's most exotic locales. He becomes accustomed to stunts and other forms of television magic that only limitless budgets can finance. Few teachers can compete with Bert and Ernie, split screens, or talking tigers.

Television is the only programmed instruction a child receives without parent, teacher, or peer group involvement. Few parents can take the time to sit and watch. With more mothers working, TV is now, more than ever, the electronic babysitter. If children have questions

Would You Believe?

A letter in a June 14, 1975, "Dear Abby" column began as follows:

"I am divorced and the mother of a sweet, four-year-old boy named Ronnie." The letter went on to explain how Ronnie and his mother were surprised by a burglar, who tied up the mother. Before being gagged, she was allowed to explain to her son that he should turn on a TV program and watch the remaining twenty minutes. He should then call for help. "Abby," wrote the mother, "my son spent the next three hours watching TV while I was bound and utterly helpless. Could [he] possibly have some hostility toward me? Should I see a psychologist? Please advise."

Or. . .

In 1975, a college professor concluded a two-year study in which he asked youngsters ages four to six: "Which do you like better, TV or daddy?" Forty-four percent preferred TV.

ABIGAIL VAN BUREN
"DEAR ABBY"

about what they see, there is rarely anyone around to answer. Nor is there anyone to contradict TV's harmful or inappropriate messages.

The most pervasive of all programmed instruction comes in the form of TV commercials aimed specifically at children. Those of us who grew up in a time when radio was the chief form of home entertainment can recall that for years one of our favorite programs was "The Shadow." We may have forgotten, but the sole sponsor of this program was the Blue Coal Company. How many of us, as a result of listening to this program, ever badgered our parents to rush out and buy us some anthracite coal?

In today's TV world, the purpose of advertising on children's television is to present toys and sugared foods so that children will feel that they are missing something important if their parents don't buy these products for them. Because TV is uniquely effective in using voice and picture to get children to understand a commercial message, American cereal, candy, and toy manufacturers have been able to turn youngsters into a national sales force for selling their goods. Certain food products are designed specifically to be pitched to children via television. This is how supermarket shelves (the *lower* supermarket shelves) come to be packed with cereals filled with purple marshmallows, cereals which are really chocolate chip cookies in disguise, or multicolored cereals with names like "Frankenberry."

Television, of course, did not invent the world of advertising. There were many commercials on radio. But the cereals that were advertised on programs like "Jack Armstrong" were the same cereals that were sold to adults. Because the sound of radio was not nearly as effective as TV pictures in selling products to children, food manufacturers did not create highly sugared products especially for the child market.

Toys are another example of the way in which products are now designed specifically to appeal to children via television. The major consideration in the design of most children's toys today is how they will look on TV. Toys are designed to make good television commercials rather than good playthings. A stuffed animal or a rag doll looks dead on TV. But battery-operated dolls that walk, talk, write their names, and perform almost every bodily function make for an exciting thirty-second message.

By far the most serious problem relating to children's commercials revolves around the issue of health. Hour by hour adults whom children respect—father figures, famous athletes, rock and movie stars, competent older children—are seen and heard encouraging children to eat candy bars, buy soft drinks, and make friends by sharing the latest munchy, sugar-coated snack. TV commercials teach children that one eats because it is fun or it is sweet or it is the way to get a prize—rather than that food is vital to health and well-being. For example:

- Nearly 60 percent of all commercials directed to children are for food products that conflict with one or more of the Dietary Goals for the United States established by the Senate Select Committee for Nutrition and Human Needs.

- Less than 4 percent of the food ads directed to children on television are for meat, bread, fruits, vegetables, or dairy products.

- In a nation where 98 percent of the population suffers from tooth decay, more than half of the food commercials aimed at American children are for heavily sugared foods.

Put simply, we sell children the worst foods we make during the critical period when they are establishing long-term eating habits.

TV advertising to children is different in another important way from adult advertising. Adults get a variety of messages from television commercials because there are so many different kinds of products that are targeted to them. But advertising to children involves a unique kind of brainwashing, since there really are only two kinds of children's products advertised: food and toys (with an occasional pair of

Dinky Donuts, Cookie Crisp, Frankenberry, Super Sugar Crisp, Honey Comb—manufacturers of children's breakfast food have learned that one of the best ways to attract youngsters to their product is to make them sound more like candy or pastry than cereal.

Warning About Dutch Treats

In the Netherlands, TV ads for sweets containing sugar cannot be aired before 7:55 P.M., may not feature children, and must show this picture insignia of a toothbrush.

While supplies last.

jeans or sneakers thrown in). The problem with this massive sales pitch to children is that it works. It sell products. There are side effects as well, not the least of which is that youngsters from families with modest or below average incomes are continually being programmed to want what only children from relatively affluent families can afford.

One reason TV has such an impact on children, and on adults as well, is that the image on the screen makes the messages so easy to "read." When radio was our *vade mecum,* we could design our own vision of reality to give meaning to the words we heard. But pictures make a difference. As Susan Sontag has written in her essay on photography, "Instead of just recording reality, photographs have become the norm for the way things appear to us, thereby changing the very idea of reality and of realism."

What, then, are the benefits for children watching television? We know, for one thing, that youngsters who see television characters solve problems in nonaggressive ways tend to solve their own problems in a similar fashion. We know that there are television characters who cooperate with each other, who openly express their feelings, who devote their energies to helping other people. There are shows in which individuals from different races demonstrate genuine respect for each other. There are programs in which hard work and dedication to a cause or task are rewarded. And there is no question that television has provided a window on the world for millions of young people, enabling them to "see" remote places, faraway peoples, and different lifestyles.

From the way children "learn" and relate to those around them, to the way adults speak and vote and spend their leisure time, television has had an impact unprecedented in world history. Perhaps nowhere is this influence more pronounced than in the way in which TV, by continuously presenting fictitious characters in real-life situations, creates a world of its own, a world often perceived as reality by millions of viewers. In our next chapter we will take a close look at this world according to television.

2 Resources

Books

Adler, Richard P., ed. *Understanding Television: Essays on Television as a Social and Cultural Force.* Grass Valley, Calif.: Cambria Press, 1981. Analyses of TV news and entertainment, critiques of specific programs and genres, evaluations of the state of TV criticism, and explorations of the future of the medium.

Comstock, George, et al. *Television and Human Behavior.* New York: Columbia University Press, 1978. A summary of research on the effects of television that covers programming, the audience, TV's role in politics and advertising, the psychology of behavioral effects, and much more.

Comstock, George. *Television in America.* Beverly Hills, Calif.: Sage Publications, 1980. An overview of the social issues raised by television, such as the power of the news, TV's impact on attention span, and its effects on family life.

Paletz, David L., and Entman, Robert M. *Media Power Politics.* New York: Free Press, 1981. Investigates the relationship between the United States press and the political elite and how it limits the public's ability to understand or respond to political events and leaders.

Films

The Impact of Television. A 16-mm color film, 20 minutes. 1980. An illustration of television's effects on its audience, this film looks at two communities—one experiencing TV for the first time, the other living without TV for a month. Also features interviews with John Chancellor, Dick Cavett, Ed Asner, John Culkin, and Linda Kahn. Available from Encyclopaedia Britannica Educational Corporation, 425 North Michigan Avenue, Chicago, Ill. 60611.

The World According to Television

The world according to television is a world of extremes. There are very few shades of gray in TV's world of fantastic feats, crucial moments, and urgent emotions. Most television characters are either beautiful or ugly, benevolent or ruthless. In TV's world neither the people nor the situations are average, for average is dull and dull doesn't draw ratings.

With the skill of the ancient storytellers, television draws us into other people's lives. We become obsessed with finding out who shot J.R., with the details of Luke and Laura's wedding, with Mork and Mindy's future. Yet there is a false sense of security in a world where even the most complicated personal or social issues are distilled and resolved in a thirty- or sixty-minute episode. For neither the people nor their lives reflect our own reality.

More than any of us realize, we are affected by the characters we see on TV. Our styles of dress, our ways of talking, our aspirations, and, most important, our attitudes and behavior are influenced more deeply than most of us would care to admit. And this exposure to the world according to television accumulates over time. Subjected to heavy doses of programmed behavior, we actively judge our own actions and environment against the standard projected on our TV screens. No matter what our better senses tell us, we come to feel that a certain brand of toothpaste will not only make our teeth white but that it will make our sex life better too. We are led to believe that women

with clean floors and ringless collars are happier; men who drink light beer are more desirable; and children who like sugary cereals are cuter and funnier. We accept sit-com family relations as the norm—and resent our own families for not being as successful, interesting, or loving as those we see on "Eight Is Enough" or "The Waltons."

> **"After watching family TV shows, I felt that my parents were inadequate and that I didn't have the perfect family life I saw on TV. It caused many fights and my growing apart from my family."**
> 17-year-old high school student quoted in *McCalls* Magazine survey

For people who watch a lot of TV, programs set up expectations that life and the process of everyday living resemble what they see on their sets. When our day-to-day existence turns out to be not as simple, not as neatly packaged, not as happy, as that portrayed on TV, frustration and tension are often the result. When the real world doesn't mesh with expectations set by watching TV, we believe there is something wrong with us. This is particularly true for those who have limited life experiences. For these viewers, television provides almost all of the information they receive about people with lifestyles different from their own. A high percentage of white children now derive most of their knowledge about blacks from a fairly limited number of TV programs. Surprising, and more than a little startling, is the fact that a significant percentage of black children now also state that it is from television that they learn most of what they know about how black people talk, dress, and behave.

Often people prefer TV reality to the real thing. Reporters at the funerals of both John F. Kennedy and Martin Luther King indicated that many of those in attendance watched the telecast of these events on their TV monitors even though they had a clear view of the proceedings directly in front of them. We seem to need the TV image to validate our experiences.

Television, with its enormous ability to send messages to so many people, has always been more than mere entertainment. TV is the most powerful teacher of our time. Because television shows are so skillfully styled, they have an air of authenticity about them that

"*Don't you understand? This is life, this is what is happening. We can't switch to another channel.*"

makes them believable. We don't have to use our visual imagination as radio demands, and without the proscenium arch of the theater we aren't always aware that what we are watching is fiction. Day after day we "learn" how the police operate, how doctors save their patients, how families communicate.

Those who are responsible for producing TV drama are in the business of creating a fantasy world of action, humor, and adventure to sell to an audience eager to escape from the frustrations and realities of the everyday world. Shakespeare's theater troupe did it; Barnum's circus did it; Broadway impresarios and the Kabuki Theater did it and still do it. But because TV daily plays to the largest, most homogeneous, most accessible audience the world has ever known, because so many people accept what they see on TV as reality, the problems brought about by the differences between the real world and the world according to television take on an unprecedented dimension.

If, for example, television through its characters would show more women leading active, forceful lives; if more minority members were portrayed as educated, self-directed human beings; if more men and women over sixty-five could appear as competent and productive people (or indeed appear at all); then the millions of people who accept television as reality would have a much more realistic range of options on which to model their behavior.

Why doesn't this happen? Television drama is controlled by a few basic formulas. The most important of these is the axiom that a program, in order to be successful, must appeal to the largest number of people possible and must attract, at the same time, the kinds of people most likely to purchase the sponsor's product. This latter consideration explains why so many significant groups in this country are ignored. Because the audience might turn away from unpleasantness associated with real life, the advertiser turns his back on the disabled, the ill, and the elderly.

There is another important factor. Because of TV's insatiable need for product, television writers are forced to turn out more programs in a single year than writers have created in a lifetime. As one producer has said, "William Shakespeare wrote thirty-four plays. That would not have carried him through two television seasons. . . . [Writing for TV] is a situation in which compromise becomes a constant companion and expediency your brother."

Faced with this dual pressure—to appeal to the broadest audience, and to produce scripts in record time—the quality of television entertainment is bound to suffer. But the entertainment factor is a fairly benign issue compared to the impact of the messages we receive from TV about ourselves and each other. In this chapter we'll look at some of these messages and the particular problems they present.

TV and the Elderly

The elderly in America are not merely misrepresented on TV; they are practically invisible. This is particularly ironic, since the elderly are the fastest-growing minority in America. There are now more than fifteen million people in this country who are over sixty-five. In fact the elderly now make up more than 14 percent of our population.

Despite these statistics, television portrays senior citizens as if they were a disappearing breed. According to the 1981 Annenberg School of Communications study, conducted by George Gerbner, only 2 percent of all dramatic characters on television are over sixty-five. This study points out that in the same week that an average viewer sees only seven elderly TV characters, he will come into contact with approximately thirty policemen, eighteen criminals, fourteen soldiers, nine doctors, and seven lawyers. In other words, although the number of lawyers in America is minuscule compared to the number of people over sixty-five, their representation on television is exactly the same.

TV has made the elderly so invisible that a youngster watching children's weekend programming has to wait five full weeks before seeing a woman over sixty-five in a leading role.

And when television drama does get around to portraying older people, it hardly does them a service: it shows them as doddering, forgetful fools, as well as victims of crime. According to the Gerbner study, three out of every ten senior citizens in TV's world are likely to be robbed or beaten (the real-world figure is less than 1 percent, which is a lower rate than any other age group). Several surveys have shown that the more older people watch TV, the more they come to believe they will be physically attacked in the real world. Thus TV not only neglects and dehumanizes our elderly; it terrifies them as well.

On those few occasions when the elderly are shown with strength and compassion, humor and humanity, the audience responds. "Summer Solstice" and "Queen of the Stardust Ballroom" are just two examples of successful shows exhibiting a renewed interest in older actors and actresses and programs about the second half of life.

TV demonstrates a clear sex bias as far as aging is concerned. Older women in dramatic roles fall victim to violence even more frequently than men. And studies show that heavy viewers actually believe that old age comes earlier in life to women. TV commercials certainly do nothing to dispel this view. While young women are usually seen selling beauty aids, their older counterparts sell drugs and other health products. Older actresses in commercials are shown having difficulty with their false teeth, suffering from constipation, and lying to their husbands about the extent of their arthritic pain. No wonder that viewers, particularly young people, get the impression that older women's bodies are falling apart.

TV and Women

Given the economics of television, it is easy to understand why more care has not been taken in the way people over sixty-five are portrayed. Older people are regarded as poor consumers. They are not, as a rule, in the high income brackets and therefore not an important target audience for advertisers. But it is not clear why women have been so misrepresented.

Rather than portraying aging as a natural, important phase of life, TV, particularly through its commercials, commonly depicts the elderly as infirm and illness-prone.

Women between the ages of eighteen and forty-nine are heavy consumers, especially now, with the added buying power that comes from working. They are, in fact, TV's most important audience as far as the industry is concerned. One would never know it from the way they are portrayed.

Women make up 52 percent of the American population. Yet male television characters outnumber females three to one. Men on TV are the movers and shakers. They are the executives, the leaders, the problem solvers. Most often they are the sole breadwinners in the family. On the other hand, most female TV characters are portrayed either as housewives or

Would You Believe?

Three out of every four male TV characters who require medical treatment recover. What about their female counterparts? Fewer than one in four gets well.

entertainers, or have no discernible occupations—this in a nation where women make up 43 percent of the labor force.

Columnist Ellen Goodman has suggested that most prime time TV series involving women can be classified into five categories: "Mating and Dating" shows, which give the impression that the only thing women are interested in is competing with each other for men; "Hair" shows, which feature well-endowed young women with trend-setting hairdos; "Role Reversal" programs, in which females like Charlie's Angels or Wonder Woman beat up men; "Titters Television" programs, where as much flesh as possible is revealed and in which two women often pursue the same man; and "It's Not My Fault, It's Historically Accurate" programs, in which blatant sex role stereotyping is featured, but excused by the producer on the grounds that that's the way things are in real life.

The programs are only part of the prob-

lem. TV commercials also present a distorted view of the American woman. Women everywhere in this country have stretched their horizons beyond the dirty dishes, the soiled laundry, the unmopped floors. It is now predicted that by the end of this decade more than 70 percent of all American women will be in the nation's work force. Yet advertisers persist in designing TV ads that show women excited about new ways to polish the furniture and the appearance of miracle cleaning liquids.

Author Jean Kilbourne has pointed out perhaps the most serious problem concerning women and the way they are depicted in TV advertisements. "Women, primarily young women," she says, "are depicted as sex objects and men as success objects. The [female] sex object is a mannequin, a shell. Conventional beauty is her only attribute. She has no lines or wrinkles (which are, after all, signs of maturity, expression, and experience), no scars or blemishes—indeed, she has no pores. She is thin, generally tall and long-legged, and above all, she is young. All 'beautiful' women in television commercials, regardless of product or audience, conform to this norm. Women are constantly exhorted to emulate this ideal, to feel ashamed and guilty if they fail, and to feel that their desirability and capacity for being loved are contingent upon physical perfection." Kilbourne further points out that the "sex object" problem is exacerbated in TV commercials that focus in on parts of women's bodies—hair, teeth, skin—that need improvement.

Some ads are changing. In some commercials women are seen opening their own businesses—and succeeding. Females are shown asking males for a date. Just as important, a husband cooks the dinner for a late-working wife, or takes the children out for a meal while Mom finishes an office report. Still, many of these ads use the working woman as a gimmick. For example, when an airline pilot's hat is removed at the end of a macho commercial we

Charles Beier/Richard Lyons

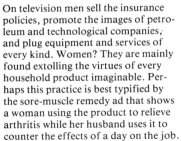

On television men sell the insurance policies, promote the images of petroleum and technological companies, and plug equipment and services of every kind. Women? They are mainly found extolling the virtues of every household product imaginable. Perhaps this practice is best typified by the sore-muscle remedy ad that shows a woman using the product to relieve arthritis while her husband uses it to counter the effects of a day on the job.

The message of this ad? Even a woman (a cleaning woman at that) can understand how this word processor works. ▶

TV commercials present messages that go beyond extolling the virtues of the products themselves. For millions of viewers the real message of the commercial is found in the way the person in the ad is presented. Is this really the way we expect women to look? ▼

find that it is a woman who has been flying the plane. The implication is often that the working woman is a novelty or that a man is never in charge of a household.

Since young viewers have less experience with real-life role models, it is particularly important that children, who are among the heaviest TV-watchers, be presented with a minimum of male-female distortion. A look at children's weekend programming reveals that quite the opposite is true. In TV cartoons, the standard fare of what *Variety* calls the "Kid-Vid ghetto," women are almost always portrayed as nagging housewives or helpless, hapless creatures. Except for the occasional "super-woman" character, the status of females is generally defined by their relationship to males. On the other hand, two-thirds of the male characters in the cartoons are lawyers, doctors, or law enforcement officers.

In Saturday morning commercials, boys are shown with toys such as cars and space vehicles, girls with dolls and makeup kits. When given make-believe occupations, more than half the female children are portrayed as housewives. If they are shown working outside the home, they are most commonly seen as models or stewardesses. On the other hand, boys are either race car drivers, soldiers, sailors, or airplane pilots.

Obviously, neither boys nor girls are given a diversity of lifestyles to choose from, but in the world according to television men hold the power, take the risks, do the interesting things, and receive the rewards. Women are primarily concerned with romance, marriage, and the care of the house and babies. The real world may have changed, but TV perpetuates antiquated notions about dominance and servitude.

Television and Minorities

The more a particular group is seen on television, the more it will be perceived by viewers as playing an important part in the real world. Conversely, a group infrequently seen on TV is regarded as insignificant. We have seen that this is the case with the elderly. It is true of other groups, such as Hispanics, who, although

It is not only in situation comedies or commercials that women are commonly misrepresented. Female cartoon characters (with the exception of a few superheroes) are most often depicted as hapless and totally dependent on men for their well-being.

living in a nation that by the year 2000 is predicted to be the third largest Spanish-speaking country in the world, are rarely seen in significant roles in TV drama. It is true also of Asian-Americans, who are most often either ignored or falsely depicted as all having the same characteristics, mannerisms, and national origins.

Research has also revealed that the more frequently a person watches TV, the more he is likely to accept stereotyped portrayals of a group as real. Thus if a particular group is portrayed in a degrading manner, viewers are likely to accept the depictions as fact, and make the TV treatment the basis for the way they feel and act toward this group.

During the last two decades there has been no shortage of attention paid to the gains made by black Americans in their struggle for equal opportunity and treatment in our society. One would hope that television, which, through its news departments, has spent so many hours recording this struggle, would be particularly sensitive to the way blacks are portrayed in regular programs.

Historically blacks have been underrepresented in television. In the early days of TV, blacks were virtually absent from the screen. When black characters did appear, it was in outrageously stereotyped roles such as the characters in "Amos and Andy." Says Bob Johnson, president of the Black Entertainment Network, "When I was growing up watching television there were only two black children on the screen, Buckwheat and Farina on the 'Little Rascals.' . . . We didn't have the reinforcement of Timmy on 'Lassie' or 'Leave It to Beaver,' 'Father Knows Best,' or any of the other programs that showed warm and cordial family ties for young white kids."

The events of the 1960s focused the nation's attention on blacks and their struggle for civil rights, and television responded by beginning to write more black characters into its programs. This trend accelerated in the 1970s, when series made up primarily of black actors and actresses presented a new set of problems.

The major issue today is not only underrepresentation but also the way blacks are portrayed. Black females are cast either as servants or in roles in which they have no discernible occupation. And more than 80 percent of all the characters on television who are obese are black women.

Black teenagers fare little better. A disproportionate percentage of TV roles for blacks go to teenagers in situation comedies. Scripts in these shows call for these characters to spend the majority of their time yelling at each other, deceiving their families and their friends, and most often playing the part of clown or buffoon (all to the roaring approval of the laugh track).

The problems connected with the way minorities are portrayed on television are made even more serious by TV's habit of recycling programming. Many of the series and movies that make up the rerun portions of the TV schedule were created at a time when people were much less sensitive to the harm that is done by stereotyping certain groups and individuals. By continually airing old programs in which Hispanics are portrayed as lazy, shiftless, and inarticulate, or American Indians are seen as drunken, cowardly savages, television is perpetuating stereotypes even if new shows make an effort to give a more balanced picture.

Minority members are not the only ones made to look ridiculous on television, of course. Many white characters appear regularly in ridiculous roles. But white characters are seen in every other conceivable kind of role as well. Until those who create TV drama become more sensitive to the harm that is done by these one-sided portrayals, the distortion about blacks and other minorities presented to an oft-believing audience will remain one of the most serious problems found in the world according to television.

Black viewers have found few positive role models in TV situation comedies or adventure shows, where black characters are often depicted as buffoons or placed in demeaning situations. One notable exception is Bill Cosby, who is seen often both in adult and children's programs and as a spokesman in a variety of commercials.

Television and the Family

In the 1950s and 60s, the typical TV family lived in a home that was always spotless, with a mom and dad who were always caring and always available, and children (always cute) whose most traumatic crises were missed homework assignments and broken prom dates. In those antiseptic TV families, mother was always around to serve cookies and milk, and father really did know best. Even on shows featuring single parents ("The Courtship of Eddie's Father," "The Partridge Family"), the families argued over issues no more meaningful than those that had troubled Andy Hardy or Henry Aldrich. Even though these typical TV families did not reflect the actual lives of most Americans, they attracted and entertained enormous audiences.

With the social upheavals of the next ten years, TV families underwent great changes. Today's so-called situation comedies deal with real-life problems: marital infidelity, unemployment, impotence, divorce, alcoholism. Norman Lear revolutionized the genre with shows that tore apart old TV clichés. "Maude" is to sentimental family fare what "M*A*S*H" is to "Dr. Kildare." Maude had an abortion, a nervous breakdown, and a facelift, and when she went through menopause on a show she helped more people to understand the crisis than most documentaries ever could.

Virtually the only happy marriages on TV exist in the past or on fantasy shows. As TV critic Jeff Greenfield has noted, "Marriage on television today is a cross between a bad joke, a bad dream, and a nostalgia trip. Finding a contemporarily, happily married couple on television is like finding an empty taxi in midtown Manhattan at 5 P.M.—possible, but not very likely."

More often than not, prime-time TV marriages are troubled with the typical soap-opera woes: infidelity, incompatibility, and incurability. Single-parents abound on shows ranging from "The Love Boat" to "Mork and Mindy" to "Hill Street Blues."

Yet with the new realism in TV comedies, even single parents on today's sitcoms have become a different breed from their predecessors. Now the mix includes a homosexual, an unmarried man with adopted children from various ethnic backgrounds, and a menage à trois. Divorce is common, but surely no more common than it is in the real world where nearly half of all marriages end in divorce.

One wonders what role models young people must be absorbing for their future family life. If children were to use TV characters exclusively as their guides, very few of our young people would ever get married at all. In the world according to television, marriage, particularly a successful marriage, simply doesn't offer enough plot entanglements. This is true even in soap operas, where the plot is continually spiced with adultery, incest, and other forms of titillation designed to hold the audience's attention. In recent years there has been a marked increase in the number of single-parent families in America. That TV pays attention to this modern fact of life is a positive attribute. But in paying so little attention to marriage, television distorts the real world.

And there is another kind of distortion. Author Richard Peck has pointed out that this generation of teenage TV-viewers has been spared the "grim and prim" adolescences of Ricky and David Nelson and the teenagers on "Father Knows Best." On the other hand, says Peck, "We seem now to be on the threshold of a new era when adolescent characters are creeping into the soap operas of daytime programming. While it's perfectly true that teenagers will cut school to watch daytime TV, they're not likely to approve of actresses impersonating teenage vixens alienating married men from

> "Most television programs are not out to corrupt adolescents, but the sex that does appear is almost uniformly seductive, furtive, out of wedlock, exploitive, or downright violent. It does not answer any of the questions about sex that kids so plaintively write to me."
> Beth ("Ask Beth") Winship

The Family Album

Today's TV families reflect many of the changes that have taken place in American society in recent years. From the childless yet blissful marriages of the Harts and Hartleys to the single-parent relationships in programs like "One Day at a Time," to the surrogate parent families in shows like "Love, Sidney," "Different Strokes," "Facts of Life," and "Gimme a Break" to the blue-collar families coming face to face with modern problems as typified in "All in the Family," to the traditional families in "Too Close for Comfort," "The Flintstones," "The Waltons," and "Little House on the Prairie," TV today may well provide viewers with the widest variety of lifestyles ever seen in the world according to television.

TV programmers have long known that in the majority of American homes, young people control the set. In the mid-70s ABC, through programs like "Happy Days," "Mork and Mindy," "Laverne and Shirley," and "Welcome Back, Kotter," began to target its prime-time schedule to this audience. The result? The network rose from a distant third in the ratings to the top of the heap.

Charles Beier/Richard Lyons

their wives. The young are markedly judge-mental about other people's standards, and they're shocking prudes. They have an innate moral code for others to abide by that would make any rating system pale. They like to look up to characters with whom they wish to ally themselves. They don't want to become clowns, addicts, greaseballs, or Lolitas.''

What teenage members of American families want most out of TV is stories that will provide strategies for coping with the adult world they are about to enter. In this they share the feelings of many older TV-watchers, especially heavy viewers who naturally feel frustrated when their day-to-day existence is so much more troublesome and complex than those of the families they identify with night after night on television.

TV and Health

We have often been told that ''we are what we eat.'' If this adage is true, then those of us who are influenced by television characters are in big trouble. The world of television is the world of the hastily downed treat. TV characters spend more time gulping down snacks than they do eating breakfast, lunch, and dinner combined. In television's world, people of all ages eat the wrong food in the wrong way most of the time (and usually in restaurants).

And yet television characters are remarkably healthy. Most of them stay slim throughout their TV lives. They hardly ever need glasses. They simply go along week by week without any discernible functional disorders. The message that we get from the world according to TV is that it is perfectly all right to eat and drink anything we want, whenever we want it. Besides, if we should get sick, TV doctors will have us on our feet in no time.

The Surgeon General's Report on Health issued in 1981 stated that the majority of the nation's health hazards are now attributable to behavior rather than disease. The report also pointed out that alcohol consumption is a major factor in more than 10 percent of all the deaths in the United States. Numerous other studies have revealed that alcoholism in America has reached near-epidemic proportions.

Yet TV characters spend twice as much time drinking alcoholic beverages as they do drinking coffee or tea. They consume fourteen times more liquor and beer than soft drinks and they drink fifteen times more alcohol than they do water. Viewers watching in prime time see a minimum of three instances of drinking an hour. And soap operas are even more alcoholic. They average six instances an hour, day after day. Contrary to what one might expect, it is not the ''bad guys'' who do most of the drinking. The heaviest TV drinkers are well-known stars appearing in regular series. TV characters seldom refuse a drink, nor do they often express disapproval of someone else's drinking. In situation comedies excessive drinking is frequently used simply as a means of getting more laughs.

Why is there so much drinking on TV? Part of it is attributable to the macho image. Beer advertisers have discovered that their most effective commercials are those in which well-known brawny ex-athletes gather together for raucous laughs, good fellowship, and free flowing drinks. And there are other reasons. Producer Norman Lear has stated that television scripts rarely call for actors or actresses to fondle a scotch or a vodka. Instead, the director or the actor himself finds that sipping a drink fills in dead time between dialogue. Lear also points out that in order to move a scene along, the director will often have a character

They all do it. From the daytime ''soaps'' to the late-night adventure shows, TV characters continually celebrate, reflect, and console themselves by reaching for one of television's favorite props—a drink.

walk across the room, step behind the bar, and pour himself a drink as he talks. It has also, says Lear, become second nature on television, as well as in the movies and the theater, for characters to express feelings of tension or anxiety by reaching into the liquor closet or heading for the nearest bar. Whatever the reasons, drinking on television is excessive and millions of Americans are being told that the way to relieve stress or to fill in time or to appear more glamorous is to pour another drink.

Even if one weren't influenced by TV characters, there are still commercial messages to contend with. The average viewer watches twenty-two thousand TV ads a year. About five thousand of these ads are for food products, and more than over half of these ads are for low-nutrition foods and snacks.

TV and Work

The world of television is one in which, according to a study by George Gerbner, policemen, doctors, lawyers, judges and law-breakers outnumber all other working people combined. On TV there are almost no clerical workers, salespeople, artists, or engineers. And blue collar workers, the largest segment of the working force in the real world, are nearly invisible. The result is that heavy TV-watchers and children come to know more about spies, coroners, and small-town sheriffs than they do about those who carry out the basic tasks in American society.

Television relies heavily on authority figures. Policemen, doctors, lawyers, and judges fill the bill. TV doctors are wise, fatherly (women on TV are not doctors; they are nurses), and right most of the time.

TV's most insatiable need is that of telling exciting stories in a simple, visual, action-packed way. That violence and crime fit neatly into this formula is one reason there is so much carnage on TV. In order to create the maximum amount of drama in the brief half-hour or hour segments allotted to them, TV writers constantly put their characters into life-and-death situations. Whether in literature, theater, or the movies, crime and violence have always been at the top of the list of subjects that will attract and hold an audience's attention. It is for these reasons that in TV's world, murders take place more frequently and crime occurs about ten

Television loves authority figures. And no TV characters are treated with more reverence than the inordinate numbers of doctors who find their way into every type of TV series.

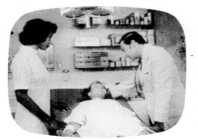

Would You Believe?

There are more gunshots fired in one evening of TV than in one year in a medium-sized American city.

Charles Beier/Richard Lyons

times more often than in the real world. Alfred Hitchcock summed up the attitude of broadcasters when he stated that "Television has brought murder back into the home where it belongs."

In television's world, according to the Gerbner study, one-third of all the characters portrayed on the screen support themselves either by fighting crime or committing it. The firing of handguns is so common that a typical night in front of the set can perhaps best be compared to an evening spent in a shooting gallery. One of the reasons for this may be that those who use the weapons need the practice. Surveys have shown that almost 85 percent of all shots fired on TV fail to hit their target. Ironically, this makes the problem of TV violence even more serious. The very fact that there is so little suffering or other damage as a result of all this human target practice makes the act of firing a weapon at another human being appear less dangerous. How can shooting a gun at someone be harmful if so few people get hurt? There are some who think that this is the most significant problem with violence in American TV. In Japan, on the other hand, characters who meet with violence in a TV drama almost always suffer bloody consequences.

In the world of television, police and private detectives alike fill their days with devil-may-care car chases, shoot-ups, and amorous adventures. The real world is far less glamorous: police handle plenty of traffic violations and domestic problems, and private detectives chase debtors, look for missing people, and shadow straying husbands and wives. Television's private eyes regularly solve crimes and bring criminals to justice; most real private detectives have little to do with the actual solving of major crimes.

And, of course, TV's men in blue always get their man, with a speed unprecedented in the annals of real life, since loose ends must be neatly tied by the close of the thirty- or sixty-minute segment. What of the long hours, mundane tasks, and many frustrations that plague real-life law enforcers, what of the bad guys who never get caught? Where are they on TV? (You can find them on "Hill Street Blues," which may account for its growing popularity.)

The typical action-adventure shows that feature private detectives, police, or other law enforcement agencies are put together by highly skilled writers, producers, and technicians. Actual police or FBI buildings are shown. Locales around the world are used and identifiable landmarks are featured. Official badges and uniforms are commonplace. Often we are told that the episode is based on some actual case (only the names have been changed to protect the innocent), and at the end of some of these programs we are even informed as to what sentence was given to the "actual criminals." All of this gives an air of authenticity to these series, increasing problems for viewers who have difficulty distinguishing between the truth and the fantasy world of TV.

These misconceptions cause trouble in the real world of lawyer's offices and courtrooms. Lawyers around the country report increased difficulty conveying to clients just what they as lawyers can and cannot accomplish. If Perry Mason can wrap up a case successfully in an hour, why can't they? And many legal officials are concerned that jurors will expect clearcut resolutions of cases as a result of TV lawyers' freeing their clients by breaking down witnesses on the stand and then pointing to the actual criminal before the startled eyes of judge and jury.

TV and the News

In the world of TV news, where a single rating point can mean millions of dollars, being first with the story is as important as it used to be in the newspaper game, where two or three city newspapers competed for subscribers. Not only do the majority of Americans now get most of their news from TV—some 40 percent get *all* their news off the screen.

Television news employs the most sophisticated system of communications the world has ever known. And besides being told what is happening—we see it take place before our very eyes. TV news is indeed our window on the world. But anyone who has ever taken part in a newsworthy event knows that there is a big difference between all that happens at such an event and what actually appears on the evening news. For viewers at home, however, what is "real" about the event is what they see on their set. And because the networks have so little

time to get all the news into their nightly telecasts, what finally does appear is less of a journalistic report than it is a headline. For there is no way that TV news can do justice to any one story in the limited time it has to cram in all the events of the day. In fact, as NBC executive Richard Salant has indicated, if all the transcripts of any one nightly newscast were cut up and pasted onto a newspaper, they would not even fill three-quarters of the front page.

Says Walter Cronkite, the dean of America's newscasters, "We attempt to include all the pertinent sides to a story, particularly a controversial one, since we are professional journalists. But not infrequently we find we must dismiss one argument or the other with barely a parenthetical phrase. The result is something not far from distortion. Not a distortion that grows from any bias, political, ideological, or sexual, but the inevitable result of trying to get ten pounds of news into the one-pound sack we are given every night."

This headline aspect of the news is but one contributing factor to the way TV news creates its own reality. For with the competition for audience so high between networks or local stations, with the rewards so astronomical for even the slightest gains in news ratings, TV newscasting has increasingly taken on many of

A standard feature of all local newscasts is the weather report. In order to keep audiences tuned in, most local stations expect their meteorologists to be as much showmen as forecasters.

The public's insatiable appetite for the news sometimes surprises even network executives. ABC's "temporary" late-night coverage of the Iranian hostage situation drew such a large audience that after the crisis was over, "Nightline" became a major feature of the network schedule.

the attributes of show business, where even bat-
tles may be staged by combatants specifically
for TV coverage. This affects not only how the
news is reported but what is reported and in
what order. "Our purpose," says one producer, "is to make information more palatable
and to make reality competitive with make-believe. . . . Of course there is a line separating
show biz from news biz. You walk up to that
line, touch it with your toe and do not cross it."

Says Paul H. Weaver, associate editor of
Fortune magazine, "In practical terms the emphasis on spectacle is revealed in the television
news organization's preoccupation with 'good
film,' i.e., film that clearly and dramatically depicts action, conflicts, ritual, or color. Faced
with a choice between two potentially newsworthy events, the American TV news organization will prefer, other things being equal, the
one for which there is better film."

Thanks to television, the public's appetite
for news continues to grow. On any given week-
day evening some fifty-five million Americans
tune in to one of the three network newscasts.
Millions begin their day watching the morning
network news shows, which now air as early as
6 A.M. And many of us are turning into night-
time news junkies as well, with the three major
networks seriously considering doubling the
length of their nightly newscasts and two of the
networks offering middle-of-the-night news
from 2 A.M. to 5 A.M. Most people watch at
least one local newscast during the day. Cable
networks showing nothing but news have been
created. (Ted Turner has two of these in operation, while ABC and Westinghouse have combined forces to create an all-news cable network
of their own.) And other cable channels feature
continuous news, weather, time, and stock
market reports that are printed across the
screen. In addition, independent news networks
have been formed to help local UHF stations
compete with their network-affiliate neighbors.

With our growing fascination with the
news, television reporters have achieved a special kind of stardom. Anchorpersons and TV

reporters, whether national or local, rank among the most visible celebrities in the nation today. They are highly paid people, eminently respectable, and credible interpreters of the world around us.

> **"It seems to me as I travel about the country that all it takes today to be an anchor person is to be under twenty-five, fair of face and figure, dulcet of tone and well-coiffed . . . that and to be able to fit into the blazer with the patch on the pocket."** Walter Cronkite

Although it has not always been true, news is now an important source of revenue for broadcasters. In 1980 the three major networks earned more than fifty million dollars in their news operations. As new technologies are introduced, the race for viewers at both network and local levels will become even more heated. The rivalry has become so intense, in fact, that many local stations are now aided by news consultants whose job it is to develop strategies, cosmetic and substantive, aimed at improving a local station's news ratings. These consultants offer advice in such matters as how an anchorwoman should wear her hair, what type of suit an anchorman should sport on camera, and what kinds of news stories should be featured in a particular community. Some of these news "experts" are on the payroll of the network to which the station is affiliated, since what is good for local news ratings is also good for the network.

On local stations and the networks more female faces are now seen than ever before. Jane Pauley ("Today"), Diane Sawyer ("CBS Morning News"), Jessica Savitch ("NBC Weekend News") all sit at a network anchor desk although there is still no female anchor for any of the nightly network newscasts.

Television and Escape:
Celebrities, Soaps, and Unreal People

Television's messages affect what we think about others and ourselves. Yet there is another aspect of TV—and that is the way millions of us use television to flee willingly from the real world, to escape voluntarily into a world of fantasy. This explains the popularity of such series as "Love Boat" and "Fantasy Island." It accounts for the phenomenal success of television soap operas and game shows. It is also one of the reasons so many viewers live vicariously through the fictitious and the real people they see on their TV screens.

Charles Beier/Richard Lyons

STEVENSON

Drawing by Stevenson; © 1981 The New Yorker Magazine, Inc.

"I'm not responsible for what you may or may not have seen on 'Love Boat,' Ma'am."

At any one time millions of people across the nation are watching the same sporting event, the same variety show, the same talk show or situation comedy or dramatic presentation. The people who appear regularly on these programs become the most recognizable individuals in the country. Far more people in the United States are able to identify Johnny Carson or Alan Alda than their political leaders. And surveys tell us that youngsters are now more familiar with Ronald McDonald than they are with Santa Claus.

The world of television is the world of the instant celebrity. There are few genuine heroes left in our culture; their place has been taken by TV figures who, through constant exposure and relentless publicity, have become more familiar to us than our next-door neighbors. We learn to care about them as we follow their adventures and problems from week to week. We get to know them well—so well, in fact, that often we confuse the actor with the role. More than one actor has failed to make the transition from one TV series to another; once an audience comes to identify an actor with the character he plays, he may be locked into that persona in the eyes of the TV viewer.

Inviting TV characters into our living rooms each week makes us not only know but trust them. We come to believe in our TV friends and consequently in the actors who portray them. This is why TV lawyers are swamped with real-life legal questions, and why more than a quarter of a million people wrote letters seeking medical advice from the fictitious TV doctor Marcus Welby. It's no wonder that Robert Young is the perfect salesman for decaffeinated coffee — would Marcus Welby, M.D., lie to you? Advertising agencies are quick to capitalize on our confusion of fact and fantasy, using TV policemen to pitch the trustworthiness of automobiles and sexy starlets to sell cosmetics and pantyhose.

Thanks to one of America's obsessions, the TV talk show, we see our modern-day celebrities not only in their dramatic roles but "up close and personal." We find out what books they like to read, who designs their clothes, and what their politics are — and often we follow suit, hoping to be more like them by copying them. We hear about their past triumphs and tragedies and their frustrations and dreams. For so many of us who live lives of quiet desperation, this association with fame and fortune may be the one bright spot in an otherwise colorless day.

Given a daily captive audience of millions of loyal viewers, talk-show hosts have assumed a role larger than life.

The Soaps

There is no contest when it comes to determining which type of TV series draws the most devoted viewers. Whether it be the long-established daytime serials like "Days of Our Lives" or "All My Children" or their relatively new prime time evening counterparts like "Dallas," "Dynasty," or "Falcon Crest," the title goes to the soap operas — hands down! Soap operas, of course, did not originate with television. Daily programs such as "Ma Perkins" and "Search for Tomorrow" dominated radio's popularity and profit charts. On TV, the soaps are more popular and lucrative than ever. In 1981 one soap opera alone ("General Hospital") attracted a daily audience of fourteen million viewers. The thirteen soap operas telecast on a daily basis by the three networks in 1981 brought in a total advertising revenue of some $700 million.

Long regarded as standard fantasy-entertainment fare for bored or unhappy women-at-home, today's television soap attracts a much

Soap Plot

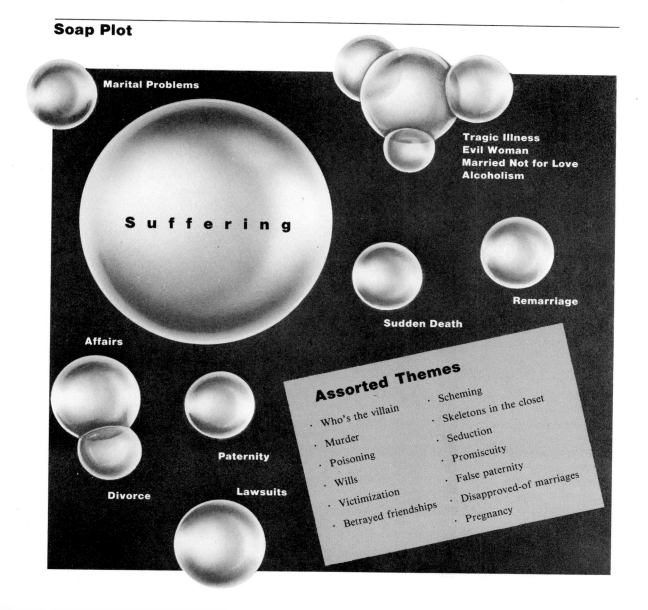

Marital Problems

Tragic Illness
Evil Woman
Married Not for Love
Alcoholism

Suffering

Remarriage

Sudden Death

Affairs

Assorted Themes

- Who's the villain
- Murder
- Poisoning
- Wills
- Victimization
- Betrayed friendships
- Scheming
- Skeletons in the closet
- Seduction
- Promiscuity
- False paternity
- Disapproved-of marriages
- Pregnancy

Paternity

Divorce

Lawsuits

different audience. Millions of men are included among the daily viewers and "soap watching" has become an established way of life in high schools and on college campuses across the nation. Appliance and TV stores are besieged by viewers seeking out a viewing spot in the middle of the day. Men and women set their TV recorders to their particular favorites before going off to work, and newspapers, magazines, radio stations, and even TV shows give daily recaps of the happenings on each of the major soaps.

The soap opera phenomenon offers the perfect example of why people watch so much television: the desire to follow a story once it has begun. The soap opera is, of course, an extreme example as the myriad of plot lines and trials and tribulations inches along day after day, week after week, year after year. Viewers get to know the characters as intimately as their own families, and when an actor is replaced fans feel betrayed; suddenly they must get used to a whole "new" Rachel.

And just as the soaps serve as a prime example of why viewers get hooked into TV, so too they offer examples of the differences between the real world and the world according to

television. In a 1981 cover article devoted to the TV soap opera as a modern American phenomenon, *Newsweek* pointed out that surveys now show that college-age soap opera addicts have an exaggerated notion of the number of lawyers and doctors in the real world and that psychologists have begun to express concern over the effects on young people watching day-by-day episodes in which no one ever performs an unglamorous task.

Ironically, there are other psychologists and sociologists who point out that in the entire world of television it is the soaps that are closer to real life than any other type of TV drama. To these observers, the fact that soap operas (exaggerated as they may be) deal with so many types of human frailties and relationships, the fact that every soap opera features characters attempting to cope with problems such as drug abuse, pregnancy, and infidelity takes them out of the category of fantasy and makes them the most true-to-life type of programming on television.

Hello! Next time you're watching your favorite show, notice how often the characters pick up the telephone (particularly on soap operas). The reason? It moves the plot along without the need for additional characters or scenery.

The Game Shows

"Contestants needed for new game show. You will be humiliated, embarrassed before your friends and a million people. And your prize will be an inexpensive item; plus the chance to appear on TV." This ad, which appeared in a California newspaper, elicited thousands of replies.

In America, as in other countries around the world, the game show has become the ultimate fantasy. The acquiring of goods via television is not confined to commercials. Among the most popular shows on TV are those which offer ordinary people the opportunity to win money or the prize of their dreams in exchange for making fools of themselves in front of huge audiences.

Most people do not go on game shows principally to win prizes. Their main motivation is simply to appear in front of the cameras, and they will literally fight with one another over the chance to appear on these shows. Says Chuck Barris, the creator of some of the most successful of all the TV games, "People will do anything, *anything* to get on television. . . . We purposely stay away from big prizes on these shows. If we introduced yachts, people would kill each other."

He is probably right. According to the producer of one game show, "Contestants are undoubtedly motivated by a wish or fantasy that, somehow, this will lead to stardom." This notion is not as far fetched as it may seem. Game shows are so powerful a vehicle of national TV exposure that talent agencies actually send clients to the game shows to audition for appearances. Many of the contestants on these shows are actually budding professional actors making the rounds.

So strong is the desire to win prizes or simply appear on television that contestants allow themselves to suffer almost any kind of humiliation to be in front of the cameras. They wear infantile costumes, affect outrageously exaggerated enthusiasm for everything that takes place, and are encouraged to speak in thinly veiled sexual innuendos, which are the stock-in-trade of so many of these programs.

> **"People here really get into game shows. Those creeps giving away tons of luxury items and trips to Honolulu. When you're deprived of everything, its fun to watch greed in action—a fantasy."** Riker's Island prison inmate

Why do so many viewers tune in to game shows? Certainly the vicarious experience of joining the make-believe world of TV motivates many watchers. But there may be deeper-rooted reasons. Says Dr. Ronald Baxter, a consultant for the BBC, "Every time a contestant bows down in abject humiliation, the viewers in their comfy armchairs lean back and grow six inches taller."

Whatever the reasons, the viewers do tune in. Despite a constant flow of criticism from groups like the National Organization for Women, the game shows continue to attract the most sought-after viewing group of all — women aged eighteen to forty-nine. And year after year these programs remain near the top of the list of the biggest money-makers in the television industry.

Programs and profits: two of the most important concepts in the world of television, a world that often presents its own version of reality. Making a distinction between TV's reality and the real world is the first step in living sensibly with television. But we cannot think clearly about what we see on TV without an understanding of why and how the shows we watch get to the screen.

3 Resources

Books

Greenberg, Bradley S. *Life on Television: Content Analysis of U.S. TV Drama*. Norwood, N.J.: Ablex, 1980. A detailed study of the content of fictional series on commercial TV, and how minorities, the elderly, the sexes, families, and social behaviors are portrayed.

McNeil, Alex. *Total Television: A Comprehensive Guide to Programming from 1948 to 1980*. New York: Penguin Books, 1980. Information on more than 3,400 series, giving network or syndication affiliation, running dates, descriptions of series (and of special programs), and casts.

Weibel, Kathryn. *Mirror Mirror: Images of Women Reflected in Popular Culture*. Garden City, N.Y.: Doubleday, 1977. A historical survey of the changing images of women in fiction, on television, in movies, in women's magazines and magazine advertising, and in fashion.

Window Dressing on the Set: Women and Minorities in Television: An Update. A report of the U.S. Commission on Civil Rights. Washington, D.C: U.S. Commission on Civil Rights, 1977. Available for sale from Superintendent of Documents, U.S. Government Printing Office, Washington, D.C., 20402. Focuses on the portrayal of minorities and women on network television and their employment at television stations.

Periodical

Media Report to Women 3306 Ross Place, N.W., Washington, D.C. 20008. Monthly. A feminist newsletter published by the Women's Institute for Freedom of the Press and subtitled, "What Women Are Thinking and Doing to Change Communications Media."

Organizations

Chinese for Affirmative Action
121 Waverly Place
San Francisco, Calif. 94108
415-398-8212
Works for increased employment opportunities for Chinese people in the communications industry, advises media on the portrayal of Chinese characters, and helps Chinese gain access to the media.

Gray Panther Media Watch
475 Riverdale Drive
Room 861
New York, N.Y. 10115
212-870-2715 or 368-3761
Monitors the media for negative stereotyping of old people and works to change attitudes of viewers of all ages toward the elderly.

National Black Media Coalition
2027 Massachusetts Avenue NW
Washington, D.C. 20036
202-797-7474
Represents local minority needs in programming and employment at the national level, helps provide technical training, and participates in the regulatory process.

National Gay Task Force
80 Fifth Avenue
Suite 1601
New York, N.Y. 10011
212-741-5800
A clearinghouse for the gay movement, focusing on the promotion of gay civil rights legislation. Media work is directed toward the generation of a positive image of gay people and for coverage of gay issues.

National Organization for Women
Media Task Force
425 13th Street NW
Suite 1048
Washington, D.C. 20004
202-347-2279
Promotes the employment and the positive image of women in the broadcast media.

Tuning In

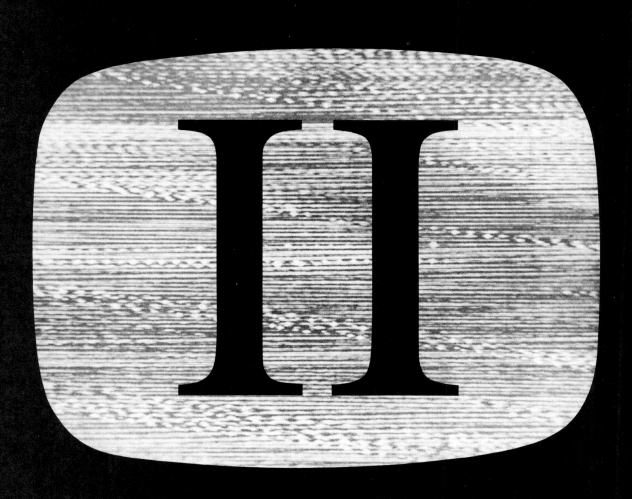

Calling the Shots

In the game of commercial television there are three major groups of players, each with its own special interests: broadcasters, the federal government, and the American public. The broadcasters (the networks, the cable operators, the videodisc and cassette makers, and so forth) are concerned with reaching the largest target audience possible and achieving maximum profits for their stockholders. Government agencies like the Federal Communications Commission are mandated to oversee how the broadcast industry works and to see that the public interest is served. Finally, there is the public, each segment of which has its own particular needs and wishes as TV is concerned.

The most important words in the broadcast industry are contained in a phrase that is part of the Communications Act of 1934. It was this act that created the Federal Communications Commission, and that agency and that act still regulate how television operates today. The seven words are part of a key sentence stating that, in exchange for free use of the airwaves, those who receive licenses to broadcast must operate "in the public interest, convenience, and necessity." This phrase, known as the public interest standard, is the main link between the broadcasters' responsibility to the Ameri-

A Hertz is Not an Avis

Frequency is a measure of the number of cycles, or complete vibrations, per second of a radio wave. A cycle is one complete performance of a vibration and is equal to a *Hertz*. Each TV channel is 6 MegaHertz wide.

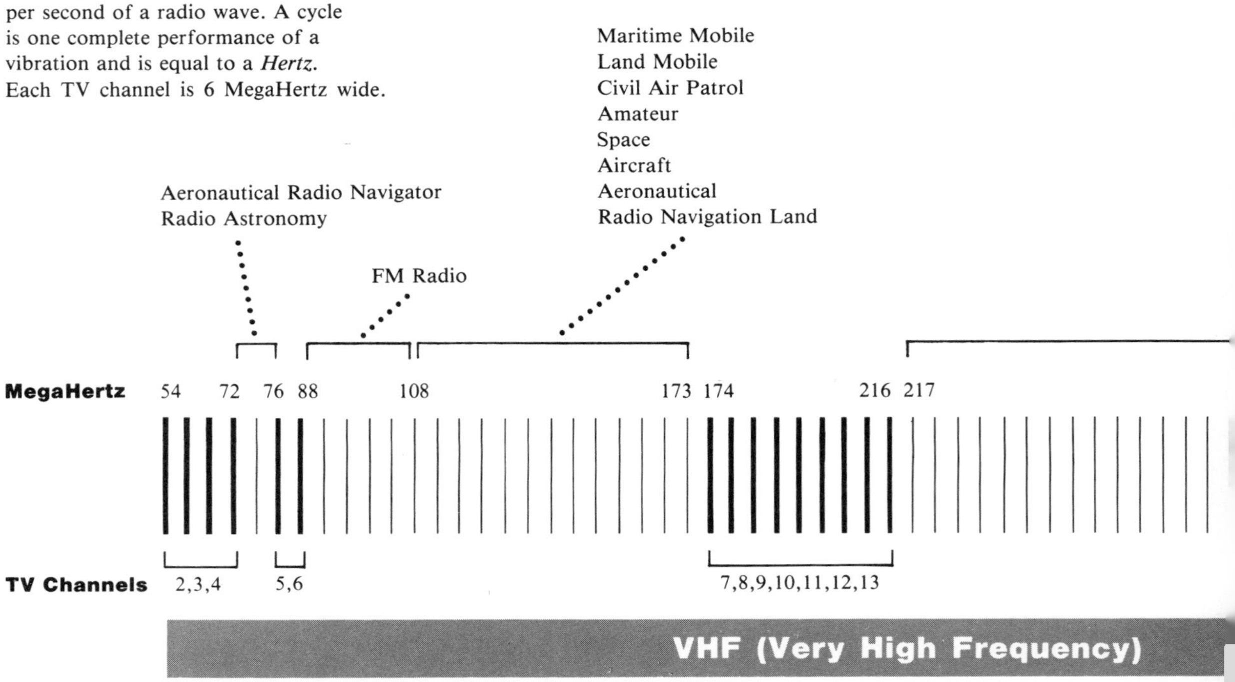

Maritime Mobile
Land Mobile
Civil Air Patrol
Amateur
Space
Aircraft
Aeronautical
Radio Navigation Land

Aeronautical Radio Navigator
Radio Astronomy

FM Radio

| MegaHertz | 54 | 72 | 76 | 88 | 108 | 173 | 174 | 216 | 217 |

TV Channels   2,3,4   5,6   7,8,9,10,11,12,13

VHF (Very High Frequency)

can public and the needs of the American people. Without the public interest standard, Americans would lose their best legal argument for responsible television service.

Yet the public interest standard has never been effectively enforced, possibly because no one really knows what the public interest is. The FCC doesn't know. Nor do broadcasters. Nor do the 226,000,000 people who make up the American public. The FCC, for example, expects broadcasters to air news and public affairs programming in the public interest. But the FCC does not (nor should it) specify what the content of these or any other programs should be. Many broadcasters believe they are serving the public interest simply by offering to the American public programs that Americans demonstrate an interest in — by watching. Finally, the American public itself, that extraordinarily heterogeneous mass of people, represents a myriad of special interests, each

clamoring louder than the next for attention and service. No single one of their demands represents the public interest.

Instead, diversity is one essential service that the television system owes the American public. Only the greatest possible variety of program types, offered through the greatest possible number of technological media, will provide the public with sufficient choice. Those who created the American television system had it in their power to set up a system with the potential for a great deal of variety. But from the beginning, decisions limited rather than expanded viewer choice. One of the major reasons there has been so little diversity in commercial television is that the number of major commercial broadcast channels is so limited.

It didn't have to be that way. The ability to transmit television pictures was developed prior to World War II. All television at that time was

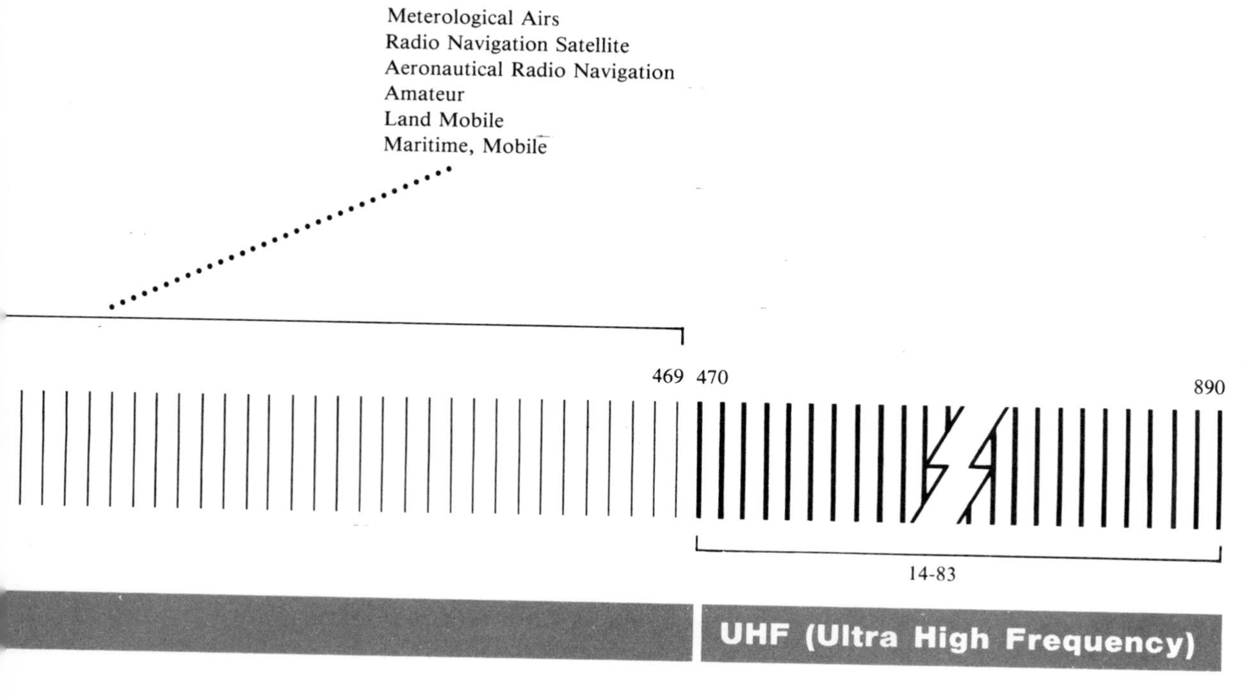

Meterological Airs
Radio Navigation Satellite
Aeronautical Radio Navigation
Amateur
Land Mobile
Maritime, Mobile

469 470   890

14-83

UHF (Ultra High Frequency)

sent out and received on the VHF (very high frequency) band. During the war the UHF (ultra high frequency) band was discovered. Many of those concerned with television in those days felt that, because the VHF band held only thirteen channels, it would be limiting to establish a national TV system on that band. Those who favored using the newly discovered UHF band, with its potential for up to seventy channels, urged the FCC to delay a decision until the practicality of UHF could be demonstrated.

Ironically, the main arguments for delay were based not on the fact that UHF would provide many more channels for broadcasters and the American public, but on the fact that CBS was frantically working to perfect a color system, one that would work only on the UHF band. RCA, CBS's chief rival, led the opposition, urging the FCC not to wait to see whether color TV was practical at that time but to push ahead immediately. The FCC took a full year to make its decision, and in March, 1947, it opted for the limited, thirteen-channel VHF system. This decision has proved to be one of the most fateful in broadcasting history. By restricting the number of available broadcast channels so severely, the FCC created a situation in which those who were able to gain initial control of these highways into the home obtained something very close to a TV monopoly. And it was an even bigger monopoly than the FCC or any of the broadcasters realized at the time. For it was soon discovered that Channel 1 was filled with police calls and other previously assigned frequencies and thus was impractical for broadcast use. Stations like the one in Trenton, New Jersey, that had been assigned to Channel 1, found themselves shut out of the system. That is why, to this date, New Jersey, the sixth most populous state in the nation, has no VHF station.

As soon as the FCC's decision was announced, hundreds of thousands of sets capable of receiving only VHF were produced and sold. The powerful corporations who were able to buy in at the beginning established a base of power that has grown so large that attempts to control it have, for the most part, proved ineffective. From that day the FCC decision was announced, UHF has been treated as a poor relative in the TV industry. It was not until 1953 that Congress passed a law requiring that all TV sets be capable of receiving UHF channels. And it was not until 1976 that Congress passed another law requiring manufacturers to equip all sets with automatic tuning devices for UHF as well as VHF.

Because airwave space on the VHF band is so limited, there are usually only three or four VHF stations in any given area. The three commercial networks have steadfastly avoided entering into any affiliate agreement with UHF stations where there are three or more VHF outlets operating. Under the American commercial TV system as it now operates, the UHF stations, because they have fewer viewers and consequently less advertising revenue, fill their programming schedule for the most part with old movies and reruns of series that once appeared on the networks. Of the approximately seven hundred and fifty commercial TV stations in this country, fewer than one hundred and fifty operate on the UHF band. How ironic—when one considers that there are only twelve channels available on very high frequency and seventy open for broadcasting on ultra high frequency.

The decision to use VHF instead of UHF was only one of a number of early decisions that limited television's diversity. It was apparent from the beginning that those who were "first in" to the broadcasting game were eventually going to make enormous amounts of money. There were those who favored charging broadcasters hefty sums for their licenses. The money collected could have been used to provide a funding base for public broadcasting so that it could become a significant part of the broadcast system. There were also those who proposed following the English example and charging the American public a tax on each TV set. This money, too, could have been used as a fund to encourage diverse programming.

Instead, TV's pioneers set up a system in which broadcasters would get free use of the airwaves. They would pay for their expenses and earn their profits by airing commercial messages. This, more than anything else, has led to the lack of variety in American television. In commercial television, it is imperative for sponsors to put the major portion of their money into those programs watched by the largest number of potential buyers for their products. And if the goal is simply to attract the largest audience day after day, then the broadcaster doesn't experiment, doesn't gamble, continues to air the same kinds of programs that have always delivered the biggest audiences.

Today for the first time there is a chance for the small audience to be served by television. Low power television stations, created to transmit within a radius of twelve to twenty-five miles, make it economical to target programs to distinct neighborhoods. Characterized by former FCC Chairman Charles B. Ferris as "the first new broadcast service considered by the FCC in twenty years," low power television (LPTV) could become a reality in the next few years.

Low power TV stations are relatively inexpensive to set up ($100,00 to $150,000, compared to $2 million for a VHF outlet). Thus it is possible for owners representing a variety of voices and interests to join the elite fraternity of broadcasters. This in fact was the purpose behind the initial conception of LPTV. In the first six months the FCC accepted franchise applications, the commission received more than three thousand requests.

Physically, low power stations are almost identical with facilities called translator stations that now exist in rural areas throughout the United States. Translator stations receive signals from a distant TV station and then rebroadcast them on a channel that is easier for viewers in the area to pick up. The difference between low power and translators is that low power is intended to originate programming.

From the beginning, public interest groups have been among the leading exponents of low power television. They see LPTV as a way for small communities to have a telecasting voice of their own. They also see the potential for minority groups to own and operate their own stations. This was one of the ideas behind the conception of the new system. However, among those requesting low power franchises from the FCC, there have been relatively few minority groups. Instead the list includes some of the most powerful corporations in the nation, many of whom are already in the broadcast industry. Requests for some one hundred and forty stations have been received from the Allstate Insurance Company, a subsidiary of Sears, Roebuck. The Turner Broadcasting System, owned by TV entrepreneur Ted Turner, has applied for twenty-five stations in such major markets as New York, Los Angeles, Philadelphia, San Francisco, and Boston. And requests have been received from ABC and NBC.

The list does include applications from public interest groups such as the National Citizens Committee for Broadcasting, a Ralph Nader organization. And an experimental station in Washington, D.C., sending out Spanish-language programs to some fourteen thousand residents of a Hispanic neighborhood in the nation's capital, is already in operation. Once the FCC has completed its final rule-making, it remains to be seen whether low power TV fulfills its promise of adding a new type of ownership and new services to television—or whether it represents merely another lost opportunity for diversity, a chance swallowed up by the moguls of the telecommunications industry.

The Birth of the Networks

In 1919, Westinghouse, GE, and AT&T pooled their communications interests to form the Radio Corporation of America. David Sarnoff, who had been working for the Marconi Company, which had sold patent rights to RCA, became general manager for the newly formed company, beginning his 50-year career at its helm. The number of radio stations grew, and by 1926 the two largest multi-station groups were competing forces for dominance in the industry. AT&T, which owned 26, was led by station WEAF (now WNBC), and RCA, Westinghouse, and GE were led by WJZ in New York and WGY in Schenectady.

AT&T made a deal with RCA to get out of broadcasting in return for the exclusive right to maintain control of transmission. RCA bought WEAF and formed the NBC Red Network in 1927, composed of the station group formerly owned by AT&T. The NBC Blue Network was formed by the original RCA chain led by station WJZ, and national broadcasting was begun through AT&T land lines.

A rival network to NBC was formed in

What's in a Name?

TV Stations name themselves subject to the approval of their applications by the FCC. All stations east of the Mississippi start with the letter *W*. Stations in the west start with *K*, except for a few that retain their originally assigned call letters (KDKA in Pittsburgh, KYW in Philadelphia).

All call names must include four letters (35,152 possible combinations) except for some early stations that have three, such as WOW Omaha, WHO Des Moines, and KGO San Francisco.

The FCC assigns about 12,000 combinations to broadcasters, and the rest are given to maritime and other communications services. If a ship gets decommissioned, a TV station can apply for its call letters and vice versa. (It's considered poor judgment to go after the call letters of a ship that has sunk!) There are five categories of names:

1. The initials or favorite slogan of the original station licensee, or of the present owner, or heroes of the owners, i.e. WCJB Gainesville: B is for Bill Marshall, the original owner, J is for his wife, Jo, and C is for their dog, Candy; WPTF-TV Durham: We Protect the Family, the slogan of Durham Life Insurance, the original owner.

2. The city or home state contracted or abbreviated, i.e.:

    WPGH-TV Pittsburgh
    WAGA-TV Atlanta
    WTOL-TV Toledo
    WATR-TV Waterbury

3. The channel assignment written in Roman numerals, i.e.:

    KIII-TV Corpus Christi (Channel 3, also known as the *I*'s of Texas)
    WLVI-TV Boston (Channel 56)

4. Words that conjure up an image of the station's coverage area:

    KAVE Carlsbad (caverns)
    KORN Nebraska (corn country)

5. Promotional or advertising stratagems, i.e.:

    WISH-TV (We wish you a . . .)
    KEZI-TV (For easy viewing . . .)

Here are a few of the more interesting call letter origins ▶

1927 by Louis Sterling of Columbia Phonograph Company, who bought out the United Independent Broadcasters and changed the name to Columbia Phonograph Broadcasting System. The Company changed hands and name (to CBS) once more before being bought out by an ad man for one of the CBS sponsors, the Congress Cigar Company, which had more than doubled cigar sales to 1 million per day in six months of radio advertising. The ad man was 26-year-old William S. Paley, who bought a lead station (WABC) in New York and reorganized the Company into a profitable network within two years.

In 1930, RCA got the GE and Westinghouse holdings of NBC because of anti-trust pressures. In 1941, the FCC, pressured by complaints from another newly formed small network, the Mutual Broadcasting System, said they would not license any station affiliated with a company that owned two networks. So in 1943, NBC was forced to sell out their weak Blue Network, bought by Edward J. Noble, the founder of Life Savers, who renamed the Blue the American Broadcasting Company. *TV Factbook*

WIOD Miami	(Wonderful Isle of Dreams)
WOW Omaha	(Woodmen of the World)
WZZM-TV Grand Rapids	(Letters chosen because upside down they read the same.)
WIS-TV Columbia	(Wonderful Iodine State)
WLS-TV Chicago	(World's Largest Store. The original radio station was owned by Sears)
WMBB-TV Panama City	(World's Most Beautiful Beaches)
WSEE-TV Erie	("See TV" as in "Watch television")
WGCD (am) Chester SC	(Wonderful Guernsey Center of Dixie)
WMTC (am) Vancleve, KY	(Win Men to Christ)
WLNE Providence	(We Love New England)
KHJ-TV Los Angeles	(Kindness, Happiness and Joy)
KOA-TV Denver	(Klear Over America. 50,000 watt clear radio channel)
KSBW-TV Salinas/Monterey	(Because of high productivity in artichokes and lettuce called "Salad Bowl of the World")
KUPK (Satellite of KAKE Wichita)	(Referred to locally as Kup-Kake)
CFL Chicago	(Chicago Federation of Labor)
KWAK Stuttark Arkansas	(Wild duck country)
WGN Chicago	(World's Greatest Newspaper, Chicago Tribune)
KALB-TV Alexandria LA	(Know Alexandria, Louisiana Better)
KGW-TV Portland Oregon	(Key to the Great West)
KVOA-TV Tuscon	(Kindly Voice of Arizona)
KWTV Oklahoma City	(World's Tallest Video, which it was in 1954 when it was built: 1,575')
KYEL-TV Yuma	(Keeps You Entertained Lovingly)
WIBW-TV Topeka	(Where Investment Brings Wealth)
WKOW-TV Madison, Wisconsin	(Called America's Dairyland)

P.D. Cue

The Providers of Television

American Commercial Broadcasters

American television broadcasters have a responsibility to entertain, inform, and educate the public. They have a responsibility to provide programming of varied content, at various times of the day, and in various formats. Programs should meet a wide range of racial, ethnic and religious interests and serve the needs of different age groups. Local broadcasters should strive to match programs to the specialized interests of their communities. At all levels of the television system, TV providers have the responsibility to encourage strong and healthy debate on controversial issues by airing all sides of

What's in a Network

	ABC	CBS	NBC
TV Stations	WABC-TV New York WLS-TV Chicago WXYZ-TV Detroit KABC-TV Los Angeles KGO-TV San Fran.	WCBS-TV New York KNXT-TV Los Angeles WBBM-TV Chicago KMOX-TV St. Louis WCAU-TV Phila.	WNBC-TV New York KNBC-TV Los Angeles WMAQ-TV Chicago WRC-TV Washington, D.C. WKYC-TV Cleveland
TV Affiliates	239	198	213
AM Radio Stations	WABC New York KABC Los Angeles WXYZ Detroit KGO San Fran. WLS Chicago WMAL Washington, D.C.	WCBS New York WBBM Chicago KNX Los Angeles WCAU Phila. WEEI Boston KMOX St. Louis KCBS San Fran.	WNBC New York WMAQ Chicago WRC Washington, D.C. KNBR San Fran.
FM Radio Stations	WPLJ New York KLOS Los Angeles WRCK Chicago KSFX San Fran. WRIF Detroit KSRR Houston WRQX Washington, D.C.	WCBS New York WBBM Chicago KNX Los Angeles WCAU Phila. WEEI Boston KMOX St. Louis KCBS San Fran.	WYNY New York WKQX Chicago WKYS Washington, D.C. KYUU San Fran.
Radio Affiliates	1,728	198	291

complex political, social, economic, and religious questions that affect television viewers on a local, regional, or national level.

This sounds like an idealized view. But it is what those who created the system had in mind when they mandated that broadcasters must operate "in the public interest, convenience and necessity." It is why the TV broadcasting system was set up with local programming paramount. Each local station is licensed for the purpose of meeting the needs of a particular community. When the system was established it was believed that a multiplicity of local stations would ensure competition and quality service for the public. It is the local station that holds the license, not the network. The network is basically a program supplier for its affiliates.

Making the local stations paramount in the television system was a good idea. As it worked out, it was a good idea that went wrong. The reason is simple: the networks have come to dominate the system because network affiliation has proved to be the most efficient and highly profitable way for local stations to operate.

Local stations can be owned by private individuals or corporations or by one of the national networks. The networks are allowed by law to own no more than five local stations. (They each do. These network-owned-and-operated stations, known as O & Os, are located in the top markets in the country.) Some corporations own a small group of stations

Tuna Fish Music—What One Network Conglomerate (CBS) Owns

CBS TV Network
CBS Entertainment
CBS Sports
CBS News
CBS TV O & O's
CBS Radio
CBS Cable
CBS Records Division
    (Records and music publishing)
CBS Records International Division
CBS Columbia House
    (Columbia Record and Tape Club, Mail Order)
CBS Video Enterprises
CBS Musical Instruments Division
CBS Specialty Stores Division
CBS Toys
CBS Educational and Professional Publishing
CBS Consumer Publishing
CBS Technology Center
CBS Theatrical Films Division

Principal Subsidiaries
April Music
CBS/Arbiter Ltd.
CBS Australia Pty., Ltd.
CBS Columbia C.A.
CBS Dischie S.p.A.
CBS International S.A.

CBS Musical Instruments, Ltd.
CBS Records Canada, Ltd.
CBS/Sony, Inc.
CBS United Kingdom, Ltd.
Lyon and Healy, Harps, Inc.
Steinway & Sons
WB Saunders Comp. Canada, Ltd.
Editora Interamericana, SA.
Interamericana Commercial S.A.
Blackwood Music, Inc.
Fawcett Input Centre (Barbados), Ltd.
5152 Ground Floor, Inc.
Riverfront Redevelopment Corp.
Gabriel Industries (Far East), Ltd. (toys)
Holt-Saunders, Inc.
Holt-Saunders Pty., Ltd.
Holt-Rinehart & Winston of Canada, Ltd.
Winston Press, Inc.
National Handcraft Institute, Inc.
World Tennis, Inc. (World Tennis Magazine)
Popular Library (paperback books)
Bond Publishing Co.
Parkhurst Publishing
Tuna Fish Music
Pacific Stereo (chain audio equipment)

Standard & Poor's, 1981

All in the Family Tree

Too Close for Comfort

Courtesy of "Too Close for Comfort"

The Love Boat

Lou Grant

Rhoda

Charles Beier/Richard Lyons

Phyllis

Courtesy of
MTM Enterprises, Inc.

The Mary Tyler Moore Show

One of television's most successful programming strategies is to spin off other series from an original hit program. The popularity of the characters in "The Mary Tyler Moore Show" led to "Lou Grant," "Rhoda," and "Phyllis." Other cast members Gavin MacLeod and Ted Knight were also given their own shows. Norman Lear's "All in the Family" led to "The Jeffersons," "Archie Bunker's Place," "Gloria," and "Maude." "Maude" in turn begat "Good Times," and Maude's neighbor Conrad Bain was rewarded with a series of his own.

Good Times

Diff'rent Strokes

Maude

The Jeffersons

Archie Bunker's Place

Gloria

All in the Family

around the country, up to a legal limit of seven. Westinghouse Broadcasting Company is one such broadcast group or mininetwork; others include Metromedia, Cox, and Meredith.

Hundreds of local television stations are *affiliated* with one of the three national networks. This means that they are paid by the network to run a certain amount of the programming generated or supplied by the network. Approximately 85 percent of all the commercial television stations in the United States are affiliated with CBS, ABC, or NBC. Each network has somewhere between two hundred and two hundred and fifty affiliates.

A network gets its stock of programs in a variety of ways: on tape from independent production companies (such as Paramount or Tandem/TAT or MTM Enterprises), live from its own studios (news, live sports, live late-night telecasts), or live from remote locations—including those beamed by satellite to the N.Y. transmitting center. Any live telecast can be stored on tape to be sent out at another time. From this range of shows, the network decides its programming schedule.

The network, in turn, acts as a distributor to the local TV stations, feeding programs via telephone lines (a service that costs each network about $15 million per year). The local affiliate stations, in turn, can accept or reject the programming the network offers, but they aren't allowed to bring in programming from the other two networks. During an average broadcast day, an affiliate station takes approximately 60 percent of its programming from the network; during prime time that figure rises to nearly 100 percent. In return for airing the programs (thereby adding to the enormous audience for national sponsors' products) the affiliates are paid by the networks at a rate negotiated individually with each station. This rate depends on the size of the market, the ratings of network programs on the station, and the competition in that particular market. Each year almost 15 percent of the total revenue from network sales advertising is paid to the affiliates for carrying network programs.

The network system has worked to the financial benefit of both the networks and the

Behind the Credits

The people behind the cameras on any given TV show far outnumber those we see on the TV screen. A full TV crew includes a producer, a director, associate producers and directors, film or tape editors, audio engineers, lighting directors, scenic designers, camera men and

The scenic crews assemble the sets.

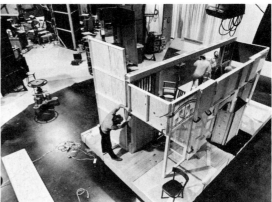

Photos: James Scherer for WGBH

The director calls the shots from the control room.

women, and a host of others. In TV, unlike the movies, the producer is the one actually responsible for making a television program. The producer takes the original idea, shapes the program and oversees every aspect of its production. The director has the job of putting the show physically on the air (choosing camera shots, directing the movement of the actors and actresses, etc.). Television production has become so expensive that it is common to have a particular show or series produced jointly by more than one company.

Television programs (pictures and sound) are recorded on the various kinds of video and audio tape and film shown here.

The below-the-scenes crew at work.

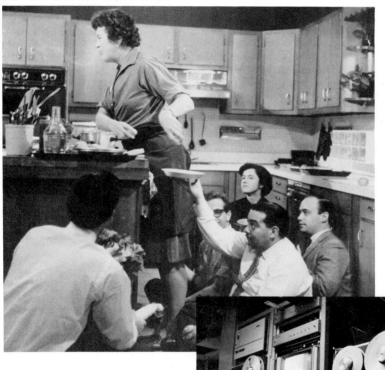

"The French Chef," Paul Child for WGBH

The videotape machine records the shows for broadcast, editing, or storage for later broadcast.

Making Up the Program Menu

It is the quantifiable audience and not the quality of programs that determines program selection. Various tactics have emerged to capture the audience and try to keep it.

Audience Flow
Once the set is on, the audience "flows" from one program to the next on the same channel, provided the programs are basically compatible to one another.

Block Programming
The attempt to precipitate a good audience flow by booking several like shows in tandem, for instance, several half-hour sitcoms. A network may book a couple of sit coms after similar hit shows on another network to divert the audience flow to their station.

Hammocking
Linking two strong shows with a weaker (or brand new) one in between. (Why get up to change the channel, it's only a half hour!)

Counterprogramming
Scheduling a different kind of show than the program on the other two commercial networks.

Blunting
Scheduling similar programs as the other networks to reduce the ratings of their programs.

Bridging
Attempting to capture the audience by choosing a show with a long running time and airing it just before the start of other prime fare.

local stations. The networks need the local stations so they can guarantee advertisers that their commercial messages will be seen across the country by large audiences. For a local station, in turn, it is easier and a great deal less expensive to push a button and "pipe in" a network offering than to create a program of its own. And the shows that are network-distributed are more lavishly prepared and promoted than most local offerings. Thus all an affiliate has to do to make a guaranteed profit is to supply air time to the network.

Not all local stations are affiliated with the networks, however. Because a network can have only one affiliate in each market, there are about one hundred and fifty commercial stations that are operated independently. These stations often host local professional athletic teams and show a hefty diet of movies, but they get the bulk of their programming from syndication services (which affiliates also use to fill out their schedules).

Such a service buys the rights to a show or, quite often, to reruns of a show, and sells them to stations. Therefore, it is possible that while first-run M*A*S*H episodes are carried on CBS affiliates only, you'll find the show's reruns on a variety of other affiliate and independent stations. Syndicated shows are usually profitable, attracting local advertisers.

Affiliate and nonaffiliate stations do provide some programming of their own. Local newscasts are big money-makers for many stations. They attract both local and national advertisers and give the local station the opportunity to create a star system and an identity of its own. But aside from newscasts, quality local programming is rare, and most locally produced shows are aired at times when audience level is at its lowest. It is with low-cost, unimaginative programs (mostly interview shows, referred to in the industry as "talking heads") that most local stations fulfill the promises upon which they base their applications for broadcast license renewal.

There are some notable exceptions. WCVB in Boston has built a national reputation based on its commitment to local programming. Some of this station's programs and series have been syndicated throughout the United States. For the past decade WCVB has been one of the most financially successful stations in the country. In 1982 Metromedia purchased the station for $220 million, the highest amount of money in television history for a sale of this kind. Whether Metromedia, the fourth largest broadcast group in the nation, will continue to pursue WCVB's commitment to local programming remains to be seen, but in any case, the Boston station has shown the industry that a local station can produce quality programs without sacrificing financial success. The Westinghouse broadcasting stations have demonstrated a similar commitment to local service. Under the leadership of Donald McGannon, this station group has developed an innovative way to add diversity to children's television. Each of its five stations is required to produce a children's

series, with an exchange process set up between the stations, so more children will benefit from these award-winning productions.

Yet such commitment is rare. In America today, a license to operate a television station is practically tantamount to a license to print money. Most local TV stations are enormously profitable. Yet they are rarely called to task for how well they uphold their responsibility to serve the public.

The one device that could be used to make station owners and managers accountable for their performance is the broadcast license renewal process. Unfortunately, the renewal of licenses has been made easier rather than more difficult in recent years. Until 1981 license renewal took place every three years. Station owners, if for no other reason than to enhance their renewal application, were aware that toward the end of the license period they needed to insert local and public service programming into their schedules. In 1981 the duration of a station's license was extended by Congress to five years, giving owners an even longer time to operate without feeling accountable.

Furthermore, the renewal process itself has been made easier. Previously, station owners

Syndication. Two of TV's most successful syndicated series have been "Gilligan's Island" and "The Lawrence Welk Show." Syndication companies own the rights to shows either specifically produced for them or sold to them after their original network airings.

Program Progeny

What do the hit series "M*A*S*H," "Alice," "Private Benjamin," and "Fame" have in common? They all originated as motion pictures. And, reversing the usual pattern, the TV series "Star Trek" has spawned two movies to date.

From the television series "Fame," © 1982 Metro-Goldwyn-Mayer Film Company.

The Art of the Spinoff

TV spin-offs come in a variety of
forms. Both ''Laverne and
Shirley'' and ''Happy Days,'' for
example, have their own TV cartoon
counterparts. And it is not uncommon
for casts of old-time favorites to be re-
united for special shows like ''The
Father Knows Best Reunion.'' The
ultimate spin-off? ''The Steeler and
the Pittsburgh Kid,'' a one hour network drama based on characters in a
soft drink commercial.

National Broadcasting Company, Inc.

Courtesy of NBC

were required to fill out long, detailed questionnaires, providing documentation of their performance under their current licensing agreements. The FCC has now eliminated this form and replaced it with questions contained on a postcard-size form. (In broadcast circles the process is now referred to as "postcard renewal.") The FCC's rationale for this change is that by randomly selecting a few stations each year to fill out a detailed questionnaire, it can keep all commercial stations in the industry on their toes, since no station will know if it is likely to be selected for scrutiny in any given year.

Many of the groups concerned about television having voiced objections to the short-

ened license renewal form. Public interest groups had succeeded in getting significant questions about children's programming included in the detailed license renewal forms. The fact that the answers given to the questions on these forms were a matter of public record meant that private citizens had access to information about the kind of service broadcasters were providing and to discrepancies in reporting. For example, it was pointed out at one public hearing on children's television that a particular station was listing the "Our Gang" comedies as an example of integrated programming—at the very time these programs were under attack by the NAACP as racist. By eliminating the detailed renewal form, the FCC has all but removed one of the public's most important opportunities to check on the performance of local stations.

The old and the new. The twenty-one-page station license renewal form, the cover of which appears on the right, has been replaced with the current short form, shown on the left.

FCC Form 303
December 1976

Approved by GAO
B-180227(RO-173)

United States of America
FEDERAL COMMUNICATIONS COMMISSION

APPLICATION FOR RENEWAL OF LICENSE
FOR COMMERCIAL TELEVISION BROADCAST STATION

INSTRUCTIONS

A. This form is to be used in all cases when applying for Renewal of Commercial Television Broadcast Station License. It consists of the following sections:

Section I — General Information
Section II — Legal and Financial
Section III — Engineering
Section IV — Statement of TV Program Service
Section V — Equal Employment Opportunity

B. Prepare and file three copies of this form and all exhibits with the Federal Communications Commission, Washington, D.C. 20554.

C. Number exhibits serially in the space provided in the body of the form. Date each exhibit. The date must be the same or preceding the date of the renewal applicant's certification of FCC Form 303. Each exhibit should set forth the name and official title, if any, of the officer or employee by whom or under whose direction the exhibit was prepared.

D. The name of the applicant must be stated exactly as it appears on the current license.

E. Information called for by this application which is already on file with the Commission need not be refiled in this application provided: (1) the information is now on file in another application or FCC form filed by or on behalf of this applicant; (2) the information is identified fully by reference to the file number (if any), the FCC form number, and the filing date of the application or other form containing the information and the page or paragraph referred to; and (3) after making the reference, the applicant states: "No change since date of filing." Any such reference will be considered to incorporate into this application all information, confidential or otherwise, contained in the application or other form referred to. The incorporated application or other form will thereafter, in its entirety, be open to the public.

F. This application shall be personally signed by the applicant, if the applicant is an individual; by one of the partners, if the applicant is a partnership; by an officer, if the applicant is a corporation; by a member who is an officer, if the applicant is an unincorporated association; by such duly elected or appointed officials as may be competent to do so under the laws of the applicable jurisdiction, if the applicant is an eligible government entity; or by the applicant's attorney, if the applicant is absent from the United States. The attorney shall, in the event he signs for the applicant, separately set forth the reason why the application is not signed by the applicant. In addition, if any matter is stated on the basis of the attorney's belief only (rather than his knowledge), he shall separately set forth his reasons for believing that such statements are true.

G. BE SURE ALL NECESSARY INFORMATION IS FURNISHED AND ALL PARAGRAPHS ARE FULLY ANSWERED. IF ANY PORTIONS OF THE APPLICATION ARE NOT APPLICABLE, SPECIFICALLY SO STATE. DEFECTIVE OR INCOMPLETE APPLICATIONS MAY BE RETURNED WITHOUT CONSIDERATION.

H. A legible copy of this application and all exhibits submitted therewith shall be kept on file available for public inspection at any time during regular business hours. It shall be maintained at the main studio of the station or any other accessible place (such as a public registry for documents or an attorney's office) in the community in which the station is licensed.

File No. BRCT-

FOR COMMISSION USE ONLY

SECTION I - GENERAL INFORMATION

1. NAME OF APPLICANT

STREET ADDRESS

CITY

STATE

ZIP CODE

Send notices and communications to the following named person at the address indicated below:

NAME

STREET ADDRESS

CITY

STATE

ZIP CODE

2. Renewal requested for following existing facilities:

Call Letters

Frequency

Channel No.

POWER IN KILOWATTS
NIGHT

DAY

HOURS OF OPERATION
☐ UNLIMITED   ☐ LIMITED

Sharing with (specify stations)

☐ DAYTIME ONLY

Other (specify)

STATION LOCATION
CITY

STATE

3. Renewal is also requested for the following:

☐ AUXILIARY ANTENNA

☐ AUXILIARY TRANSMITTER

☐ ALTERNATE TRANSMITTER

SECTION II - LEGAL AND FINANCIAL

1. Is applicant's Ownership Report (FCC Form 323) filed with this application?

☐ YES   ☐ NO   If NO, give the date of filing of the last Ownership Report _____ and the station's call letters _____ of the renewal application with which it was filed.

2. Is the applicant in compliance with the provisions of Section 310 of the Communication's Act of 1934, as amended, relating to the interests of aliens and foreign governments?

☐ YES   ☐ NO

3. Is the applicant or any officer, director, or principal stockholder (any person owing 25% or more of applicant's stock) an officer, director, or 25% or more stockholder in a newspaper publishing company, a CATV company, or a company engaged in broadcasting related activities?

☐ YES   ☐ NO   If YES, attach as Exhibit No. _____ a complete listing and description of those interests.

4. Since the filing of the applicant's last renewal application for this station or other major application, has an adverse finding been made or final action been approved by any court or administrative body with respect to the applicant or parties to the application concerning any civil or criminal suit, action, or proceeding, brought under the provisions of any federal, state, territorial or local law relating to the following: any felony; lotteries; unlawful restraints and monopolies; unlawful combinations, contracts or agreements in restraint of trade; the use of unfair methods of competition; fraud; unfair labor practices; or discrimination?

☐ YES   ☐ NO   If YES, attach as Exhibit No. _____ a full description, including identification of the court or administrative body, the proceeding by file number, the person and matters involved, and the disposition of the litigation.

5. Attach as Exhibit No. _____ a detailed balance sheet of the applicant as at the close of a month within 90 days of the date of this application.

Public Broadcasting

In 1967 a Carnegie Commission report recommended that educational television should be expanded into a public broadcasting system that provided an alternative service to that provided by commercial TV. The report stated that the creation of this system would be in keeping with the true purpose of television, which ". . . should serve more fully both the mass audience and the many separate audiences that constitute in their aggregate our American society."

The Carnegie report was received enthusiastically by Congress and before the year was out the Public Broadcasting Act of 1967 was passed, creating the Corporation for Public Broadcasting, with the task of setting policies for a national public broadcasting service and channeling funds for programming to the individual stations.

Today, less than twenty years after its creation, supporters of public broadcasting point with pride to a variety of programs the system has brought to the American audience. Series such as "Masterpiece Theater," "Nova," "The MacNeil/Lehrer Report," and "Sesame Street," have been some of television's finest moments.

Yet despite these accomplishments, public broadcasting today finds itself in a major crisis. Seriously short of funds, facing severe challenges from cable TV and other new technologies, and finding itself the target of criticism from both sides of the political spectrum, public broadcasting's situation is grave. There are those both inside and outside the broadcast industry who believe that its very existence is in jeopardy.

By far the biggest problem that public broadcasting faces concerns money. There are

Public broadcasting has brought a wide variety of programs into American homes. Shows like "The MacNeil/Lehrer Report," "Sesame Street," "Brideshead Revisited," "The French Chef," "Crockett's Victory Garden," "The Scarlet Letter," and "The Dick Cavett Show" have provided viewers with some of television's finest moments.

Don Perdue for "The MacNeil/Lehrer Report"

"Brideshead Revisited," Granada Television International

"Crockett's Victory Garden"

"The Scarlet Letter," William Baker for WGBH

"The French Chef," Paul Child for WGBH

three models that can be used to describe the way public broadcasting stations get their programs. In Model A, programming is supplied free of charge to all public broadcasting stations in the country. This is made possible by the fact that the cost of this programming is paid for by a single source. For example the entire tab for "Masterpiece Theater" is picked up by the Mobil Oil Corporation. Similarly, "Washington Week in Review" is paid for by the Ford Motor Company, and the National Geographic specials are totally underwritten by the Gulf Oil Corporation. In a variation of Model A, multiple funders provide the finances for a particular program or series. The series "Cosmos" was funded by the Atlantic Richfield Corporation, the National Science Foundation, and the Corporation for Public Broadcasting.

In Model B, public broadcasting stations around the country decide that certain programming is so important that they will put their own money into seeing that it gets on the air. Under a system called Station Program Cooperative (SPC), stations vote on whether or not money from their cooperative pool (some $30 million in 1981) should be used to produce certain shows or series. Voting influence for the various programs is based on station size (WNET in New York had 5 percent of the vote, whereas certain small stations have less than 1 percent). Even after a majority of the stations have voted to underwrite a series, there is often not enough money to fully fund the production. Outside funds are then sought to make up the difference. The series "Nova" is funded with $4 million from the Station Program Cooperative and $1 million from the Johnson & Johnson Company. "The MacNeil/Lehrer Report" is produced with over $5 million from the SPC and another $1 million each from Exxon Corporation and American Telephone and Telegraph. Sometimes, as in the case of "Great Performances," outside funders actually contribute more money than SPC. That series re-

ceives $1.3 million from the cooperative and $3 million from Exxon.

Model C is employed when the stations themselves put up the entire cost of a program. Examples of this type of financing are few and far between, but the popular series "Sneak Previews" was funded in this way.

In a time of economic hardship, in a nation governed by an administration openly committed to slashing PBS funding to the bone, public broadcasting finds itself cutting back programs, laying off employees, and searching desperately for ways to survive. There are many who now believe that the Carnegie report's vision of a workable alternative to commercial television was doomed when Congress failed to appropriate the enormous amount of money needed to allow public broadcasting to compete effectively with commercial TV. PBS has always suffered from the fact that only 107 of the system's 274 stations operate on the VHF band. There are those who contend that if the PBS outlet in Washington D.C. had been a VHF rather than a weak-signaled UHF station, United States senators and congressman would have been better able to judge for themselves the merits of PBS programs, and the system would have had a better chance of getting the funding it needed.

Whatever the reasons for the lack of support for PBS, the money raised by public broadcasting from private viewers, corporate underwriters, and the federal government is simply not enough to meet its present and future needs. Even a $150 million grant ($10 million a year for fifteen years) from *TV Guide* publisher Walter Annenberg to develop college courses for credit on television is not enough to ease the financial burden.

Educational programming has always been one of PBS's most important functions. And the quality of the educational fare offered by the system is first-rate. Yet here too there is a real financial problem. Money for educational children's programs has become increasingly difficult for PBS to get. Corporations, in general, have no incentive to reach children with a message designed to improve their corporate image, and the Office of Education, which has always been a chief funder of educational programming, faces a highly uncertain funding future of its own.

The issue of the direction in which PBS should now be headed in this new economic climate has become the subject of much debate. Critics of the system have stated that public broadcasting, particularly in recent years, has focused too heavily on national programming. A recent Carnegie Commission report criticized PBS for its lack of commitment to local programs and issues. Yet many supporters of PBS maintain that the only way it will survive is by putting even more emphasis on nationally acclaimed programs such as ''Life on Earth'' and ''Masterpiece Theatre.'' Michael Rice, senior fellow of the Aspen Institute, who worked for thirteen years as a station executive in public broadcasting, takes the position that ''. . . apart from the occasional special, local programming on public television has not per-

suaded viewers of its indispensable value. Except in rare instances [the programs] are of marginal value and disproportionate expense.''

Public broadcasting has been the target of other criticism that upon close examination is unfair. PBS has been charged with elitism, with concentrating on programs that appeal to what has been termed the American aristocracy. Yet according to a 1980 Nielsen survey, more than 68 percent of *all* American households watch public television for some part of a week and almost 60 percent of these households are families with incomes under $15,000. Other critics point to the fact that PBS's programs consistently draw a smaller audience than the shows on the three commercial networks. This too is unfair. Those who criticize public broadcasting because they feel it doesn't measure up in the ratings game fail to take into account the fact that public broadcasting is playing a different

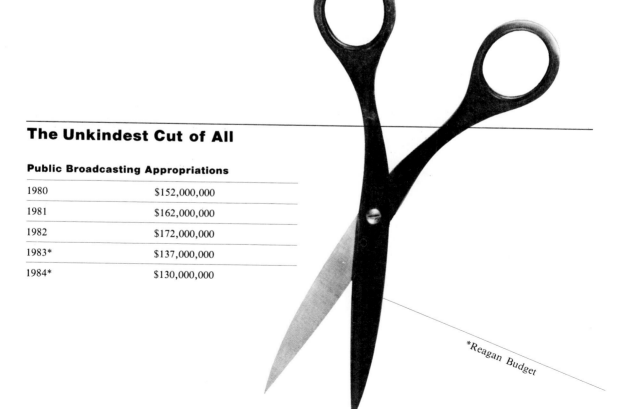

The Unkindest Cut of All

Public Broadcasting Appropriations

1980	$152,000,000
1981	$162,000,000
1982	$172,000,000
1983*	$137,000,000
1984*	$130,000,000

*Reagan Budget

Among the most heralded of all of television's ongoing series, PBS's "Masterpiece Theatre" has brought some of the world's best actors and stories to the TV screen. Shown here are scenes from "Upstairs, Downstairs," "I, Claudius," and "A Town Like Alice."

Henry Crawford Associates, New South Wales, Australia

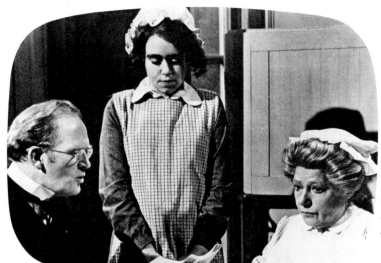

London Weekend Television Photo

BBC/London Films

game. It was created as an alternative to the commercial networks, not as a competitor.

If it is to survive, public broadcasting must find a way out of its financial dilemma. What can be done? Some of the larger PBS stations are setting up divisions to sell programs to cable TV and to videodisc and video cassette companies. There have been increased calls for the imposition of a spectrum-use tax (a fee for the use of public airwaves) on commercial broadcasters by those who feel that, if PBS is to be properly funded, then the time has finally come for the use of such a tax to guarantee its existence.

In 1982 Congress authorized an eighteen-month experiment whereby ten PBS stations were permitted to raise funds by airing low-key forms of commercial advertising. The stations were allowed to sell time for ads that look much like those on commercial stations and were also permitted to offer expanded corporate underwriting credits to companies that fund PBS programs. Previously, if the Burpee Seed Company underwrote a program, its credit was limited to a simple "Funding for this program was provided by the Burpee Corporation." Under the new arrangement, the company's logo can be shown and a brief tagline— ". . . manufacturers of seeds for gardens all across America"—can also be included.

While it could indeed help ease the financial situation, the new policy would, in the long run, cause additional problems. The appearance of ads in public broadcasting would erode PBS's two major funding sources. There would no longer be a public policy rationale for giving federal grants to the system, and the appearance of commercials could cause some of PBS's audience to stop sending its dollars to the so-called viewer-supported network. In addition, ads on public broadcasting might subject the system to the same ratings pressures as those of its commercial counterparts.

In what is probably the most far-reaching plan to date to solve the financial crisis, PBS President Lawrence Grossman has proposed the establishment of a new cultural pay-TV service to help fund PBS. Called the Public Sub-

scription Network, it would offer theater, art, dance, and opera to subscribers for somewhere between $10.00 and $13.00 a month. It would also sell these programs to cable, low power TV stations, and other subscription services. Says Grossman, "If the pay service can throw off enough money, it could subsidize the rest of the public television system."

Whatever the solution, public broadcasting's present and future are tied directly to its chief funder and regulator—the federal government.

There are several ways in which the government has a direct influence on public broadcasting. First of all, some of the PBS stations in this country are directly run by either state or local governments. Second, the members of the Corporation for Public Broadcasting are appointed by the President of the United States and are subject to confirmation by the Senate. This, combined with the fact that so much of PBS's funding comes out of the federal budget, means that public broadcasting is always directly affected by the attitudes of the administration in power.

There is no clearer example of this than the events that took place during the presidency of Richard Nixon. Documents now available through a Freedom of Information Act inquiry reveal that Mr. Nixon, convinced that public broadcasting was much too liberal, was determined to undermine it during his time in office. In 1971, speaking to a convention of public broadcasters, Clay T. Whitehead, director of the White House Office of Telecommunications Policy, openly stated the administration's displeasure. He warned the public broadcasters to give up any idea of becoming a "fourth network," and stated that any system that received public funds had no business airing news or public affairs programs.

Two months later President Nixon vetoed an important two-year funding bill for public broadcasting on the grounds that the system had become too centralized. Freedom of Information Act documents reveal that the President took this stance in response to a memorandum

Who Watches Public Television

Public TV distribution figures dispel
the myth that the Public Broadcasting audience is disproportionately
highbrow, high income, and white.
PBS, 1981

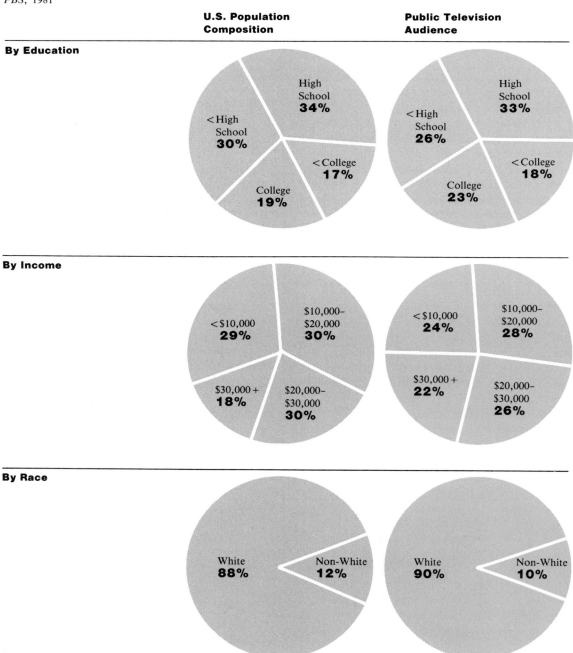

U.S. Population Composition   **Public Television Audience**

By Education

U.S. Population Composition:
- High School **34%**
- <College **17%**
- College **19%**
- <High School **30%**

Public Television Audience:
- High School **33%**
- <College **18%**
- College **23%**
- <High School **26%**

By Income

U.S. Population Composition:
- <$10,000 **29%**
- $10,000–$20,000 **30%**
- $20,000–$30,000 **30%**
- $30,000+ **18%**

Public Television Audience:
- <$10,000 **24%**
- $10,000–$20,000 **28%**
- $20,000–$30,000 **26%**
- $30,000+ **22%**

By Race

U.S. Population Composition:
- White **88%**
- Non-White **12%**

Public Television Audience:
- White **90%**
- Non-White **10%**

from Mr. Whitehead suggesting that decentralization would successfully weaken the system. "Exploiting the diverse issues that plague relationships in public broadcasting," Mr. Whitehead stated, "provides an opportunity to further our philosophical and political objectives for public broadcasting without appearing to be politically motivated." In desperate need of federal funds, public broadcasting responded by revamping its system so as to weaken the powers of the Corporation for Public Broadcasting, giving more power to local stations, which in the eyes of the Nixon Administration were more conservative.

In January, 1981, a Reagan transition team stated, "In this time of trying to balance budgets, putting a freeze on federal hiring, and getting a grip on inflation, it doesn't seem to be proper for the taxpayer to support the public broadcasting system. . . . There is no more basis for the federal government to play a leading role in supporting public television than there is for the government to play a similar role in the publication of novels or textbooks or in theatrical production."

Later that year the Reagan Administration's Office of Management and Budget, ignoring the fact that well over half of the nation's TV households watch some public television in any given week, stated, "The audiences of CPB-supported stations tend to be wealthier and more educated than the general populace; they certainly possess the personal resources to support such stations, and they should do so, if they want to enjoy the benefits of public broadcasting. Taxpayers as a whole should not be compelled to subsidize entertainment for a select few."

The 1979 Carnegie Commission declared that "Public broadcasting tried to invent a truly radical idea, an instrument of mass communication that simultaneously respects the artistry of the individuals who create programs, the needs of the public that forms the audience, and the forces of political power that supply the resources." There are millions of Americans who would agree with the Boston *Globe*'s editorial assessment that "public television is good at what it does. It is no more elitist than the public library. . . ." Television would suffer an extreme blow should public broadcasting be forced out of existence or weakened beyond recognition.

Religious Broadcasting

One of the most striking developments in television in recent years has been the appearance of a host of articulate, energetic religious leaders who have used the airways as a nationwide pulpit to put forth their messages and solicit funds for spreading their gospel. TV evangelists such as Jerry Falwell, Jim Bakker, and Pat Robertson have been able to attract enormous TV audiences while garnering more than $50 million apiece each year in the form of cash contributions sent in by their followers.

Religious broadcasting is, of course, not new to the airwaves. Radio provided an important outlet for preachers of every religion. And at the beginning, Sunday morning television featured religious broadcasters of every denomination. What *is* new is the fact that because these "prime time preachers" attract such large audiences and are so well financed, they have power unprecedented in the history of religious broadcasting.

The ministers of the electronic church have become live television professionals. Their studios, their equipment, their broadcasting facilities rival those of the major networks and independent stations. They have found that the talk show format is the most successful way for them to get their messages across and to appeal for the millions of dollars that come into their coffers on a regular basis. Talk shows are not the only types of programs that the new religious broadcasters have copied from their commercial counterparts. There are already fundamentalist Christian news and game shows, and the Christian Broadcasting Network (CBN) has developed "Another World,"

Prime Time Preachers (America's Top Television Evangelists)

Rank	Show	Preacher	Households
1	Oral Roberts & You	Oral Roberts	1,362,000
2	Hour of Power	Robert Schuller	1,255,000
3	Rex Humbard	Rex Humbard	1,247,000
4	Jimmy Swaggart, Evangelist	Jimmy Swaggart	947,000
5	Day of Discovery	Richard De Haan Paul Van Gorder	791,000
6	Old-Time Gospel Hour	Jerry Falwell	691,000
7	Insight	Drama by Paulist Fathers	523,000
8	Gospel Singing Jubilee	Gospel Music Entertainment	455,000
9	PTL Club (Praise the Lord)	Jim Bakker	413,000
10	It is Written	George Vanderman	368,000

Nielsen, May 1981

a Christian soap opera. Looking ahead to what they see as the unlimited future of religious broadcasting, television preachers have established special schools of communications, designed to develop Christian broadcasters who will spread their gospel with an ever-increasing degree of TV professionalism. CBN University already has a School of Communications, and telecasting skills are being taught at Jim Bakker's Heritage School of Evangelism and Communication, at Jerry Falwell's Liberty Baptist College, and at Oral Roberts University.

In their solicitation of funds the new religious broadcasters have discovered that the computer is as important to them as the television set. Highly sophisticated lists are kept of each contributor or potential contributor, as well as every person who writes to the program. Computers allow the religious broadcasters to mount enormous direct-mail fund-raising campaigns, crusades that bring in more than enough money to cover the multimillion-dollar costs of producing their TV programs.

Yet with all of the sophisticated techniques available, the basic method used by TV preachers to raise funds is the direct over-the-air appeal. Nationwide fund-raising telethons in which viewers are asked to ''save the ministry from imminent bankruptcy'' are held on a regular basis. Appearances by famous athletes and entertainment figures are featured (often accompanied by testimonials of miracles achieved through prayer). And week by week, millions of dollars are raised through the sales of books, records, tape recordings, and religious jewelry and art.

Most of these television evangelists represent fundamentalist, New Right, conservative religions. There are many observers, including a host of mainline religious leaders, who are deeply concerned about the stance these TV preachers take. They are disturbed primarily about the fact that the new TV evangelists seem —like Father Coughlin in the early 1940s—to be less proreligion than they are anti so many other things: certain books in school and public libraries, certain programs on television, and certain political candidates. Says Lutheran leader Reverend Charles Bergstrom, ''I don't think it's right to question someone's relationship with God on the basis of their political opinion.'' And Balfour Brickner, rabbi of the Stephen Wise Free Synagogue in New York City, writes of ''the incredible speed with which the new religious and political right has corralled the power they have to transform the American political process. . . . Advanced technology has given these crusaders an electronic horse on which they can reach any home and hamlet in America.''

The ideological battle concerning the New Right preachers is bound to escalate. New avenues of reaching television audiences, represented by the new TV technologies, are already being utilized by TV ministers. Perhaps the most alarming element in religious broadcasting is the fact that these developments could mean the end of religion as a public service on television. Instead, the airwaves would be dominated by those religions able to pay the most for access. And too often, the religions that can afford to pay are the ones that use air time to raise money.

The Role of Government

The Federal Communications Commission

As one of the institutions jointly responsible for the public interest, the government has the duty to encourage a diversity of highways for communication; to promote new technologies that will bring the public greater access to information; and to favor widespread ownership of communications services. Throughout the years there have been examples of effective government intervention in these areas. In 1962 the Federal Communications Commission ruled that all television manufacturers had to build click-dials for UHF channels into their television sets, improving the competitive position of UHF technology and guaranteeing increased public access to information. In 1981, the state cable commission in Connecticut barred the firm that owned the only newspaper in Hartford, Connecticut, from owning also the two cable television systems that serve the city. Continued government funding of public broadcasting is another way of increasing diversity by supporting alternative communications systems with program services not provided by commercial broadcasters.

The key government player in the game of television is the Federal Communications Commission. This agency traces its roots to the chaos that developed over the airwaves during the golden age of radio. By 1927 there were so many radio stations operating on so many uncontrolled frequencies that signals from one station constantly interfered with signals from another. To put order into the situation, the United States Congress established the Federal Radio Commission. This agency was given exclusive authority to license all radio stations and to require them to use a specified amount of power, to operate on a specified broadcast schedule, and to stay within an assigned frequency. Seven years later the Federal Radio Commission Act was amended and was replaced by the Communications Act of 1934. The name of the agency administering that act was changed to the Federal Communications Commission. It is this agency, headed by seven commissioners appointed by the President, that carries the government's responsibility for regulating how broadcasting works.

The FCC does not have unlimited powers. It cannot tell stations what they should broadcast. Actually, the only way in which the real extent of the powers of the FCC can be determined is through test cases in the courts. For example, in 1969, in the landmark *Red Lion Broadcasting Company* v. *The FCC,* the Supreme Court ruled that the FCC has a duty to *make certain* that broadcasters give adequate coverage to public issues and a duty to make

sure that both sides of an issue are presented. This case also established the concept that because the number of channels on commercial TV is so limited, and because there are so few broadcasters and so many viewers, broadcasters do not have rights that are ". . . comparable to the right of every individual to speak, write, or publish." In the case of television, said the Court, ". . . it is the right of the viewers and listeners which is paramount."

The FCC and the broadcasters have always had an interesting relationship. Through the years there has been criticism that the FCC has seemed friendlier to the TV industry it is supposed to regulate than to the public it is supposed to protect. The broadcast industry spends an enormous amount of money each year lobbying the FCC and other federal agencies and congressional committees. Almost all the major TV stations in the country are represented by Washington-based lawyers who, besides providing expert counsel, also do a great deal of lobbying.

There is, of course, nothing illegal about lobbying. It is a legitimate and time-honored way of operating within the political system. The problem is that the public as a whole is usually unfamiliar with FCC procedures. Thus the broadcasters are almost always at an advantage when dealing with this agency in matters that concern the "public interest." And concerned private citizens have neither the time nor the money it takes to counter the efforts of the broadcasters by lobbying on behalf of the public. In his landmark book, *Television: The Business Behind the Box,* Les Brown summarized the problem by stating that broadcasters have always felt that the FCC ". . . is wicked when it attempts regulation that interferes with the pursuit of maximum profits, requires the broadcaster to program for the poorer classes who are unattractive to advertisers, makes it a condition of licensing that he prove his attempt to ascertain community needs through meetings with civic groups, and insists that he present both sides of any issue according to the Fairness Doctrine. But on the other hand, the commission is the parent to whom the broadcaster runs

The FCC

The Federal Communications Commission has the responsibility for regulating radio and TV broadcasting, telephone, telegraph, and cable TV operations, two-way radio and radio operators, and satellite communications. The scope of FCC responsibilities can be seen in this brief outline:

Broadcast
FCC regulates:
- AM radio
- FM radio
- television
- ITFS (Instructional TV)
- International Shortwave

FCC issues:
- construction permits
- operating licenses
- license renewals and transfers

FCC oversees:
- compliance by broadcasters to all of its policies

Cable
FCC makes rules that:
- govern broadcast signal carriage, quality of services delivered, and access to cable for nonbroadcast programs
- limit delivery of interstate programming

FCC regulates:
- all new cable systems

FCC enforces:
- all its rules regarding cable

FCC is responsible for:
- maintaining relations with state and local authorities who share responsibility for local regulation of cable TV systems

Common Carrier Communications
Common carriers are companies, organizations, or individuals who provide communications to the public for hire. They must, at established rates, serve all who wish to use them.

FCC regulates:
- interstate and international common carriers including:
  telephone
  telegraph
  microwave radio
  land mobile radio
  high frequency radio
  satellite
  ocean cable

Non Broadcast
FCC regulates:
- all forms of private radio service
  aviation
  marine
  amateur
  public fixed station in Alaska
  public safety (police, fire)
  industrial
  land transportation (railroad, taxi)
  citizens bands
  radios at sea

In addition the FCC constantly monitors all its airwaves to detect unlicensed operations, and to provide such services as radio bearings for airplanes in distress. The FCC regulates CB broadcasting, assigns call letters to new radio and TV stations, oversees the Emergency Broadcast Service and performs a myriad of other functions.

to protect him from new competition and from the new technology that could make him obsolete.''

Since FCC chairmen are presidential appointees, their attitudes toward rules naturally reflect the feelings of the administration in office. Never has this been more apparent than with the FCC chairman selected by Ronald Reagan in 1981. At the outset of Mark S. Fowler's tenure in office, the commission put forth proposals calling for revisions in the Communications Act of 1934, declaring that ''. . . it is the telecommunications policy of the United States that the public interest is served by. . . relying upon competitive marketplace forces rather than administrative regulations.''

In a major speech delivered to broadcasters in September, 1981, Chairman Fowler made it clear that under his regime, government regulation of the broadcast industry would be kept to a minimum. Said Mr. Fowler, ''I believe that we are at the end of regulating broadcasting under the trusteeship model. . . . Under the trusteeship model, the commission fashioned rules to dictate how the broadcaster was to serve his community. In return for adhering to its pronouncements broadcasters could expect commission policies that protected protectionism. Under the coming marketplace approach, the commission should, so far as possible, defer to a broadcaster's judgment about how best to compete for viewers and listeners, because this serves the public interest.''

In his speech Mr. Fowler went on to question the wisdom of such established policies as the Fairness Doctrine, the limit on how many stations a single person or company can own, and the requirement that individual stations ascertain the needs of the public they are licensed to serve.

Mr. Fowler's remarks were received with great enthusiasm by the broadcast industry. On the other hand, his words brought consternation and apprehension to those wary of a new government policy in which the few checks on broadcast industry power were to be removed. Nothing in television's brief past would seem to justify this unbridled confidence in the ability of broadcasters to ascertain and meet the public's needs.

Other Governmental Agencies

The FCC is not the only government player in the game of television. There are other agencies and departments that have watchdog responsibilities over TV. It is the responsibility of the Federal Trade Commission to check on unfairness and deception in TV advertising and to take appropriate action when necessary. In 1976 the FTC, acting upon a complaint filed by Action for Children's Television, ordered the Hudson Pharmaceutical Company to stop advertising candylike Spiderman vitamin pills on television programs aimed at children. According to the FTC ruling, these advertisements were ''unfair or deceptive'' because they tended ''. . . to induce children to take excessive amounts of the vitamin supplements which may cause injury to their health.''

Yet, like the FCC, the Federal Trade Commission under its current administration has shown clear signs of adopting a hands-off policy as far as the regulation of broadcasters is concerned. In 1981, the FTC halted its three-year-old proceedings to investigate whether the more than $800 million a year worth of advertising targeted to children was unfair or deceptive. At issue was the question of whether children's advertising deceives youngsters because they are too young and too unsophisti-

Vive Quebec!

On April 30, 1980, Quebec passed a law that prohibits television advertising aimed at children under the age of 13. The law is based on the argument that children are vulnerable and easily deceived and should not be the target of advertising especially designed to attract them.

cated to understand the vested interests behind the ads. The commission said it could not ". . . justify sacrificing other important enforcement priorities" in continuing its inquiry.

One of the most important government players in the TV game is the United States Congress. As the overseeing body for the FCC and the other regulatory agencies, it has a powerful influence on the rules these agencies make. Congress created the agency that set up television in the first place. And it was Congress that legislated the ban on cigarette advertising on TV. In 1981 alone Congress introduced more than ten bills to deregulate broadcasting.

Perhaps the most visible way Congress maintains its role in the game of television is as a target for various lobbying groups. On the children's television issue, for example, broadcasters joined with the cereal, sugar, and toy industries in a heavy lobbying campaign that convinced Congress to force the FTC to stop the children's advertising rulemaking.

Government responsibility in TV is a Catch 22 situation. Without government involvement there is not enough funding for alterntive programming, yet government funding does not come without strings attached. Can government always be counted on to encourage robust debate on controversial issues, or are there some subjects it would prefer kept off the air? Without government supervision officials are susceptible to political favors and even bribes in the form of political contributions. Perhaps the biggest "catch" is the dilemma of the elected official who gets on the wrong side of the most important communications channels in the country when he is so dependent upon them for publicity at election time.

Government and Cable

Government involvement in cable is limited primarily to the local level, where city and town governments are the cable franchising authorities. Initially, the federal government used its influence to prevent cable from developing. However, a much different stance is maintained today and Washington's reins are much looser. Now the doors have been opened for the networks and powerful groups in other media to

enter the cable field. This move toward conglomerate control, not only of commercial TV and cable but of newspapers, magazines, and books, poses the danger that a small number of companies will control what America sees, hears, and reads.

Cable systems in any community operate as monopolies. Cable service in a community is determined by the contract that is negotiated with the cable company. The contract is a valuable tool. It makes possible a second chance for individuals to control their own telecommunications environment. Whatever cable company is awarded the franchise for a city or town controls the channels. In many communities the franchising authorities involve community organizations from the beginning, making sure that the cable company that eventually wins the franchise is one that gives the best indication it will meet the needs of the community. This is important because the public interest standard in the Communications Act does not apply to cable.

The Viewing Audience

Of the three groups who call the shots in television, all of us who make up the American audience have, in some ways, the most profound responsibility for our viewing experience. We have the ultimate control over television: we can turn it off. We must remind ourselves that turning off television does not mean tuning out the world. We have access to other forms of information and entertainment: we can read the newspaper or a book, go to the movies, talk to friends, play with our children, or walk the dog. We can choose to change the channel, we can select programs from the weekly television schedule and watch only those shows that match our interests. If we are worried about our children's television viewing habits, we can keep them from watching so many hours of television and allow them to see only programs that we help to choose.

Concerned citizens can make sure that local broadcasters are carrying out their licensed responsibilities. They can participate in the cable franchise process and can gain access to cable channels and produce their own shows. Under the Fairness Doctrine, members of the public can demand the airing of opposing points of view on controversial issues. In short, we can pretty well determine all there is to determine about television. Right? Wrong. For while this ideal exists in theory, the reality is that only a small percentage of the American public controls the television sets in the home and speaks out in the community in favor of television diversity. The vast majority do not have (or find) the time, money, energy, interest, or information they need to be actively involved. Most Americans flip on the television when they come home without bothering to consult the TV schedule or change the channel. They do not know about FCC rulemaking proceedings, broadcaster license renewal challenges, cable franchising agreements, or the Fairness Doctrine.

The American television audience has become little more than a pawn in the business

> **"I believe the quickest way to kill broadcasting would be to use it for direct advertising."** Herbert Hoover, 1924

of television. They, more than a single program or special or series, represent the product, the valuable commodity, the prize of the television industry. It is relatively simple. Broadcasters target programs to the largest possible audience. The size of the audience determines the popularity of the show, and the popularity of the show determines the amount of money that can be charged for each advertising minute. The popularity of the show also determines its clout in scheduling. In the eyes of commercial broadcasters, a good show is one that attracts a large enough audience to command the highest possible advertising rate. A bad show is one which, because of its ratings, cannot bring top dollar. That is why so few documentaries make it to the air in prime time. That is why the needs of minority audiences, always small by definition, are seldom addressed.

Because commercial TV exists as a vehicle to deliver customers to sponsors, it has become

Program-Free TV

A company called On-Line Media now markets six-minute repeating cassettes of videotaped, sound-free commercials that play on TV sets mounted above supermarket cash registers.

The estimated 1982 audience is 25 million viewers a week—but may reach upwards of 100 million viewers before long. Another challenge for the Nielsens!

Tom Hopkins

important for advertisers and broadcasters to attract the "right kind" of audience as well as the largest possible number of viewers. Through the highly sophisticated science of demographics, advertisers and TV executives can now determine not only whether enough people are watching a particular program but also whether they are the kind of people most likely to buy the products promoted on the show. This is the reason a program like "Gunsmoke," which appealed primarily to older viewers, was taken off the air when its ratings were still comparatively high. Advertisements are not a by-product of television; they are the reason for it.

The nature of television advertising has changed significantly since the early days of TV. Originally major corporations paid for an entire program. Shows like the "Texaco Hour" or "Kraft Music Hall" contained commercial messages from a single source. The advertisers of some sponsored programs actually produced the shows and dictated program content. Following the quiz show scandals of the 1950s, when it was proved that particularly attractive

contestants were being given answers in advance to ensure their success and heighten interest in the program, the networks began to take control of programming. Today the networks either totally own and produce the shows they air or they have significant money invested in their development.

Even if there had been no scandals, the nature of the program sponsorship would have changed. It is now simply too costly for one company, even a major corporation, to pay the freight for an entire program. Besides, in their search for the largest number of customers possible, advertisers have learned that it is better to scatter their commercials on different programs throughout the broadcast day. In fact the whole psychology of TV advertising has changed over the years. Today ad agencies favor short commercials with messages that seek to convince viewers that a particular product will help them live the good life. The audience is often thrust directly into the commercial. "You've just put out the world's biggest oil well fire." (Naturally it's time for a beer.) Whereas slogans have always been a common feature of radio and TV commercials, today they are designed to symbolize a whole way of living rather than merely to describe a product ("It's Miller Time"; "You Deserve a Break Today").

Since selling products is the *raison d'être* of commercial TV, the production of some TV ads is approached more seriously than the programs themselves. Filmmaker Stanley Kubrick, speaking in 1977 at a time when production costs were considerably lower than they are today, noted that "A feature film made with the same kind of care as a commercial would have to cost $50 million." And actors and actresses today earn more money from their participation in commercials than from stage appearances and motion pictures combined.

Few viewers have to be reminded that many TV ads are abrasive or in poor taste and that the constant repetition of certain commercials is particularly irritating. The claims made in many of the ads are, upon close scrutiny, misleading and downright ridiculous. "Two out of three doctors recommend. . . " Does

> **"Commercial broadcasting seeks instantly to capture audiences and to hold their attention without flagging. To allow the magnet of attention to grow weak for an instant is to risk the falling away of millions of human iron filings—a disaster immediately translated into severe economic loss. "Hold that audience!" is the first commandment of the lords of broadcasting to their faithful priests who shepherd their anonymous multitude to the green pastures of high Nielsen ratings."** Robert Lewis Shayon, "The Maintenance Men, or Reflections on the Art of Broadcasting", Hósó-Bunka Foundation Symposium, 1979

Some of the most powerful commercials promote not only a specific product but a whole way of life.

Top Ten TV Advertisers (1981)

1	Proctor and Gamble $392,800,000	Camay, Coast, Downy, Dreft, Cascade, Cheer, Comet, Dash, Ivory Soap, Ivory Snow, Ivory Liquid, Joy, Lava, Mr. Clean, Oxydol, Safeguard, Spic N Span, Tide, Top Job, Zest, Biz, Gain, Era, Bounce, Crisco, Duncan Hines, Jif, Pringles, Puritan Oil, Crest, Gleem, Head & Shoulders, Lilt, Prell, Scope, Secret, Sure, Wondra, Pert, Bold, Charmin, White Cloud, Puffs, Bounty, Pampers, Luvs, Folgers, High Point Decaff.
2	General Foods Corporation $238,100,000	Birds Eye Frozen Foods, Minute Rice, Shake N Bake, Good Seasons Salad Dressing, Stove Top Stuffing, Jell-O Gelatin, Pudding & Pie Filling, Calumet Baking Powder, Baker's Chocolate & Coconut, Dream Whip, Swans Down Cake Flour, Alpha Bits, Post Toasties, Grape Nuts, Grape Nuts Flakes, Raisin Bran, 40% Bran Flakes, Super Sugar Crisp, Honey Comb, Cocoa Pebbles, Fruity Pebbles, Post-Tens, C.W. Post Family Style Cereals, Log Cabin Syrups, Log Cabin Country Kitchen Pancake & Waffle Mix, Awake Frozen Concentrate, Tang, Orange Plus, Instant Postum, Kool-Aid, Gaines Meal, Gaines Burger, Prime, Prime Variety, Top Choice, Cycle Canned Dog Food, Gaines Puppy Choice, Gravy Train, Maxwell House, Yuban, Sanka Brand, 97% Caffein Free, Brim Decaffeinated Coffee, Maxim, All the Freeze-Dried Versions, (Sanka, Brim), Electra-Perk (Maxwell House, Sanka, Yuban, Max-Pax) Max-Pax Electra Perk Ground Coffee Filter Rings, General Foods International Coffees, Mellow Roast Coffee & Grain Beverages, Burger Chef.
3	General Motors Corporation $146,900,000	Cars, trucks, buses, diesel locomotives and engines, aircraft engines, earth moving equipment, missile components
4	American Home Products $131,400,000	Drugs, foods, household products, housewares
5	Ford Motor Company $113,900,000	Cars, trucks, tractors, and implements
6	Bristol Myers $109,900,000	Toiletries, pharmaceuticals, hair care and coloring products, beauty appliances, household products, nutritional and vitamin products
7	Philip Morris $99,500,000	Cigarettes, beer, soft drink beverages, freeze dried products, frozen fruit juice, labels, glassine and greaseproof papers, technical and fine printing papers, napkins, and disposable tabletop products, adhesive and liquid coatings, specialty chemicals, industrial powder coating, insurance and real estate.
8	Johnson & Johnson $97,800,000	Surgical dressings, medical, baby and allied products
9	Lever Brothers $95,000,000	Soaps, detergents, shortenings, margarine, marinades, pancake mixes and syrup, dentifrices, toothbrushes, toiletries, glycerin, and other household and industrial products
10	Sears Roebuck $86,800,000	General merchandise retailer

Broadcast Advertising Reports

If they buy it, why shouldn't we? Television's most popular way of selling is to use established and easily recognizable stars to plug sponsors' products. The financial rewards for their participation are so great that some of TV's and movies' biggest personalities have become regular pitch men and women. In a relatively recent advertising development, ad agencies have begun to use the heads of certain corporations on air to peddle their wares. The most famous owner/salesman on TV? It's no contest: Frank Perdue and his chickens ▶

Would You Believe?

Brooke Shields was paid $250,000 for a 60 second Japanese TV spot. James Coburn's 1977 Schlitz commercial earned him $250,000 a word ("Schlitz Light")!

Is it any wonder that TV advertisers are able to lure stars into making the sales pitch.

this mean that in the entire country *three* doctors were polled? "Experts agree that our product is better." What is the advertiser's definition of an expert? What is meant by "better"? Better than what?

Advertising rates are based on the size of the audience. With fifty-five million people watching the evening news and shows such as "Dallas" or "M*A*S*H*" drawing audiences of thirty to thirty-five million, any new adult program that fails to draw sixteen million viewers is considered a failure. The cutoff point for children's programs is three million. The art of gauging this audience size is a lucrative business in itself. In an industry where a single rating point in prime time is worth more than $10 million and advertiser decisions are based on

exactly who is watching each show, the people who determine the ratings and assess the audience makeup are indispensable.

The best-known and most widely used of all the TV rating systems is that compiled by the A.C. Nielsen Company. (While the name Nielsen is synonymous with television, this organization actually gets most of its revenue conducting customer surveys for various American corporations outside of television.) To compile its television index the Nielsen Company places a small black box called an Audimeter in twelve hundred households across the nation. The latest census figures are used to get the most representative sample possible. Every time one of the wired television sets is turned on, the Audimeter records the time of day, the channel being watched, and how long it is watched before a switch is made. The Audimeter compiles its record minute by minute. All of the information it gathers is relayed to a central computer, which collects the data from all twelve hundred Audimeters twice a day.

In addition to the Audimeters, the Nielsen Company also asks twenty-three hundred additional households to keep a written log of their TV-viewing. The purpose of these diaries,

1980 Commercial Prices for 30-Second Spot	
Disney's Wonderful World	$ 70,000
Soap	$ 90,000
Laverne & Shirley	$100,000
Happy Days	$110,000
Monday Nite Football	$115,000
Taxi	$115,000
Little House on the Prairie	$125,000
Dallas	$145,000
M*A*S*H*	$150,000
60 Minutes	$150,000

Ad Age, 9/1/80

The Bottom Line of Television

Television is big business. Big expensive business. Here's a breakdown of the expenses and income of some of your favorite shows in 1980.

1980

Broadcast:	$9,100,000,000		
Cable:	$1,693,000,000		

Jan-Feb Averages per show	Net Revenues	Cost	Profit
Late Night			
Tonight	$190,000	$ 59,000	$131,000
Saturday Night Live	$455,000	$295,000	$160,000
Daytime			
Another World	$230,000	$ 71,000	$159,000
Days of Our Lives	$131,000	$ 52,000	$ 79,000
Hollywood Squares	$ 34,000	$ 18,000	$ 16,000
Password	$ 30,000	$ 16,000	$ 14,000

Reprinted with permission from *Variety*, 5/16/80

The cost for a 30-second commercial spot during the Super Bowl:	
1973	$ 90,000
1974	$100,000
1975	$110,000
1976	$125,000
1977	$125,000
1978	$185,000
1979	$180,000
1980	$234,000
1981	$275,000
1982	$345,000

called Audilogs, is to supply information on such things as the age, sex, and income of individual viewers of specific programs. Every year one-fifth of the households involved in the Nielsen sample are replaced. Still, this means the same household is monitored for five years, a span of time considered too long by critics of the system.

The Nielsen Audilog system is but one of many polling and survey operations that reveal not only how many people are watching a particular program but who they are, where they live, how much they earn, how much education they've had, what they like to buy, and what they like or don't like about every aspect of television itself.

How accurate are these ratings? Throughout the years the Nielsen system has been the target of repeated criticism. By monitoring twelve hundred families in a nation where there are more than eighty million TV households, the company actually samples only one of every sixty-two thousand homes. Does this really mean that every time one of the twelve hundred monitored families races home to watch "That's Incredible," sixty-two thousand other families in the country are doing the same thing? More than just the reliability of the Niel-

sen rating system has come under attack. Former FCC commissioner Margita White spoke for many when she stated that the rating system, ". . . by encouraging the imitative rather than the innovative, by overemphasizing 'the numbers' at the expense of quality and encouraging bland programming to the lowest common denominator, may be the single major obstacle to better-quality programming."

Despite the relatively small sampling upon which they are based, the Nielsens, like the election-day political polls we have become so accustomed to, may well reflect actual audience size more accurately than critics of the system would like to admit. But they determine *only* the size and makeup of the audience. They say nothing about the attitude of the audiences toward the shows. The mere fact that millions may be watching a program is no indication that they all like it. The audience may be tuned in because that particular program is the best of a bad lot. Or many may be tuned in and not paying much attention to the screen. What is needed is a way of measuring how the audience feels about a show as well as how many people are tuned in. The United States lags far behind

The Ratings

The size of the audience "delivered" by a station to the advertiser during a given show determines how much the broadcasters charge for commercial time. The bigger the audience, naturally the more profitable in the long run it is for advertisers to buy time on that show, provided the viewers match the characteristics of their proven customers.

The industry speaks of this money as CPM or cost per thousand, that is, the cost to the advertiser per thousand people seeing the commercial. If the CPM is too high it's likely the commercial will be dropped. In order to determine commercial rates for local stations Nielsen conducts "*the sweeps*" also known as sweeps week, when station programming goes bananas with blockbuster shows trying to win the highest ratings.

Second Season is the midyear introduction of new shows to replace fall failures. Second season introductions have often done remarkably well ("All in the Family," "Barney Miller," "Dallas," "Happy Days," "Laverne & Shirley," "Dukes of Hazzard," "Jeffersons").

A rating point means the percentage of total TV households watching the show; a *share* is the percentage of TV households with their sets turned on or the percentage of actual total viewers. One rating point is about 12 Nielsen Households and one Nielsen house represents about 65,000 real houses, which as one critic has pointed out means that if one Nielsen man gets up for a beer 65,000 people follow.

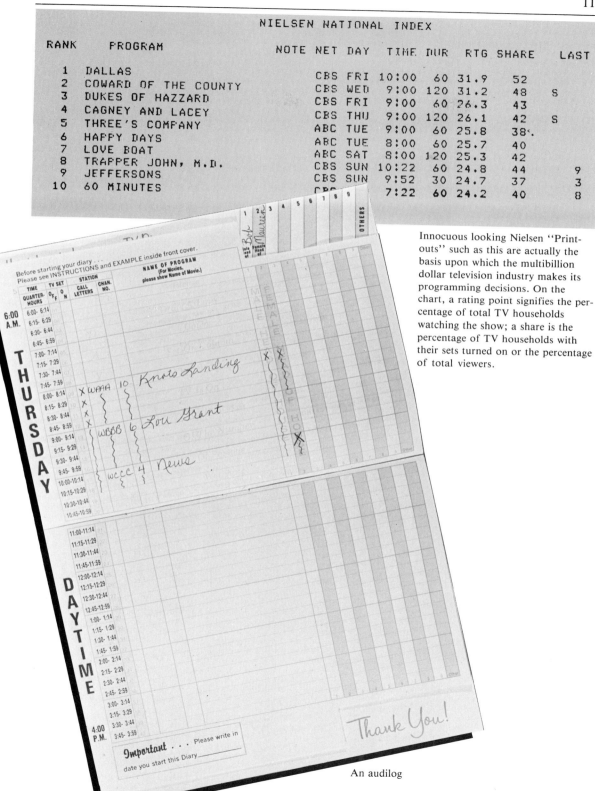

NIELSEN NATIONAL INDEX

RANK	PROGRAM	NOTE	NET	DAY	TIME	DUR	RTG	SHARE	LAST
1	DALLAS		CBS	FRI	10:00	60	31.9	52	
2	COWARD OF THE COUNTY		CBS	WED	9:00	120	31.2	48	S
3	DUKES OF HAZZARD		CBS	FRI	9:00	60	26.3	43	
4	CAGNEY AND LACEY		CBS	THU	9:00	120	26.1	42	S
5	THREE'S COMPANY		ABC	TUE	9:00	60	25.8	38<.	
6	HAPPY DAYS		ABC	TUE	8:00	60	25.7	40	
7	LOVE BOAT		ABC	SAT	8:00	120	25.3	42	
8	TRAPPER JOHN, M.D.		CBS	SUN	10:22	60	24.8	44	9
9	JEFFERSONS		CBS	SUN	9:52	30	24.7	37	3
10	60 MINUTES		CBS		7:22	60	24.2	40	8

Innocuous looking Nielsen "Print-outs" such as this are actually the basis upon which the multibillion dollar television industry makes its programming decisions. On the chart, a rating point signifies the percentage of total TV households watching the show; a share is the percentage of TV households with their sets turned on or the percentage of total viewers.

An audilog

several nations (England, France, Canada, the Netherlands, Sweden) who have for years been measuring qualitative as well as quantitative responses in the belief that it is more important to increase viewer satisfaction than it is to increase the number of hours spent in front of the television set. British law, for example, has mandated since 1973 that ''Appreciation Indices'' be compiled for commercial programs.

Recently, serious attempts have been made in this country to institute a qualitative rating system. The Arbitron Company, for one, has initiated a system in which it mails out to sample households diaries that require participants not only to indicate what programs they are watching but also to make qualitative judgments about the shows they watch. And the Public Broadcasting System has begun testing a new qualitative TV rating system to measure the extent to which viewers find a program ''entertaining,'' ''useful,'' ''informative,'' and ''different'' from other TV shows.

Sometimes it seems that television will never be more than, at best, a money-making leisure machine and, at worst, a tool for economic and political propaganda. It is clear that although joint responsibility among broadcasters, the government, and the public is the ideal guarantor of the public interest, this joint effort has been a hope rather than a reality. What is apparent is that only an actively involved audience can see to it that both conventional TV and the new technologies will provide the diversity that is so badly needed.

4 Resources

Books

Arlen, Michael J. *Thirty Seconds*. New York: Farrar, Strauss & Giroux, 1980. An enlightening and entertaining discussion of the making of American Telephone & Telegraph's famous ''reach out and touch someone'' commercial.

Barnouw, Erik. *The Sponsor: Notes on a Modern Potenate*. New York: Oxford University Press, 1978. The rise of broadcast advertising, its current dominance and prospects for future change.

Bergreen, Laurence. *Look Now, Pay Later: The Rise of Network Broadcasting*. New York: Doubleday, 1980. An excellent history of the radio and TV national networks and how they grew.

Brown, Les. *Television: The Business Behind the Box*. New York: Harcourt Brace Jovanovich, 1971. A vivid, anecdotal documentary of a year in the television industry that explains how programming decisions are made and how the business really works.

Cole, Barry, and Oettinger, Mal. *Reluctant Regulators: The FCC and the Broadcast Audience*. Reading, Mass.: Addison-Wesley, 1978. Behind the scenes at the Federal Communications Commission; a clear, thoughtful look at its operations, the players, communicating with the FCC, regulatory functions, and the kidvid controversy.

Cowan, Geoffrey. *See No Evil: The Backstage Battle over Sex and Violence in Television*. New York: Simon and Schuster, 1979. The attorney who organized the landmark legal challenge to TV's ''Family Hour'' describes the case in detail and shows how policy is made at the networks and in government.

Friendly, Fred W. *The Good Guys, the Bad Guys, and the First Amendment: Free Speech vs. Fairness in Broadcasting*. New York: Random House, 1976. A lucid analysis of the Red Lion case and others that have helped define the Fairness Doctrine.

Kahn, Frank J., ed. *Documents of American Broadcasting*, 3rd ed. Englewoods Cliffs, N.J.: Prentice-Hall, 1978. A handy sourcebook of basic papers relating to American broadcasting, including public laws, regulatory codes, cases and decisions of the

FCC, Congress, and various courts, arranged chronologically.

Levin, Harvey J. *Fact and Fancy in Television Regulation: An Economic Study of Policy Alternatives.* New York: Russell Sage Foundation, 1980. Provides background information on federal broadcast regulation, a critique of current policies and assessment of selected alternatives. The author makes a compelling case for diversification of station ownership and other changes that would help to bring about greater program diversity.

Taishoff, Sol, ed. *Broadcasting Cable Yearbook.* Washington, D.C.: Broadcasting Publications, Inc., published annually. The most comprehensive directory to the business of broadcasting. Lists individuals, companies, stations, professional services, and associations.

Films and Tapes

Buy, Buy. A 16-mm color film, 20 minutes, 1973. A wry look at the methods and motives of the producers and agency people who make TV commercials. For junior high level up. Available from Churchill Films, 662 North Robertson Blvd., Los Angeles, Calif. 90069.

Marketing the Myths. A 16-mm color film or video cassette, 25 minutes. 1976. An informative and entertaining collection of 24 TV commercials from around the world, designed to assist in the study of TV advertising in relation to the myths of modern-day culture. Available from Phoenix Films, 470 Park Avenue South, New York, N.Y. 10016.

The Television Newsman. A 16-mm color film, 28 minutes. 1976. An entertaining, fast-paced look at a day in the life of a big-city TV newsman that takes us behind the scenes at a TV station. Available from Pyramid Films, Box 1048, Santa Monica, Calif. 90406.

Organizations

National Association of Broadcasters
485 Madison Avenue
New York, N.Y. 10022
212-759-7020
Provides a Television Information Office, lobbies on behalf of the industry before Congress, initiates broadcasting research.

Association of Independent Television Stations
1140 Avenue of the Americas
New York, N.Y. 10036
212-575-0577
Association of unaffiliated independent stations and related organizations.

Corporation for Public Broadcasting
111 16th Street NW
Washington, D.C. 20036
202-293-6160
Nonprofit, nongovernmental agency promotes and finances development of noncommercial media. Supports the Public Broadcasting Service (PBS).

National Cable Television Association
918 16th Street NW
Suite 800
Washington, D.C.
202-457-6700
Cable industry trade association.

National Federation of Local Cable Programmers
3700 Far Hills Avenue
Kettering, Ohio 45429
513-298-7890
Provides assistance in local access efforts and serves as an advocate at the federal level. Sponsors conferences, maintains video library and information referral services. Publishes quarterly newsletter.

Public Broadcasting Service (PBS)
475 L'Enfant Plaza SW
Washington, D.C. 20024
202-488-5000
PBS is the service and representative organization for public television stations.

Home Tech

By the end of the 1980s watching television will be a far different experience from what it is now. With gasoline prices and the cost of entertainment caught in the inflationary spiral, more and more of us will be staying home, spending less money on tickets to the theater and to sports events and more on what is already

Would You Believe?

In 1979, Americans spent more money ($1,948,000,000) *repairing* TV and radio sets than they did attending all manner of live performances combined ($1,551,000,000).

called our "home entertainment center." Given the new technologies that are proliferating all around us, it will probably be a "communications center" as well.

Receiving broadcast programs will be but one function of our "home tech" system. The system will probably also include equipment for playing videodiscs and cassettes and for recording anything that appears on the screen from a myriad of sources. Our TV set will have attachments to plug us into such services as a home computer, two-way cable, and videotext. The set itself will have a much different look. Many of us will own flat, wall-size screens upon which the picture, now freed from the tube, will be projected. And the landscape of America, crisscrossed by TV antennas in the 1950s, will be dotted by dish-shaped receivers that will allow us to pick up programs and services from satellites cruising in space.

Most of the technology for these services and features is already in place. Perhaps the most far-reaching is cable television, which is

bound to have a major effect on our lives and on the way we deal with TV's virtues and its vices.

The prospects for the new television are exciting. We're in the midst of the video revolution. Never have we been in such a good position to protect what is good in television and remedy what is bad. To do so, however, requires a familiarity with the new technologies. That's what this chapter is all about.

Direct Satellite

On the day when Americans learned that the Russians had a satellite named Sputnik floating through space, most of us were concerned only about the major setback in the space race that this represented. Nearly a quarter of a century later, it is clear that the most exciting by-product of space exploration has been the development of new communications techniques. Today the future of much of the "new" television is linked directly to the use of satellites that relay pictures across the nation and around the world. Commercial and public broadcasting, major cable and pay-TV companies are already using satellites to transmit their programs to subscribers.

Satellites are unaffected by atmospheric conditions and are a less expensive way of transmitting television signals than almost any other method. In order to pick up satellite signals, a dish-shaped antenna is needed, and today there are almost two thousand such receivers throughout the United States.

Originally the cost of these antennas—called earth stations—was so high (about $100,000) that only cable companies and other communications corporations could afford them. But the cost has dropped to around $10,000, and it is predicted that by the middle of this decade much smaller earth stations will be available for as little as $300. It is also safe to say that the FCC will continue to modify its space regulations, paving the way for dozens more transmitting satellites to be launched in the future.

Already the number of individuals with earth stations of their own is growing. (Even the Nieman-Marcus catalogue for 1980 featured one at Christmastime). Owners of these dish antennas pick up programming from as far away as Brazil, receive network "feeds" from correspondents long before newscasts reach the air, receive an ever-increasing number of programs from every broadcast source available, and even get, direct from NASA, pictures of explorations of distant planets.

As with many other new technologies, the legality of private earth station owners' picking up free signals from pay-TV broadcasting is now being challenged in the courts, and the ultimate legal rights of broadcasters and the pub-

lic are still to be determined. Meanwhile, major broadcasters such as RCA and CBS have announced plans to develop direct broadcast satellite systems that will supply programs designed specifically for earth station owners. There are many who feel that direct satellite broadcasting will eventually compete significantly with cable and over-the-air TV for a majority of the audience.

Video Recorders

Although video cassette recorders (VCRs) are now the vanguard of the new technology, they were actually introduced in 1956. Despite a price tag of what in today's inflated economy would be $200,000, more than eighty of these early recording units were sold to television stations around the country.

In 1975, the Sony Corporation introduced a home model (called Betamax), which sold for

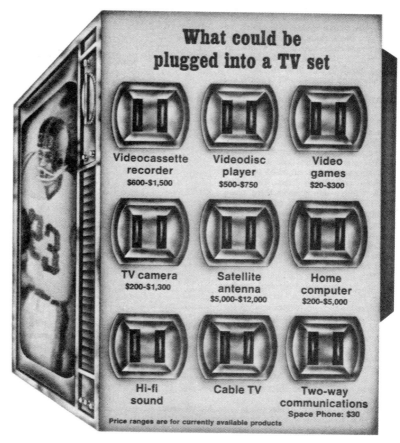

What could be plugged into a TV set

Videocassette recorder $600–$1,500	Videodisc player $500–$750	Video games $20–$300
TV camera $200–$1,300	Satellite antenna $5,000–$12,000	Home computer $200–$5,000
Hi-fi sound	Cable TV	Two-way communications Space Phone: $30

Price ranges are for currently available products

Bill Purdom. Reprinted from *Business Week;* © 1981 McGraw Hill, Inc.

Have Picture, Will Travel

How does television work? Light reflects off the objects on the set and is picked up by the camera shooting the scene to be broadcast (or taped for later broadcast). Once inside the camera, the light hits an electrified target that is composed of 525 lines of 367,000 photosensitive dots. Each dot lights up as brightly or dimly as that part of the scene it mirrors. On the other side of the target, still inside the camera, is an electron gun that scans the lines of dots (every other line is read in two sweeps of the beam) 30 times in a second and essentially memorizes the brightness of each dot in order and sends out the information down the camera cable to a TV screen in studio control. If there are several cameras, there are several pictures and it is the director's job to choose which one to put on the air (or on the tape to air later.

From the studio's Master Control to the station's transmitting tower, the television signal (the picture and sound converted into electronic information) is joined to a powerful radio wave and broadcast to you.

Master Control

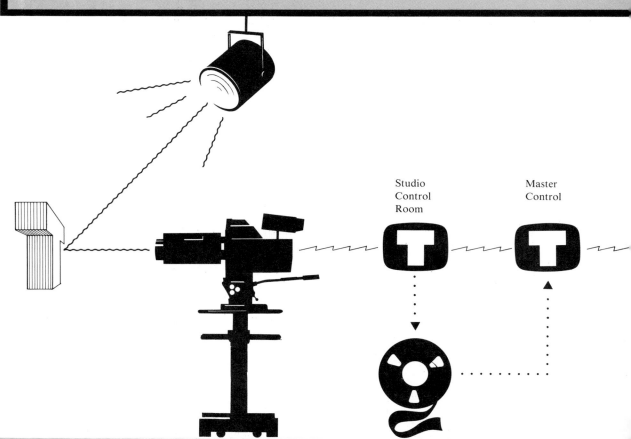

Studio Control Room

Master Control

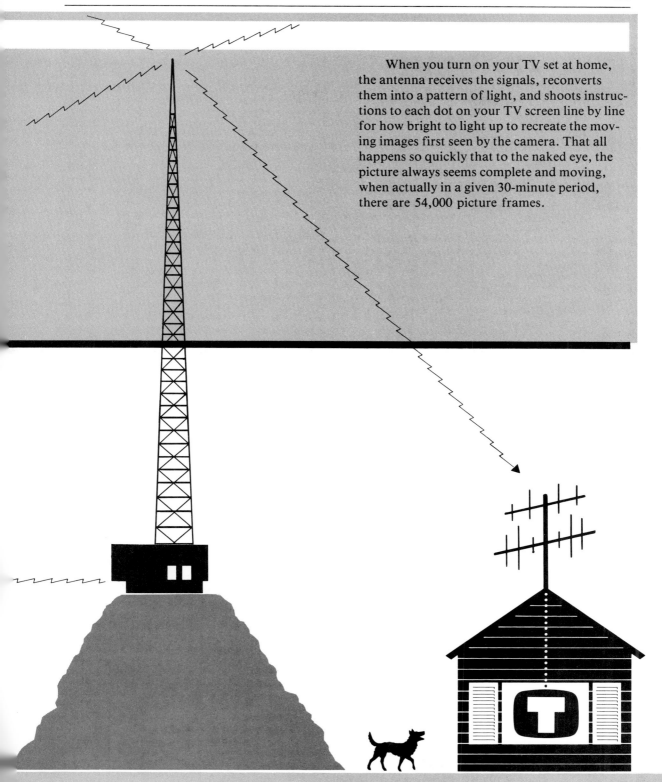

When you turn on your TV set at home, the antenna receives the signals, reconverts them into a pattern of light, and shoots instructions to each dot on your TV screen line by line for how bright to light up to recreate the moving images first seen by the camera. That all happens so quickly that to the naked eye, the picture always seems complete and moving, when actually in a given 30-minute period, there are 54,000 picture frames.

Mega-Vision

The development of Projection TV has brought with it extraordinary changes in screen size so that in your home you can now watch TV on screens as large as 20 feet, depending on your passion for television and your pocketbook. There are some facts to know before you invest.

First there are two basic types of projection TV: the single-tube system and the multiple-tube system. Obviously a system that projects three colors separately is going to give finer picture quality. The single tube projector, a magnification system with less sharpness and brightness, is considerably cheaper and more compact than the three-tube system and may suit the needs of the less exacting viewer.

Viewing problems are magnified when projected on to a large screen. If TV reception in your area is poor, remember that it will look even worse on a jumbo screen. Models differ in how far to the right or left you can move before the picture disappears. Be aware that large audiences will have to sit grouped together in front of the TV screen, unless you select a model that specifically allows for wide angle viewing.

Video Review, June 1981

Large-screen projection TV

Ralph Bogartman/NOVABEAM® Model One Projection TV

Pee-Wee Vision

At the same time that TV screens are getting bigger they're also getting smaller. Sinclair Research in England is coming out with a flat-screen black-and-white TV set measuring 6 inches wide, 4 inches high, and 1 inch thick, and weighing only a few ounces. The flat screen is three times brighter and uses four times less power than conventional TV.

Still More

Three-screen TV sets that allow you to watch three shows at once. And a color set that shows you an instant ten-second replay at the press of a button.

$2,300. A year later another Japanese electronics firm, JVC, began to market a rival model known as VHS (Video Home System), and the battle for supremacy of the home video recorder market began. The Beta and the VHS systems are incompatible. A viewer cannot play a VHS cassette on a Beta machine and vice versa. Most experts agree that there is little difference in the quality of these two systems, and although other competitors have entered the field, Sony and JVC have the most popular models in the growing market.

Video recorders allow viewers to create their own prime time. Once a show is recorded it can be played at any time, not only when a network or local station schedules it for airing. And a VCR owner does not have to be home to record a show. By presetting the timer, she can record up to eight hours of programming using VHS and up to five hours on Betamax. Both can be programmed to record from a variety of stations and at a variety of times.

Video recorders are operated in much the same way as tape recorders. Sophisticated models allow the viewer to speedscan a videotape while the images flash by on the screen, to freeze independent frames for close study, to advance the tape frame by frame, and to play back action in slow motion. They also come equipped with remote controls. The price range for most one-half-inch home VCRs today is from $600 to $2500.

Industry executives promise that the future video recorders will feature even greater playing precision and editing capabilities and that prices will continue to drop. Cameras and other equipment that can be used with the VCR to make home movies will undoubtedly also become less expensive to buy and easier to operate.

In addition to the programs they record off their TV set or make on their own VCRs, owners can rent or purchase a wide variety of prerecorded cassettes featuring everything from gardening to hard-core pornography. There are cassettes that show how to cook Italian, Japanese, Chinese, Jewish, French, and American dishes. Video cassette catalogues feature tapes that give expert instruction on the fine points of tennis, golf, soccer, hockey, skiing, baseball, basketball, and football. Dr. Benjamin Spock has prepared a cassette called "Caring for Your Newborn" that, along with the "Video First

Home video cassette recorder

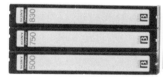

Sony Corporation of America

Satellite TV—Dish 'N' Data

There are 16 satellites operating in fixed orbits 22,300 miles above the earth's equator. Five are owned by Western Union, four by AT & T, five by RCA American, and two by Telesat Canada.

The launching of communications satellites has revolutionized TV. The signals can cover the whole continent with incredible speed, and "feed" more than one show at once, since a satellite has either 12 or 24 transponders capable of transmission, unlike the conventional network line system that can distribute only one show at a time.

Western Union Corporation

An earth-station transmitter with a powerful antenna beams up a signal to a satellite. The satellite relays the signals back to earth to a waiting earth-station (or dish). The signal is then transmitted to television sets by cable or microwave.

James Scherer for WGBH

RCA American Communications, Inc.

Earth satellite dish

Satellite Services

Black Entertainment Network	Entertainment
Cable News Network	24-hour news
C - Span	Live coverage of U.S. House of Representatives, some Senate hearings
Christian Broadcasting Network	Religious & variety
ESPN	24 hour sports
Modern Satellite Network	Movies, interviews, specials, women's programs
Reuters News-View	Sports, financial general news, features, horoscopes, weather and ski information
Satellite Program Network	Interviews, consumer awareness, exercise
Spanish International Network	Spanish language programming
USA NETWORK	Pro & college sports from Madison Square Garden, Calliope (Children's films)
Warner Amex Satellite	Children's shows
The Movie Channel	Movies, specials

Superstations

There are 3 local TV stations which use satellite transmission to broadcast their signals to cable systems across the nation. Because of the cable audience they reach they are called superstations.

WGN-TV	Sports, movies, comedy
WOR-TV	Movies, sports, entertainment
WTBS	Movies, Atlanta Braves and Atlanta Hawks sports, comedy

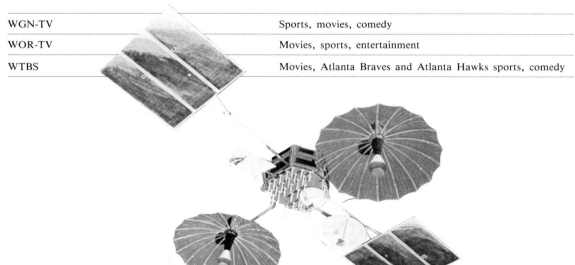

Hughes Aircraft Company

Aid Kit'' and the "CPR" tape, gives the VCR owner a start toward a video home medical library. Performances on video cassettes range from Evel Kneivel (demonstrating the proper rules of motorcycle riding) to Meryl Streep (narrating a series called "Coping with Illness").

But for most owners it is the VCR's ability to record TV programs while they are being aired that remains its most important feature. Says one young mother, "It's been a lifesaver with our Jeremy, who is seventeen months old. I taped 'The Muppets,' and every time he's crying I put it on. It does wonders." Says psychiatrist-author Dr. Theodore Isaac Rubin, "If my video recorder stopped working today, I would think we had gotten our money's worth. It's more than a gadget; its an instrument. I've been able to save several programs that I love to see, like the oldie *Pygmalion* and a National Geographic special on Russia. Sooner or later, everyone will have one of these things."

Videodiscs

A videodisc looks like a phonograph record and works on a player plugged into a TV set. A single videodisc can hold 54,000 picture frames of information, making it the greatest form of information storage yet invented for the home market.

Despite many setbacks in the development of the videodisc, many communication experts believe that the future undoubtedly will belong to the disc.

There are three distinct videodisc formats. One, which is employed by RCA in its Selectavision System, uses a stylus to pick up audio and visual information. A second, used in the Pioneer and Magnavox systems, employs laser beams. A third system (called VHD) preferred by several Japanese manufacturers employs a stylus but claims to feature all the advantages found in the laser system. The fact that all of these videodisc systems are incompatible has kept the quantity of videodiscs that have found their way into American homes from even closely approaching the rarefied numbers that

many in the industry had predicted. The lack of a wide variety of programming available on discs has also limited sales up to now.

With laser discs, more than with any other type of TV now available, viewers have control of the way they watch programs. Each of the 54,000 frames on a laser disc is numbered, and at the touch of a button viewers can call up any of the images. They can go back and forth, stop the action and study a particular segment, or replay a section to see it again.

The possibilities for videodiscs seem endless. The contents of an entire museum could be stored in full color on one disc. An encyclopedia could be housed page by page on a single disc. Some of the nation's largest corporations are already recording their catalogues on videodiscs so that customers and employees can see every piece of their merchandise and study individual items at the touch of a button.

Some of the disc technology that has already been developed is truly exciting. At the Massachusetts Institute of Technology, engineers have perfected a disc in which a map of Aspen, Colorado, is flashed on the screen. The screen is touch-sensitive—by running a finger along any route on the map, the viewer is taken on a visual trip along the chosen route. Details of buildings can be studied and short histories of a particular location can be selected. If the viewer wishes to go in a different direction, he or she simply "calls back" the map and traces a different route with a finger. Similarly, there are discs that begin by showing all the parts of a machine. By touching one particular part of the picture on the machine, the viewer sees and hears what the maker of the disc has to tell him about that particular part.

One of the most promising features of the videodisc is its interactive capability. When hooked up to an external minicomputer, a videodisc can become a learning, shopping, or business center. The chairman of a business firm that has been studying videodisc technology has stated that a system combining a videodisc player and a minicomputer "combines the strength of the three most powerful educational technologies—the book, the television, and the computer—and outperforms any one of them." Programming is being developed that will allow children to interact with what they see on the screen instead of merely sitting passively in front of the TV set.

Probably the most important aspect of videodisc technology is its potential for increasing program choice. Whereas millions of viewers are necessary to ensure the success of a commercial TV program, for a videodisc to break even, only a few thousand need be sold. Whole libraries of children's books could be dramatized and put onto videodiscs. Children's

concerts and visual lessons in painting or skiing or nature studies will be available in a format a child can actually control. The possibility exists that at long last young people will be able to watch programs that are not only worthwhile but suitable for their age level.

Videotext

The basic ingredient of videotext is old-fashioned print—right across your television screen. What will the print tell you? If the prognosticators are right, everything you could ever possibly want to know. In a videotext system, a special decoder is plugged into your television set. At the touch of a key-pad device, airline schedules, stock market reports, news, weather and traffic reports, book and movie reviews, TV and theater schedules, classified advertising, or home-study courses flash across your screen.

The system has two-way capability, so you can bank, shop, send and receive mail, and play

How Videodisc Works

The videodisc is basically a TV record—a storage system using TV playback equipment. There are different types that are incompatible with one another because of the method of conversion of the disc data into video. The videodisc offers the storage capacity of a 30-minute video program per side (that's 54,000 frames) and incredibly fast random access to the data contained anywhere in the disc. The two types currently available are put out by RCA and Philips–MCA. The RCA model is "pressed" using lasers, with a tracking stylus for playback. The Philips player uses laser technology both for recording and for playback.

RCA Consumer Electronics Division

an endless variety of video games through this one system. Videotext has particular advantages for disabled people, who will be able to conduct much of their business without leaving home. And it allows for effective communication with the deaf.

Videotext was initiated by the British Broadcasting Corporation, and already more than fifty thousand homes in Great Britain receive it. The BBC System, called Teletext, sends out some eight hundred ''pages'' of printed material that runs simultaneously with regular programs. The pages are invisible until the viewer punches his keyboard and brings them into view. In the United States, both American Telephone and Telegraph and the General Telephone and Electronics Corporation have begun experimenting in this technology. And other corporations such as Sears, Roebuck, Federated Stores, RCA, CBS, American Express, and Dow Jones are entering the field. According to an industry survey, videotext decoders will be incorporated into all new color TV sets by 1985.

Videotext presents a challenge to some existing institutions, particularly newspapers. The system could significantly affect classified advertising, since viewers could find more information more specifically targeted to their needs at the touch of a button. The computer-based data can be continually corrected and kept up-to-date. Already AT&T is converting its Yellow Pages into videotext. And proponents of the system foresee a time when the vast majority of print advertising will be carried not by magazines and newspapers but by the TV set in your communications wall.

Here are some examples of teletext services being developed across the country.

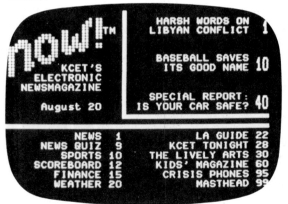

Courtesy of KCET/Los Angeles Teletext Project
Photos by Mitzi Trumbo

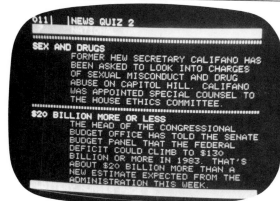

Designed by Gene Mackles
Photos by Jeff Dunn for WGBH

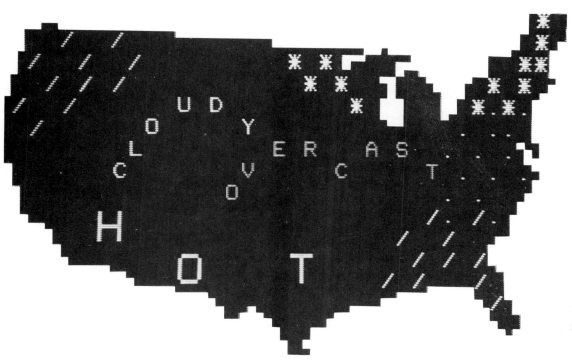

Map by Tom Sumida
Photo by Alan J. Brightman for WGBH

Closed-Captioning

For most viewers the airing of the movie *Force 10 from Navarone* by ABC on March 16, 1980, was hardly a landmark telecommunications event. But for the deaf people in the country it signified a new world of television viewing. *Force 10 from Navarone* was the first TV presentation to be accompanied by closed-captioning, a system that allows the hearing impaired, through the use of home decoders, to watch television programs complete with printed captions. The number of closed-captioned network programs has been steadily increasing and today almost all the most popular shows offer this important service. In addition many live events, beginning with President Ronald Reagan's 1981 inaugural address, have been closed-captioned. Viewers can find which programs are scheduled for closed-captioning by checking in a program guide; the initials CC are usually inserted beside the shows that offer this service.

Video Games

Like television itself, video games burst on the national scene almost without warning. Americans already spend close to 1 billion dollars on video games each year—more money than they spend on movies and records combined!

Like their pinball-playing ancestors, youngsters—particularly teenage boys—comprise the greatest number of video game fanatics. But the craze has captured the attention and participation of Americans of all ages. These machines are now located in executive dining rooms, beauty parlors, restaurants, and arcades throughout the country, but soon even this excuse for going out of the house may be unnecessary. In 1981 the number of households

PAC-MAN manufactured by Atari, Inc., under license from Namco America, Inc. Trademark of Bally Midway Mfg. Co.

Atari Pac-Man—America's most popular home video game

purchasing video games quadrupled from 2 percent of the country to 8 percent, a modest jump compared to what will happen in the next few years.

Utilizing the latest developments in electronic technology, video games, with their moving, often lifelike figures and their realistic sound effects, are a challenge to eye, hand, and

Would You Believe?

Mattel and M. A. Kempner, Inc., are now marketing a game that allows viewers in separate locations to compete with each other via TV.

By watching the displays of spaceships or other "invaders" on their sets, callers can zap the enemy's forces by yelling *pow, pow, pow* into the telephone. The popping sound of *pow* is programmed into a station's game control to release a "shot." Each contestant's voice separately activates the laser for his team.

brain coordination. They give players the opportunity to repel invaders, land airplanes through a maze of obstacles, escape from the clutches of monsters and villains, and compete with themselves or friends and relatives in every type of athletic contest imaginable. The games require dexterity and skill to win—but the biggest winners are unquestionably the manufacturers of the product. In 1981 alone, Warner Communications' subsidiary Atari, Inc., the leader in the industry, garnered revenues

exceeding $1 billion, while the Bally corporation grossed more than $130 million.

Video games, like television itself, have come under strong attack from a variety of sources. Parents have criticized their ubiquity, not to mention their expense. Psychologists have expressed concern that many of the games glorify violence even more than the TV programs children watch. They worry because the number of hours young people spend with these games further removes them from reality and human contact. Perhaps even more significant is that Gamblers Anonymous has criticized the games, claiming that gambling compulsion can begin with children as young as ten years old.

There are, however, those who feel that there are positive aspects to this phenomenon. They claim that the games help children develop hand-eye coordination and that future generations raised on these games will be better drivers, athletes, and mathematicians. They say video games are preparing youngsters for the technologically dominated world of the future. "Most adults are afraid of computers," says one engineer, "but with these video games even the youngest kids are learning to cope with the kind of machines they're going to have to live with for the rest of their lives."

Cable

Cable television was developed in the late 1940s to serve communities unable to receive clear TV signals because of their terrain or their distance from television stations. Cable companies erected antennas in areas that had good reception in order to pick up broadcast systems and distribute them to subscribers for a fee. That is why cable is also called CATV or Community Antenna Television.

For a long time many people believed that the full development of cable would do away with the concept of "free" television in this country, and would be contrary to the public interest. The networks, fearful of losing their long-standing hold on the industry, applied heavy pressure on the Federal Communications Commission to put brakes on the new system. In the late 1960s the FCC responded by imposing a strict set of regulations on cable operators. Cable companies were prohibited from carrying programs that aired the same day on local over-the-air stations. They were prevented from bidding on the telecasting rights to major events such as the World Series. And FCC regulations dictated that cable companies could not bring any signals into a major market from more than seventy-five miles away without first obtaining FCC permission.

In the mid 1970s, however, the FCC did a complete about-face and, amid an atmosphere in which TV competition from every source was suddenly encouraged, lifted restrictions designed to protect local stations from cable. As far as the government is concerned, cable TV is now free to develop without interference. In 1981 more than twenty-three million American homes (28.3 percent of the country) were already hooked up to cable, and it is predicted

Would You Believe?

There are now plans on the drawing board for an electronic locator button that can be sewn into the clothing of your toddlers. When you're wondering where they are, simply press the locator key of your video terminal and a map of the neighborhood comes up on the screen—a tiny colored dot reveals the location of each child.

Would You Believe?

For a quick, peaceful getaway you can now surround yourself with gentle waterfalls and lapping tides—cassettes marketed as tranquil Video Wallpaper.

that by the end of the decade half the nation will be wired. CATV systems now operate in every state of the nation and in several other countries, including Australia, Canada, Belgium, Germany, Great Britain, Italy, Japan, Mexico, Sweden, and Switzerland. All cable systems constructed in the United States must now, by FCC regulations, have a minimum twenty-channel capacity. Some systems already offer over a hundred channels for programming and other services.

The main differences between cable TV and conventional television is that with cable, programs are transmitted through wires rather than than over the air, permitting cable to have a greater channel capacity. The number of channels in over-the-air transmission is limited by interference between channels. But up to fifty-two channels can be transmitted at the same time through one coaxial cable. When two cables are set in place next to each other, channel capacity increases to 104. Cable systems have another advantage: the protected cable shields the TV signal from atmospheric conditions. That is one reason cable reception is so much clearer than conventional TV.

Cable systems have three basic components: the headend, the distribution system, and the subscriber terminal. The headend, which is usually constructed at the base of a master antenna, receives signals from a variety of sources. These signals come from local and far-away stations, from communications satellites circling overhead, and from other cable systems. Most cable systems in America today are still one-way. Signals are transmitted from the headend "downstream" via the distribution system (the cable) to the subscriber. However,

in two-way systems, such as QUBE (see page 000), signals can be transmitted not only "downstream" to the subscriber but "upstream" from subscribers back to the headend. Sophisticated cable systems such as the ones in Reading, Pennsylvania, and Lansing, Michigan, actually allow viewers in different locations throughout these cities to see and talk to each other via the television set.

The major arteries of a cable system are

New Technology

Broadcasting
Radio or television signals sent through the airwaves for public use.

Cable Television
Cable systems transmit signals through copper wire cable (instead of over the air) to television sets, providing interference-free pictures.

Coaxial Cable
A double axis cable that conducts electronic signals when an electromagnetic field is created between the concentric copper wires and the insulator separating them.

Fiber Optics
Transmission lines of thin glass fibers to transmit light signals that can be converted to carry audio and visual information of a very great channel-carrying capacity.

Franchise
A contract between a local government and a cable company to use public property to install and operate a cable system, with specifications for services.

Headend
The brain center of a cable system, the headend facility receives, converts, and retransmits incoming signals to the subscribers.

Interactive
A cable system capable of two-way communication (home to station and station to home), so that subscribers may "talk back" to their TV sets.

Microwave
High-frequency transmission of TV signals in a narrow line-of-sight path. This short wave part of the spectrum is greatly affected by obstacles.

Multipoint Distribution Service (MDS)
A short-distance (under 25 miles) transmission for data and non-broadcast programs to businesses, individual homes, or apartment complexes.

Multiple Systems Operator (MSO)
Any cable company that owns more than one cable system.

Pay TV
Television services offered to subscribers on a monthly subscription or a pay-per-view basis.

Subscription TV (STV)
Services using standard broadcast channels and offered for a monthly or per-program fee through the use of a scrambled broadcast signal, decoded by the subscriber.

the trunk lines that carry the signals, which are then diverted into feeder lines bringing sound and picture into the subscriber's home. The connection point between the feeder line and a television set is called the subscriber terminal.

In order to operate a cable system within a community, a cable company must have the official permission of the local government to lay cable lines within the community and to send signals into homes and public buildings. Local authorities have the power to grant the franchise to whatever cable company they feel will best serve the community. The franchising procedure, described in detail in Chapter 9 (see pages 000 to 000), is a complex and most important process for any city or town considering a cable system.

Superstation
A local TV station that beams its signal via satellite across the nation to cable subscribers (WTBS, Atlanta; WOR-TV, New York; WGN-TV, Chicago).

Tiering
Extra cable services packaged to appeal to special interest viewers for an additional monthly fee.

Satellite Glossary

Communications Satellite
A signal reception center keeping pace with the earth's revolutions in a fixed orbit 22,300 miles over the equator, which retransmits the TV and audio signals to receivers located on earth (also called a "bird").

Dish
A spherical shaped antenna that collects satellite transmission as part of an earth station.

Direct Broadcast Satellite (DBS)
A satellite service whose signal is delivered directly to homes equipped with a collecting dish, bypassing cable and local broadcast systems.

Downlink
The signal sent from a satellite to earth; often the term is used to refer to the equipment that receives this signal.

Earth Station
The equipment used to receive or transmit satellite communications.

Footprint
The term used to describe the territory on earth covered by a particular satellite.

Transponder
The functional unit of a satellite (there are 12 or 24 transponders depending on the satellite model), which receives the earth signal, modifies it, and retransmits it back to earth. Each transponder can handle one color TV program or 12 radio broadcasts.

Uplink
Part of the satellite communications system transmitting signals from earth to satellite.

How Cable TV Works

TV is transmitted in two ways: through the air to the set (conventional broadcast TV) or through a cable that is physically connected to the set (nonbroadcast cable TV).

Cable systems have certain standard parts: a master antenna that receives the TV signals from the air; a brain center called the headend, which houses all of the signal receivers and converters, distribution equipment, and sometimes program production equipment; and a series of coaxial (copper) cables called trunk lines (the main drag), feeder cables (down your street) and drop cables (to your house).

Depending on the level of sophistication of a system, the brain center may house microwave equipment for the relay of signals from TV stations and satellite receivers for the collection of signals from satellite trans-

mission. Some systems are equipped with production facilities so they can produce their own shows. They may also be equipped with satellite "uplinks" so that locally originated programs can be sent up to one of the orbiting satellites for transmission across the nation. Some systems have cables that are capable of carrying signals both to and from the home, so that interaction becomes possible.

In general, cable TV gives better television reception because signals are not subject to interference from other airwaves. More channels (and thus more diversity of programming) are possible than with conventional TV because a single coaxial cable can carry 52 channels at once. New developments in fiber optic cables promise even more channel-carrying capacity.

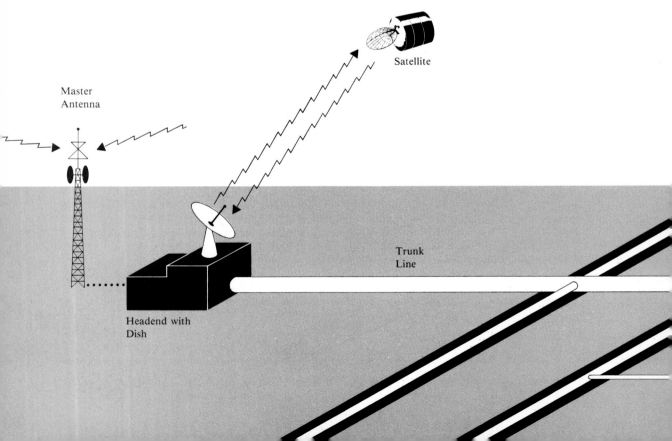

Satellite

Master
Antenna

Trunk
Line

Headend with
Dish

A cable subscriber not only can tune in to any one of the multiple channels that cable supplies as basic service, but he can also, if he is willing to pay for it, avail himself of the several pay-TV services that cable offers. Pay-TV companies send out a scrambled TV signal on certain channels and subscribers, for a fee, can view special programs such as first-run movies, live telecasts of theatrical productions, and sporting events by attaching a device to their set that unscrambles the picture. The money-making potential of pay-television is staggering. Says one sports cable executive, "Say we have ten million sets in five years. We could charge as little as $8.00 for one sporting event and still gross $80 million." *Sports Illustrated* has pointed out that "It takes no talent for addition to extrapolate from these figures a wildly optimistic view of the megabuck possibilities for

Cable Stats

- Cable laying costs range from $8,000 to $12,000 per mile but can jump to $80,000 per mile if underground cable is indicated.

- The 4,400 systems operate in 10,400 communities.

- Currently there are 22,000,000 subscribers or 27.39 percent of all TV households.

- Revenues for the industry increased by $1 billion in one year to total $2.3 billion in 1980.

- Most of the nation's systems offer 12 channels and cost $8.50 per month for the basic service.

- One seventh of all systems accept advertising on locally originated channels (costing from $1 to $200 for a 30-second spot), but most derive less than 50 percent of their revenues from advertising.

- One-third of all cable systems have broadcasting ties (down by 6 percent from last year).

Broadcasting Cable Yearbook, 1981

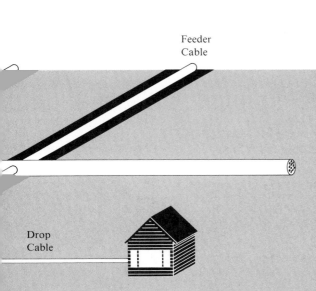

Feeder Cable

Drop Cable

pay-per-view on a national scale. Think of it. At $15.00 a head, the Super Bowl draws $1.5 billion. A seven-game World Series, $2.1 billion. The Kentucky Derby, $496 million. It's like trying to visualize infinity.''

Cable companies can also create programs. Local governments have made the awarding of franchises contingent on the establishment of a certain number of public access channels on which citizens can telecast free of charge. In addition cable, through a separate institutional loop, can link schools, libraries, hospitals, and businesses within a community or across the nation.

With its multiplicity of channels and its potential for offering access time to private citizens and groups, cable represents a radically different approach to TV programming and viewing. With so many programs from which to choose, viewers become their own programmers. Television has been a medium addressed to a mass market, a market defined by the largest number of views likely to buy the sponsor's product. A multichannel cable system can address smaller audiences virtually ignored by commercial TV. As one observer has noted: ''When hundreds of channels are available, scientists can create programs for scientists, poets for poets, women's groups for women's groups, socialists for socialists, conservatives for conservatives. Instead of the relentless, desperate search by the producer for the lowest common denominator, cable encourages another kind of search, closer to the kinship that exists in a conversation between friends, or between essayist and reader.''

Would You Believe?

There is now a microwave oven that, via a built-in TV receiver, teaches you how to cook, shows you what ingredients to use, gives you instructions verbally, shows you what the recipe should look like, cooks the meal for you, and, when it's ready, announces *madame est servi*. What next? The same TV in the same oven will be able to give you a closed-circuit view of children's rooms or the front door.

The threat to the networks and the local TV stations posed by cable is real. Predictions of how much audience the networks will have lost to the new technologies by the end of the decade range from 10 percent to 50 percent. A 1981 Nielsen survey found that in homes wired to pay-TV, network ratings were 10 percent lower than the national average. Now convinced of the reality of the challenge of the new technologies, the networks have abandoned their policy of denying cable's potential effect and have jumped into the revolution themselves. ABC and CBS have formed their own cable networks and have set up divisions to create special programming for cable systems around the world. In addition, ABC has purchased the Eastern Sports Cable Network and CBS has been taking a serious look at Ted Turner's all-news cable network with an eye toward acquiring it.

But cable is not without its problems. Much of the public has always believed that cable, because of its monthly subscription fees, would come into the home free of commercials. But increasingly cable executives are focusing on the potential advertising revenues available to them. Says Edward N. Ney, chairman of Young and Rubican, one of the world's largest advertising agencies, ''If you are looking forward to the much-proclaimed video revolution, with its cable and satellite transmission, as a way of escaping the constantly increasing advertising clamor in your life, forget it. Advertising is going to follow you right along.'' According to another cable entrepreneur, cable

Pay TV

Pay TV is an extra TV service delivered for an extra monthly or per program charge to cable subscribers. It works through the use of a converter which unscrambles the channel, or, if the subscriber prefers his selections a la carte, the channel decoder is activated by the viewer on a program-by-program basis.

Some pay channels now available or on the way:

Bravo!
Cultural events

Cinemax
Variety, Movies including cult and foreign films

Escapade
Action/adventure movies, R-rated movies

Galavision
Spanish language entertainment from Latin America & Spain, movies, dramas, soaps, comedies, musicals

PRISM
Family entertainment, live sports events

Rainbow
3 part package:
1. Escapade   2. Bravo!   3. Sneak Preview (movies 1st released on pay TV)

Nickelodeon
Children's programming 14 hours/day

HBO
First run movies, some sports, entertainment specials

Home Theatre Network
Movies, specials

The Movie Channel
Recently released movies 24 hours/ day

Private Screenings
Adult entertainment, action/adventure, R-rated movies

Show Time
Movies, Broadway and Off-Broadway specials, plays, nightclub acts, musicals, comedy series, Southwest regional sports

advertising presents opportunities that go beyond the world of commercial television. Advertising on cable, he said, ". . . is going to be the great equalizer. Even mom-and-pop retailers will be able to afford time at the local level, adjacent to a special-interest program that relates to their product. And long-form commercials might just be a copywriter's dream. Just think of all the things that can't be adequately sold in thirty or sixty seconds."

Already some 20 percent of all cable systems accept commercials on their local origination channels. And although revenue from advertising by cable companies to date is tiny when compared to the $11 billion grossed by the networks in 1980, several TV executives have predicted that by 1990 cable advertising could bring in more than $2 billion. Some of the nations's biggest corporations are cable advertisers. Bristol-Meyers has allocated funding to sponsor a health program on the USA Network, a precedent that disturbs many who question the propriety of a drug manufacturer's underwriting a series on health. Even "Calliope," the children's show on that network, is aired with commercials. The idea of cable's becoming dominated by advertising is a serious issue for those who feel that any TV system that relies heavily on revenue from sponsors will ultimately become captive to the very ratings game that cable, through paid subscriptions, has the potential to avoid.

As cable grows, the offerings on the pay-TV channels will become more varied. The American public has already demonstrated its collective inability to resist most highly promoted TV fare. Will it be be able to say no to attractive pay-TV programs that can come at the push of a button? And if events such as the World Series, the Super Bowl, or the newest Broadway play are shown exclusively on pay-TV, will our monthly pay-TV bill be as high as our mortgage payment? Will we, through paid subscription TV, be setting up a communications system where only the rich can take advantage of its services?

Subscription TV

Special interest programs (entertainment films, sporting events) are available to non-cable subscribers through the use of over-the-air-transmissions that are scrambled except to paying customers who have decoders. As with pay cable, these programs are billed for on a monthly or pay-per-view-basis.

The programs are broadcast on a UHF channel, which operates commercially during the day and as subscription TV during prime-time hours.

Interactive Cable

Interactive or two-way cable TV is one of the most intriguing of all the new television technologies. Actually it is not all that new. Since 1977 Warner Communications, Inc., has operated a two-way TV system in Columbus, Ohio. Called QUBE (the letters have no meaning), the system provides subscribers with a small console that allows them to receive thirty channels of programming from various sources. The console also contains five buttons that allow viewers to answer multiple-choice or yes-or-no questions or "ask" for further information. For example, during a political debate carried by QUBE, viewers are asked to indicate whether they agree or disagree with a point made by a particular candidate. Responses are tabulated instantly, and viewers are able to see how the audience as a whole reacts to that particular issue in the debate.

Ahead lies the opportunity to tie the interactive aspect into entertainment programming. Whodunits will be created where viewers, with the aid of a more sophisticated response capability, will actually choose from a variety of preprogrammed options and create their own plot lines, follow whatever clues they feel are essential, and solve the "case" for themselves.

"Touching-in" **On Qube**

Featured Highlights

T-1 Special Events

*denotes program was video taped at an earlier time

Sunday November 1	Monday November 2	Tuesday November 3	Wednesday November 4	Thursday November 5	Friday November 6	Saturday November 7
6 am Front Row with Flippo*	11 am Dateline Columbus — Candidates Night*	8:30 am Dateline Columbus — Candidates Night*	11 am How To Use Your Qube*	9:30 am Qube At Your Service — encore from November 4*	10 am Columbus Alive — encore from November 5*	10 am The Magic Touch — encore from November 3*
9 am Dateline Columbus — Candidates Night*	3:30 pm Columbus Alive — encore from October 29*	9:30 am Holiday Handcrafts — Ornament Painting*	1 pm Holiday Handcrafts — Ornament Painting*	2:30 pm Holiday Handcrafts — Ornament Painting*	12 nn Front Row with Flippo*	11:30 am High School Football — Dublin vs Grandview*
11:30 am Holiday Handcrafts — Natural Wreaths*	5 pm Holiday Handcrafts — Ornament Painting*	11 am Dateline Columbus — Candidates Night*	3:30 pm Columbus Alive — encore from November 3*	4:30 pm The Magic Touch — encore from November 3*	3 pm How To Use Your Qube*	2 pm Columbus Alive — encore from November 2*
12 nn Columbus Alive — encores from October 26-29*	6 pm Dateline Columbus — Candidates Night*	6 pm Dateline Columbus*	6:30 pm Qube At Your Service — LIVE	7 pm Columbus Alive — LIVE	4:30 pm Qube Football Review — encore from November 2*	6 pm Qube At Your Service — encore from November 4*
4 pm Dateline Columbus — Candidates Night*	7 pm Columbus Alive — LIVE	7 pm Columbus Alive — LIVE	7 pm Columbus Alive — LIVE	8 pm Qube Football Review — encore from November 2*	7 pm Holiday Handcrafts — Ornament Painting*	6:30 pm High School Football — Dublin vs Grandview*
7 pm Holiday Handcrafts — Natural Wreaths*	8 pm Qube Football Review — LIVE	8 pm The Magic Touch — LIVE	8:30 pm Dateline Columbus*	9 pm Dateline Columbus*	9 pm Dateline Columbus*	9 pm OAC Soccer Championship*
12 mn How To Use Your Qube*	12 mn Dateline Columbus — Candidates Night*	1 am Front Row with Flippo*	9 pm Columbus Amen — LIVE	10:30 pm High School Football — Dublin vs Grandview*	10:30 pm High School Football — Dublin vs Grandview*	1 am Front Row with Flippo*
				9 pm Dateline Columbus*		
				10:30 pm Holiday Handcrafts — Ornament Painting*		

Warner Amex QUBE

Using the QUBE Interactive TV System

While the development of interactive TV adds a new dimension to the video experience, there is the question of whether or not it is truly interactive. As the technology now exists, participants in two-way cable can respond only to questions framed by employees of the company that controls the system. Already much concern has been raised about an immediate feedback procedure in which political decisions and electoral strategy are based on a system in which serious reflection is replaced by momentary whim. There have already been several instances in which politicians and the media have presented as significant viewer "preferences" made to satisfy the time-frame of a television poll and based on inadequate sampling techniques.

The Question of Privacy

The most serious problem brought on by the new interactive technologies has to do with privacy. As the lines between major American industries are becoming blurred, it will become increasingly difficult to make distinctions relating to the functions of television, telephone, and computer. As writer Anne Branscomb has said, "In the good old days the provider was as distinctive as the service. Western Union typed telegrams, the Post Office delivered mail, the New York Times Company published the daily paper. CBS, ABC, NBC, and PBS broadcast television shows, Ma Bell sent the phone bill, and reading a best-seller meant a trip to the library or the bookstore. Now, with Dial-a-Bird, Dial-a-Prayer, and even bedtime stories just a few digits away, it's hard to tell who's responsible for what. The New York *Times* arrives via a computer terminal, movies sell at the corner video market, and Federal Express brings the mail."

Would You Believe?

A British Broadcasting consultant to developing nations, along with an inventor friend, have attached silicon cells to a TV set to convert sunlight to electricity. The electricity is stored in a battery for powering the TV, two hours of sun roughly converting to one hour of viewing pleasure. The idea came about when the inventor, Kurt Lewenhak, watched a how-to show on agriculture on a visit to Ghana and realized how few Africans could ever see such programs and benefit from them. What do they call their new solar-powered TV receiver? A "sunset" of course.

Who is going to see to it that the price we pay for all these new services is not the loss of one of our most prized possessions—our privacy? One potential nightmare is the misuse of the personal information that is compiled as a matter of course by many of these new technologies. We will be able to do our banking via TV, but will our financial records be available to credit companies, government agencies, and whoever wants to use it to advantage? We will receive our mail electronically, but what safeguards will there be to guarantee that our personal correspondence will not be seen by others?

The new technologies will make our homes more secure, but all of our comings and goings will be a matter of record. We will be able to let our voices be heard as to whom we like in an election and what types of programs we like to watch, but those data will be accessible to a lot of people with whom we might not want to share this information. Says one cable executive, "With the sophisticated equipment we have, we can tell just about what you eat for breakfast. It's real George Orwell out there."

The privacy issue is serious because traditional ways of protecting individual or business privacy are ineffective in the face of new ways of compiling, storing, and sharing data. It is folly to expect help in this area from the companies that will control the new technologies. The most they seem able to promise is that they will face the issue once a more significant number of American homes are equipped with interactive TV or videotext or multichannel cable.

And from all indications the federal government won't be much help either. In a paper released in 1980, two FCC staff members proposed that the marketplace should decide just how much privacy those who control the new technologies should provide. In other words, it is their opinion that participants in interactive home TV should pay for assurances of privacy the same way they pay for special programming. This "pay for privacy" idea is totally unacceptable, if only because it protects the rich and not the poor.

What then can be done? What can you do to ensure that your privacy will be protected? Chapter 9 offers detailed guidelines for establishing a cable franchise, but there are a few general tips to mention here. Before subscribing to a cable company you should know just what that company's policy is regarding privacy rights. The cable company should agree in writing that it will not include your name on any list of subscribers it gives to another company or individual without your consent. Where interactive cable is involved, you should have the right, upon reasonable request, to see your own records, and the company should agree that after a certain amount of time has passed it will destroy all records of your viewing and voting preferences. You should work to see that your local cable contract makes the meeting of certain privacy requirements a necessary adjunct to franchise renewal. Your local government can follow the example set by Massachusetts guidelines. It can:

- Conduct an educational campaign designed to inform all the citizens in your community about the privacy issues involved in cable.

- Prohibit any cable operator from sharing any information about the viewing habits of any individual subscriber with any third party.

- Require cable operators to provide all subscribers with a clear written explanation of their privacy rights, how these rights will be protected under the law, and what the individual company has done in the past to protect privacy rights.

- Require cable operators to agree that before *any* survey that identifies subscriber behavior or preference is undertaken, each subscriber will be notified and have the unconditional right not to participate in such a survey.

- Ascertain whether or not your state has privacy legislation comparable to the Federal Privacy Act of 1974. If not, the leaders of your community should work with their counterparts in other cities and towns to induce your state legislature to adopt such legislation.

Although it is easy to be captivated by the glitter and the games of the new technologies, we should not forget that the role of a communications system is to communicate. No matter how dazzling it is to operate a battery of buttons or to watch newsprint appear as if by magic, we must not ignore the need for people to exchange information, to debate issues, and to develop new strategies for the spaceship earth.

Living with Television

Television and You

Everyone watches television. Everyone. Whether it's on a daily basis for hours on end, or only once every few months for a special program, we all watch television. And whether we admit it or not, most of us like television. It's entertaining. It's informative. It's great companionship for the person alone; it's a casual social activity for a group. TV watching is easy to do and, compared with the cost of movies or the theater today, it's inexpensive.

Perhaps because watching TV is so available, we have come to abuse television. First of all, we watch too much—almost seven hours a day, on the average. We are in danger of becoming a culture reliant exclusively on the electronic media for many of our needs. As the video revolution captures more and more of our attention (it's estimated that by 1990, nine out of ten homes will have video/computer systems), we will spend even more of our waking hours in front of a television screen.

Is this bad? Neglecting other important activities—books, exercise, hobbies—in favor of sedentary TV viewing certainly is undesirable. Equally disturbing is that most of us do not watch *television programs;* we simply watch *television*. We may turn the TV set on for a specific show we consciously decide to watch, but all too often the set stays on after the program has gone off. Thirty minutes of "M*A*S*H" turns into three and a half hours of programming. Before we know it the news is over and the late movie has begun: where did the evening go? We were going to read the latest magazine, pay some bills, write a letter, or spend a quiet evening at home with our family. "Television," says psychologist Peter Crown, "in addition to being a source of entertainment and information, has taken on the role of the electronic fireplace of our time. Just as gazing into a campfire can be absorbing and hypnotic, so can gazing at the TV screen. It doesn't matter what's on, it only matters that there is something emitting light patterns."

Broadcasters know our disinclination to turn the set on and off for specific programs, and they take advantage of it. The most popular shows frequently are shown in the first prime time slot. And then we're hooked. The networks also know that flipping on the set is a habit for most people. Even if we have no particular show in mind, we're likely to turn on the TV "just to see what's on." Once the TV is on, we switch channels looking for something interesting (or familiar) to watch. Chances are we won't find anything that genuinely interests us but will settle on the program we find least objectionable of the choices offered that hour.

The danger of our habitual manner of watching television is that it means we are approaching television with passivity. And if we are accepting of what we see on television, we are overlooking our personal responsibility to ourselves. Unless we become more discerning viewers, we place ourselves at the mercy of television's messages.

Most of us probably watch television because we like to be entertained in the comfort of our home and we want to escape from the hassles, disappointments, and routines of everyday life. This desire to escape to a simpler world where problems are solved by familiar formulas explains why millions of viewers will, week after week, watch a detective series in which the pattern is always the same. Somehow the uncomplicated ritual of watching the hero break down the alibi, discover the motive, and identify the culprit without deviating from what we know is going to happen allows us to relax and soothes our souls. The "escape" provided by TV also contributes significantly to why children are so enamored of it. Because children can watch television without having to accommodate to parents, teachers, or even peers, youngsters have found in TV an uncomplicated, nondemanding world into which to escape.

Another important reason we find ourselves, children and adults alike, unable to turn off the television set is that most television tells a story. Whether we're watching "Dallas," "60 Minutes," "Upstairs, Downstairs," or even many commercials, there is a conscious plot line to be followed. We need to "stay tuned" or we will never know what happened.

There is also an important vicarious aspect to our television watching. Millions of us—men as well as women—watch soap operas, dramas, and situation comedies because these shows allow us to participate in a world that for one reason or another has been denied us in our own lives. We identify with the pains and pleasures of TV characters, sympathizing with them as they cope with divorce, death, or illness, rejoicing at their good fortune—putting ourselves in their shoes. We may do this consciously, fantasizing about an opulent style of living or a more exciting existence. Sometimes the identification with TV characters is unconscious, and we come to love or despise them, forgetting they are fictional. We may begin to emulate those we admire, picking up their mannerisms. We even allow their values and ethics to influence ours. If we see TV characters repeatedly lying or having extramarital affairs and not suffering for

their deceit, we tend to think our own punishment for the same actions wouldn't be so harsh . . . so why not do it? At some level, countless viewers have chosen television to be the new arbiter of moral issues, and they turn to it for approbation of their actions.

Television, by design, divides the world into winners and losers, and many people watch TV because of the pleasure they derive from "the thrill of victory, the agony of defeat." The spectacular success of televised sports is one of the most phenomenal aspects of the television experience. Viewers identify with the athletes and project themselves into the "life or death" situations that TV not only reports, but often creates. Whether the challenge is the eighteen-foot putt on the final hole, the last-minute field goal, or even the last water ditch in a meaningless battle of celebrities, millions of viewers will be tuned in. This "winners and losers" phenomenon carries over to other areas of TV besides sports. It is at the heart of the success of the countless quiz and game shows that dominate large blocks of TV programming time, and it explains our fascination with a growing number of televised contests, from the Miss America Pageant to the Oscars, Emmys, Grammys, and so on. These competitions allow us the pleasure of resolving anxieties in a matter of moments. We wait anxiously for the envelope to be opened, for the drumroll to subside and

the winner to be crowned. And then we sit back, relieved to know now who is "the best."

Television is used in many other ways to relieve anxiety. In many homes TV watching reduces the discomfort of having to discuss difficult or unpleasant family problems or having to talk at all. Instead of dealing with these issues, families engage in conversation (during commercial breaks, of course) about the one thing they can converse about amicably and without anxiety—the TV show they are watching at the time.

Knowing why we watch television— and understanding its effects on us—are essential tools in becoming better television viewers. As television matures and grows into the single most indispensable tool of the twenty-first century, it will be even more important for us to be better viewers. Being better at watching tele-

"The Image Orthicon Camera Tube Awards"

The TV industry's trophy for excellence was originally named by TV engineer Harry R. Lubcke, then president of the Academy of Television Arts and Sciences, which bestows the awards. Emmy stems from "Immy," which was the nickname for the image orthicon camera tube.

vision doesn't mean watching fewer (or more) hours every week. It doesn't mean watching the "MacNeil/Lehrer Report" instead of "General Hospital." It simply means being conscious of what we choose to watch and critical of what we see. In fact, coming to terms with the simple

Would You Believe?

In Indiana, a man dropped his bowling ball through his television set when it wouldn't switch on. In Illinois, a man watching a boxing match in a tavern got upset with the decision, threw a bottle of beer at the tube, injuring the bartender with the flying glass so badly that he had to be hospitalized. A Californian who fell off his roof while trying to repair his TV antenna vented his rage by kicking in his television set. In another California community, police were called in when a viewer pumped 17 bullets into his set. His first words to the constabularies: "Didn't *you* ever want to shoot *your* television?

Then there was the furor that was aroused over the results of a sporting event on TV. A Swedish viewer, displeased by the 4–1 score of a Czechoslovakia-Sweden hockey game, threw the set out the window. In a fit of remorse he started to drive the TV to a repair shop, but in the process crashed into another car, totalling his own.

Finally, a California company has come upon a creative solution to all these expensive fits of temper—a TV brick. A piece of foam rubber that looks like a brick, it will bounce off leaving your set unharmed. And for $2.99 plus shipping, it will leave your pocketbook relatively unscathed.

fact that you like to watch television may be the first and best step you can take to being a better television viewer. Unlike any other cultural medium—and TV *is* a medium of culture, both high and low—there seems to be a reverse snobbism in operation. Many people, particularly those with advanced educations, are reluctant to admit that they watch anything other than ''Masterpiece Theatre'' or ''NOVA'' or a live Pavarotti concert. (''Mary Tyler Moore'' re-runs are acceptable.) What is the result? A nation full of closet ''Love Boat'' devotees.

How do you know, then, if you abuse television? If you watch too much television or if television has an addictive hold on you? The quiz here can help you judge the extent of television's grip on your life.

We're not recommending that everyone go on a strict TV diet. For the elderly and shut-ins, TV is not only a welcome companion—it may be the only companion. If you do choose to cut down on the amount of television you watch, there are several practical tips we can offer. Even if there aren't others around to encourage you, you can kick the TV habit. One suggestion is to wean yourself gradually. Pick only shows that you know you genuinely want to watch, and turn the TV off when those programs end. If you find it difficult to turn the set off for the half hour between ''Happy Days'' and ''Three's Company,'' try turning off just the sound at first. When we have the television on simply for companionship, we don't need both the audio and video portions. Pick a no-TV night—an evening on which there aren't any programs you particularly want to watch. Make other plans for that evening every week, so that you don't feel you're missing the action on those shows (which you're probably watching out of sheer habit anyway). Start a weekly poker group, or a reading circle. Join your local Y and make one night a week a workout night.

You can cut down on television indirectly by becoming a more critical viewer. We wouldn't dream of going to the movies or the theater without first reading or hearing a critique that made us think we might like the event. Yet night after night we sit and watch television with no more recommendation than

the three-line plot summaries we find in our newspapers or *TV Guide.* Nor would we attend any other cultural event without analyzing it after the fact. Were the actors good? Did the play make sense? What was the movie trying to say? Television deserves that type of critical questioning from us as well, particularly now, as the lines between TV and other cultural media have begun to blur. We probably watch as many full-length movies on television as we do at a movie house. And cable and public television stations now bring theater, dance, and music to our home screen.

You might want to become your own TV critic, asking yourself some questions:

- Why am I watching this program?

- What are the direct messages of the program (or commercial)? How does the message I see compare with the message I hear?

- What are the hidden messages in the program? Is it expressing a particular bias?

- What in the program is fact, what is opinion, and what is plain fantasy? (This question isn't intended to apply only to programs like ''Star Trek'' but to the news as well.)

- Does this program use any ''tricks''—with the camera work, the music, the laugh track—to enhance the story or influence my reactions?

- Do I notice anything interesting about how this program is made? The casting? The makeup and costuming?

- What do I think is good about this program? Bad? Why?

The programs aren't all we see on television, of course. Commercials have an enormous influence on us. They account for as much as 20 percent of air time and, as we've pointed out before, are often produced with

Some Questions to Ask Yourself About Your Own TV Watching

- Are you upset with the amount of time you spend in front of the TV set? How much time *do* you spend with TV? How does this compare with national viewing statistics? (The average American watches 6 hours and 44 minutes per day.)

- What kinds of things have you stopped doing because of your TV watching?

- Do you find yourself watching selected programs that you look forward to, or do you simply watch whatever is on?

- Has television affected your life positively? Negatively?

- Do you find that your buying decisions in the supermarket or the department store are helped by TV commercials? Hindered?

- Do you *automatically* turn on the television set when you walk into your home? Is the TV set on in your bedroom right up until the time you fall asleep? When else do you *automatically* turn on TV? For example, as soon as you enter a hotel room? Whenever you're home alone with a couple of hours to kill?

- For the most part, do you watch TV alone or with other people? When you watch with others do you ever discuss what you have seen with them? When you have finished watching a program alone do you ever ask yourself what you liked or did not like about it?

- Do you feel yourself adjusting your own personal schedule in order to watch TV? Do you avoid going out on Friday evenings so you won't miss "Dallas"? Do you show up late for engagements because you had to see the end of "60 Minutes" or "Family Feud"?

- Has television affected the quality of time you spend with your family? Do you do less together because of televised weekend sports? What about mealtimes? How many meals do you eat in front of the tube?

- Is television a major irritant in your home? Do you fight about what to watch, about turning it off?

- Do you have cable or a video recorder? If you do, do you find that you're watching even more television than you did before? Have the increased options made your TV viewing more enjoyable?

more resources than the television shows they interrupt. For one thing, commercial advertisers have a great deal at stake. In ten or fifteen or thirty seconds they must (a) tell you what their product is and what it does; (b) convince you that you need the product; and (c) show you how it is better than any other competing product.

Often advertisers show you that you need their products by implying they will deliver far greater intangible benefits than could possibly be true. This assertion is most often made by association. Celebrity endorsements imply you will be just like your favorite athlete or movie star if you wear Brand X underwear. Beautiful models prey on our desire to be more socially and sexually successful and tell us the secret is to use Brand Y toothpaste. Parents are given the message that they will get along better with their children if they all eat at Restaurant Z. The world of TV ads has become a world of fantasy, and it is just as important to know the difference between fantasy and reality in TV commercials as in the programs themselves. A good commercial helps you make a rational buying decision in the marketplace. Remember that when you are watching messages that try to sell you a new lifestyle with a money-back guarantee that your dreams will come true.

Being a critical viewer is only the first step: becoming a responsible viewer is the ultimate goal. On a personal level this means taking responsibility for your TV choices, enacting the decisions you've made about the quality and quantity of television you should watch. On a social level it means standing up for what you believe about television and protecting its diversity.

Today in America there are a number of organizations whose avowed purpose is to protest specific television programs. The most powerful of these are part of a movement by ultraconservative religious groups to censor television. This religious New Right worries a lot about television. The Reverend Jerry Falwell, of Moral Majority, Inc., calls TV a ''ven-

Sometimes a TV ad becomes as popular as the program it accompanies. The James Garner–Mariette Hartley commercials for a major camera company have ranked among the most popular advertisements ever shown. Can you name the company? If you can, the ad has really worked.

dor of perniciousness.'' The Reverend Donald Wildmon, founder of the National Federation for Decency and chairman of the Coalition for Better Television (CBTV), has been monitoring television programs and rating them and their sponsors for decency since 1977. The same people who would deny women equality under the law and who want to take away our choice of books, our decisions about procreation, and our ability to teach our children about evolution now want to control television content.

The New Right is trying to determine what the rest of the American public—the real majority—may or may not see on television. This vocal minority brings organized economic pressures to bear on sponsors of programs it doesn't approve of, in an attempt to force broadcasters to take certain programs off the air. Perhaps the first program removed in the interests of the New Right morality would not be missed. But what would the next target be? How long would it be before the news is censored?

Once we allow Reverend Wildmon, or anyone, to impose his standards on us, we have created a disease far worse than the one his group aims to eradicate. America knows that disease firsthand. It's called censorship, and we suffered a serious bout of it during the 50s, thanks to another dedicated guardian of morals named Senator Joseph McCarthy.

The product of those who are out to "clean up" television is hit lists: hit lists of programs, commercials, advertisers, networks. Behind most of these hit lists is the veiled, and sometimes not-so-veiled, threat that if the programs are not taken off the air the sponsors of these programs will be made to suffer. Blacklists are nothing new to the communications industry. *Red Channels: The Report of Communist Influence in Radio and Television* was published in 1950; it listed 151 well-known writers, directors, and performers. Within a short time, many of them had lost their jobs and were unable to get others. The fact that the accusations against these people were untrue or

The purpose of a television commercial is to get your attention, persuade you to buy the product, and have you remember the product once you're at the market or store. TV ads fall into several categories such as: ads that use special effects, product comparisons, commercials that tell a simple story, testimonials, and statistical claims.

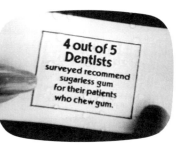

irrational (actor Philip Loeb was accused of helping Communism because he had sponsored an ''End Jim Crow in Baseball'' committee) was immaterial. The blacklist made the accused controversial and that was enough for advertisers and broadcasters, who quickly dropped them.

What we seem to be threatened with by the New Right is another kind of blacklist, a blacklist of ideas. At the height of the McCarthy era in the 1950s, no one dared mention Communism over the airwaves unless he railed against it in the next breath. Are we coming to a time when television will not dare to mention abortion, homosexuality, or the E.R.A. for fear of scaring away sponsors?

The television reform tactics of the Coalition for Better Television may be censorious, but it is important to point out that these tactics are not against the law. Groups have a legal right to deliver harangues against what they consider immoral television, to publish lists of the programs they find offensive and of the industries that sponsor these programs, and even to promote consumer boycotts against these companies' products. But being legal doesn't make these tactics any less harmful to the American public. Television reform does not have to mean censorship and repression. It does not have to mean interference with program content, which violates the public's right to know.

When someone with power over the channels of communications decides that it is ''better'' for the public not to hear about a dangerous or disturbing new development, a vital public right is taken away. No one has the right to decide that it is better for the people *not* to know. What it boils down to is that the thing we

Censorship has become a serious issue on television today. One of the major targets of pressure groups determined to control TV content has been the series ''Love, Sidney'' in which the main character was originally intended to be a homosexual.

have to worry about is not what we are getting on television; it's what we're not getting.

Television censorship of sorts already comes from a variety of sources. First of all, there are advertisers. No company is going to spend huge sums of money to advertise its products on a program that it feels will offend a large number of potential customers. For this reason, most advertisers avoid controversial programs. This explains why you see so many programs on TV that can only be described as banal. It also explains why so few of the nation's best writers write for television: it's simply impossible for them to deal with real human issues in a medium that so often screens out real issues and relies night after night on violence and titillation to move its stories along.

The networks are another source of censorship. They decide which programs to air and one of their prime concerns is to make sure that they don't upset advertisers by telecasting "offensive" shows. Since almost all network programs are on tape, the opportunity exists to "bleep out" what is, to the networks, offensive material on programs that do make it to the air.

Up to now, the television industry as a whole has policed itself with still another kind of TV censorship. The networks and the local stations around the country subscribed to the National Association of Broadcasters' television code, which prohibited certain practices in

The NAB Code's specific guidelines for underwear commercials ensure that viewers will never have to see bras and girdles on live models such as Jane Russell.

both programs and commercials. In TV shows, for example, crime could not be rewarded, profanity could not be used, and nudity could not be shown. The television code set down specific guidelines for the advertising of certain products such as alcoholic beverages or ladies' undergarments. (No hard liquor could be advertised; beer and wine ads were allowed but the actor could not be shown actually drinking it. Bras and girdles could be advertised but the models showing them had to be fully clothed.) The Code has been challenged by the Justice Department as anticompetitive, and the NAB has canceled its caveats. We must wait and see whether this action will mean a return to the ads of the snake-oil salesmen.

Even the First Amendment does not protect deception in television commercials. Nor does it protect libelous statements, or the equivalent of shouting "Fire!" in a crowded theater. And a recent Supreme Court decision specifically exempts pornography involving children from constitutional protection. But for protection against almost any other kind of content, language, or ideas, the best solution is using the off switch on the television set.

6 Resources

Books

Logan, Ben, ed. *Television Awareness Training*. New York: Media Action Research Center, 1977. Thought-provoking articles on aspects of the TV-viewing experience and worksheets to encourage critical viewing.

Norback, Craig T., and Norback, Peter G., eds. *TV Guide Almanac*. New York: Ballantine Books, 1980. A handy directory and source of facts and information on TV topics ranging from audience research to becoming a contestant on game shows.

Television and the Family

A great many people in this country and overseas are disturbed about the relationship of children to television. They're upset because there is so much on TV that they don't like. They're disturbed because adult-only films find their way into the living room. They worry about what children are missing when they spend so much of their leisure time with TV.

There are, of course, some bright exceptions to the generalizations about mediocrity, some creative, delightful, challenging alternatives that prove the potential of the medium.

Television for children has the power to enhance the magic of words with the wonder of pictures. It could be a Whole Earth Catalogue, a shopping list of strategies for coping with an increasingly complex world. One has merely to sit down in front of a television set any Saturday morning to realize how much more needs to be done.

The main reason so many families have a television problem is that in most homes the television set is on too much of the time. It is on through dinner; it remains on during family conversations; children have it on while doing their homework. It is an omnipresent member of the family. If this were not true, the average American youngster would not watch twenty-five to thirty hours of television a week. And that's too much television: too much good TV; too much bad TV; too many cartoons; too much "Sesame Street." It's just too much time in front of an electronic box.

It's a serious problem. For as much as we should be concerned about what our children watch day after day, we should question what they are *not* doing because they're spending so much time in front of the TV set. It's a difficult problem. America in the 1980s is not the America of the forties or the fifties. Today there are millions of working mothers in this country. Single-parent households have become commonplace. The structure of the family has changed and parental control has become more difficult to maintain than ever before.

Even in families which, by yesterday's standards, would be regarded as traditional, the problem of dealing with children's viewing habits is difficult to manage. And with good reason. It's so easy for youngsters to watch TV. And all their friends, schoolmates, and young relatives spend the major part of their leisure time watching television and talking about what they see.

Some families have chosen to wait until the children are ten or eleven years old before bringing a TV set into the home. They find it easier to do without some of television's most wonderful moments in the interest of avoiding the issues and conflicts about TV-watching that often disturb family peace and quiet. These families employ a number of ways of handling the problem of total abstinence. When a space shot or a special series like "Shogun" is being shown they rent a TV or arrange to watch with friends.

But doing away with TV is an extreme solution. And it is going to get more difficult to do. As we have seen, the day is fast approaching when the TV set will be part of a whole communications center in the home, and it will be much harder for those who can afford these new services to do without television.

The main reason most people resist the idea of abstaining from TV is simply that they like television. They don't want to lose the opportunity to see the world's greatest entertainers, to attend sporting events, to watch first-run movies, to get the news as it happens—all in their living rooms. Most parents don't give up riding in cars with a child because it's potentially dangerous. They get a car seat. They don't empty the house of furniture when a child begins to walk. They put cotton on the corners of the coffee table. Instead of doing without television, these parents try to figure out how to handle TV problems in the home.

This chapter makes a number of concrete suggestions about changing your children's TV habits and offers ideas to help them become selective viewers while providing them with the time and the incentive to do other things. It's important that you understand that these are only suggestions. You may find some of them helpful. Perhaps they will start you thinking about other ways in which you can get your family on a TV diet—in which they watch TV programs instead of merely watching television.

Looking at TV with Your Child

The first question parents concerned about the effects of television on their youngsters should ask themselves is "Have we ever seen the programs that our children are watching?" There is no way you can help your children deal with what they view unless you watch the programs with them. This doesn't mean you should watch

"... I didn't know a thing about children's TV, so I spent three Saturdays from nine o'clock in the morning until one-thirty in the afternoon in my study watching TV. By the time one-thirty rolled around, I was crazy." Dick Salant, vice-chairman, NBC

all the time. But if your children spend every Saturday morning watching cartoons, it is important that you spend at least part of one Saturday morning watching with them. One of the reasons there is so little variety in children's weekend programming is that the industry knows very few adults are watching. The adults who are in front of their sets at this time tend not to be concerned parents but people seeking mindless entertainment in the form of cartoons.

Most parents spend a lot of time worrying about what's going on in their children's

Jimmy Jet and His TV Set

I'll tell you the story of Jimmy Jet—
And you know what I tell you is true.
He loved to watch his TV set
Almost as much as you.

He watched all day, he watched all night
Till he grew pale and lean,
From "The Early Show" to "The Late Late Show"
And all the shows between.

He watched till his eyes were frozen wide,
And his bottom grew into his chair.
And his chin turned into a tuning dial,
And antennae grew out of his hair.

And his brains turned into TV tubes,
And his face to a TV screen.
And two knobs saying "VERT." and "HORIZ."
Grew where his ears had been.

And he grew a plug that looked like a tail
So we plugged in little Jim.
And now instead of him watching TV
We all sit around and watch him.

(from *Where the Sidewalk Ends*, by Shel Silverstein)

schools. They quiz their youngsters on what happens in the classroom; they skim through their children's textbooks; they even visit the school periodically. But few of us question our children about what they have seen on TV and what they think they've learned from it. And remember, children spend more time in front of the tube than in the classroom.

Look at TV with your children. Look for behavior your child is likely to imitate. Look for TV characters who care about others. Look for women who are competent at a variety of tasks. Look for people from a variety of cultural and ethnic backgrounds. And—look for ideas for what to do when you switch off the set.

Applauding and Booing

There is a great deal we could have learned from Shakespearean audiences in Elizabethan England about how to watch TV as a family. In those days when something happened on the stage that offended a viewer's tastes or values, he did not hesitate to express disapproval verbally. When something took place that delighted him he was quick to applaud. It is important for us as parents to let children know what our values are, what we approve or disapprove of. Actually we do it all the time. We do it about food: most of us let our children know that candy is not particularly good for their health.

One of the most significant ways we can help our children cope with what they see on television is by watching with them and letting them know what we think about what is happening on the screen. Think about a football game or a Saturday movie matinee from the good old days. Very few of us are reluctant to express our opinions at football games, and many of us over forty remember the hissing, the booing, and the raucous applause that took place in the movie theaters every Saturday as we watched the heroes and villains in the serials and adventure flicks.

You don't need to turn your TV-watching experience into Saturday afternoon at the ball park. But you can make your family's TV-viewing a participatory experience—participatory to the point where expressing your feelings out loud becomes an important part of the experience itself.

And you might want to go into it more deeply than merely hissing, booing, or applauding. When your family is watching the news and there are stories of wars, or portrayals of children suffering in foreign countries, or reports of murders, it is appropriate to make comments that will help your children deal with these issues. The sense that your youngsters get of your response and your attitudes will help to counter the TV education they get when they watch alone. You are terribly important to your children. Although sometimes you would never know it from their behavior, most of them would rather have you than the TV set. By participating in their TV experience you can use the issues brought up on the screen to let them know what you think is important and to help them distinguish between fact and fiction in what they are seeing.

As you watch the programs, talk with your children during the commercial breaks or after viewing. Talk about programs that delight them. What in particular do they find amusing or rewarding? Talk about programs that upset them. What in these programs disturbs them? Do they really believe that there is an Incredible Hulk and that he turns green? Is it better, perhaps, if they don't watch these programs at all? If there is violence in a program, point out the ways that violence in real life is painful. Discuss the ways in which TV characters could solve particular problems without violence. Talk about how TV shows cavity-producing foods both in programs and ads. Talk about TV toys that can break too soon, and explain what the disclaimers in small print on the screen really mean.

Most important, as you watch the programs, talk to your children about the differences between the make-believe world of television and real life. What about the special effects they see? Do they understand that those are really professional stuntmen and women smashing up all those cars or falling off roofs or staging those brawls? Do they realize that real-life people get hurt in fights or smashups or shoot-outs? Are they aware of the fact that most of the audience laughter they hear on the comedy shows and cartoons is "canned," and that there's nothing wrong with not finding the shows as funny as the audience seems to think they are?

Be specific with your comments. If you see a succession of ads in which women are waxing poetic about various mops, detergents, and brands of toilet paper, ask your youngsters if they think that most women really talk and act that way. Discuss with them why these ads appear in the first place. What about the black characters in the situation comedies they are watching? Do they think that most black people act like George Jefferson or Fred Sanford? Do your children really believe that teenagers prefer smashing up cars to almost any other activity?

If you are offended by certain programs, let your children know why. Let them know specifically what it is that disturbs you. If your children continue to watch the program, make sure that you occasionally drop in and watch some of the program with them. Do the same thing about programs that you think are good for your youngsters. Let them know why you think they're good. If a child gets to the point where he can say something like "Mom, you'd like this show because the people in it really seem to care about each other," you've not only succeeded in letting them know how you feel about things, but you've started them on the road to becoming critical viewers.

A special strategy: if you have young adolescents in your family, you don't need to be told how difficult it is to talk to them directly. Most parents of teenagers find that it is hard to get their ideas across to young people who are trying to establish their independence. However, if you are watching TV together as a family you can always make your comments to your husband or wife or to a younger child, hoping that the older one is going to get the message. Who knows? Enough of these stage whispers might even draw the teenager into a real discussion.

A final point: as you discuss specific issues or programs, as you point out the differences between fantasy and real life, let them know that TV is a business and what that means. If they can begin to understand such things as the role of the profit motive in broadcasting, who calls the shots, why there are so many commercials and how programs are aimed at certain audiences, they will be better able to handle what they're looking at.

Neighborhood TV Guide

Remember when one of the more popular toys on the market was a miniature printing press? Children used to love seeing their stories in print and distributing their own newspapers. Why not revive this absorbing activity? Your sons and daughters could write and distribute a newspaper with a TV section including their recommendations, or they could concentrate on the subject of television and produce a TV guide for their peer group. They could involve their family or their friends in writing reviews of series, editorials, comments about commercials, and stories about their favorite actors. Any artist in the family could draw caricatures or "connect-the-dots" puzzles. Jokesters could make up TV riddles or crossword puzzles. They would be proud of their work, and they'd be away from the set and developing critical viewing skills at the same time!

Choosing TV Programs with Your Child

It would never occur to most families simply to head out to the movies, to wind up in whatever theater they happen to stumble upon first. We check the paper to see what's playing in nearby movie houses and then we choose. This is also the way most of us pick which play, concert, or sporting event we attend. Yet when it comes to television, many parents are content to let their children (and themselves) flip the dial and watch whatever program they stumble upon.

Once a week look at a TV schedule, either in the Sunday newspaper or in a publication like *TV Guide,* and draw up a list of programs

Dissatisfied with the various guides to TV programs on the market? How about helping youngsters in your neighborhood create their own guide? Here's a sample.

March 13-19, 1982

Maple Street TV Guide

Weekly Trivia Quiz

1. What is the name of the newest Orkan and who plays the role?

2. Who is Bob Keeshan?

3. What is Fonzie's real name?

4. What does Miss Piggy call herself?

This Week's Poll

What's the dumbest commercial on television? (Call 222-2222 Tuesday between 7 and 9 pm.)

Last week's winner: Best program theme song - "One Day at a Time"

High School Sports on Cable

- Sunday at noon, channel 7
- Tuesday at 8:00, channel 4
- Friday at 7:30, channel 4

Help Wanted

Movie Buffs: Go to a lot of movies? Our TV Guide needs you to write reviews of movies that went from the movie theatres to television, like "The Champ" and "Oh God!" We want to find a few people we can call on to give their opinions. If you're interested, write to us and send us a short review of a movie. (We are an equal opportunity employer; movie fans of all ages may apply.) You, too, can see your words in print!

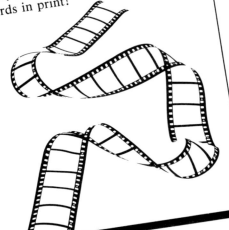

2

Weekend Best Bets

If you speak Spanish a little or a lot, you can practice with ''Carrascolendas'' - but only if you're up early.	Saturday, 6:30 am, channel 4
You've read the book . . . ''Huckleberry Finn'' is also a tv movie.	Saturday, 4:00 pm, channel 56
Check out the music of the Miami Sound Machine on ''Checking It Out.''	Saturday, 6:00 pm, channel 2
''Lights! Camera! Annie!'' - How they made the musical into a movie.	Saturday, 7:30 pm, channel 2
''Dallas'' freak? See Linda Gray on ''Kids are People Too.''	Sunday, 8:00 am, channel 5
Kermit has a birthday on ''The Muppets.''	Sunday, 7:00 and 7:30 pm, channel 4

Cable Calendar

Teens Talk to the School Board	Wednesday, 7:30 pm
Carver Jr. High Musical Theater	Friday, 7:00 pm

for that week. If you subscribe to cable television, you probably receive a weekly listing of programs from the company that has the franchise in your community. Using these guides you can, as a family activity, design a TV schedule that makes a great deal more sense than the hit-or-miss, uncontrolled TV schedule that your youngsters probably now follow.

In setting the schedule you will need to examine the guides carefully. Remember, some adult programs may be better than the standard children's offerings for your family. You know your children's interests. You know if a program about dance or underwater exploration will hold their attention long enough to inform or delight them.

Make your viewing list an attractive one, and make the weekly preparation of it an activity that's fun for the whole family. Your children will sense that you care about what they watch and that you're willing to spend the time to work with them to develop a sensible schedule, and that's important.

Children like to talk about television. Some families run the weekly TV scheduling like a town meeting. It gives everybody the chance to talk about specific programs, and it becomes an activity that everyone actually looks forward to. You can even bring neighborhood children into your scheduling sessions: turn the event into a party.

Preparing the schedule will bring out the reasons individual family members watch a particular program and what other options are available at that time. Another suggestion: if the majority of the family wants to watch a program like "The Dukes of Hazzard" that you find objectionable, don't veto the idea out of hand. You can use this opportunity to discuss the issue of reckless driving with your youngsters. Most important, you've created the opportunity to discuss how the program differs from the real world. And again, the fact that you have set the stage for a discussion may be even more important than the issue itself.

By planning a weekly schedule, you will help your children develop the habit of watching programs rather than just watching television. If they think about the schedule in terms

of programs and time allotments, they have to start thinking about turning the set off when the program is over. One of the reasons children view so much TV is that the set is turned on for whatever program they want to see and then is left on until they go to bed.

The key to creating a family TV schedule is the use of the program guide. As cable brings more and more channels into the TV picture, the use of these guides will become even more important. Once there are fifty or a hundred channels on cable, it would take you the length of an entire program just to check on all the shows by switching the dial. Increasingly we are going to have to depend on information in the program guides. Perhaps these guides will provide children with a new motivation to learn to read.

In any case, television program guides should be put together with more care and more detail than at present. You might want to let the editors of whatever guide you use know that to be a more responsible parent you need to have more detailed information about the content of shows, and about whether or not they are appropriate for children. Most editors respond positively to letters from readers. By contacting the people responsible for the program guides you can become a lobbyist for your own family.

One final suggestion: in making your schedule, make sure that you don't overlook local program listings. These local programs may be of special interest to your youngsters; this is particularly true of cable TV and those cable channels that televise local high school plays, athletic events, and community activities. Since these programs are aimed at a narrow audience, you won't find many ads for them. You need the local listings to find out what televised events in your community are worthwhile for your children to watch.

A TV Diet

In helping your children choose which programs they view, you will have to deal with another major issue. No matter how attractive the programs are, how many hours a week should children be allowed to watch? You will have to be the final decision-maker on this one.

And once you decide on a figure you must make sure that it is adhered to. Many parents feel that ten hours a week (an hour a day on weekdays and two hours a day on weekends, with an hour reserved for an irresistible special) is appropriate. With the national average for children's viewing between twenty-five and thirty hours a week, you would make a major contribution to your children's welfare by putting them on a TV diet. By making a weekly schedule and involving children in the selection of the programs, you may find that this significant accomplishment is not as difficult as you think. But you'd better be prepared for at least two side effects. First, when you limit your children's viewing hours you can expect to be asked questions as to why you watch so much television yourself. Second, you have to start thinking about what your youngsters will do once their time in front of the set is significantly reduced. This isn't easy, particularly for two-career couples and single parents. But unless your children have special problems, there is nothing better you can do to aid their development than helping them plan activities away from the TV set.

Be flexible in enforcing your schedule. For example, what do you do about television if your child is home ill? If your youngster is lying in bed with nothing to do, you may not want to spend the day trying to soothe or entertain him. If you have the time, reading aloud together or playing a board game or cutting magazines into collages is an alternative for sick days, but that time is a luxury most of us don't have. This is one time that TV, if used properly, can be a blessing. It is a time when you can legitimately bend the rules of your schedule. We aren't recommending that your child spend the day watching soap operas and game shows. There are other programs worth watching. The Public Broadcasting System airs shows designed for in-school use during the day. For the most part these are creative and delightful programs, not just the teacher-in-front-of-the-blackboard. Call your local PBS station to find out when they are aired.

Did You Ever Stop to Ask?

- Is television practically a member of the family?

- Is television doing most of the talking at your house?

- How many TV sets do you have at home?

- When and where do you watch TV?

- Is TV watching a private thing reserved for the bedrooms or do you watch as a family?

- When and where do your children watch?

- Does TV disrupt family mealtimes?

- Is TV the babysitter in your house?

- Do family members turn on the TV as soon as they walk in the room?

- Does the TV stay on even if no one is in the room?

- Do you use TV as a reward?

- Do you decide to watch a certain show, or is the decision just to watch?

- Does your family watch TV instead of talking to each other?

- If you think you watch too much TV ask yourself why.

Would You Believe?

An ingenious physician from Scotts Valley, California, has a cure for his family's TV addiction. He calls it "pedal vision."

Electricity to run his TV set is stored in a battery pack, connected to an alternator wheel, connected to an exercise-bike tire, connected to a would-be TV watcher. One hour of pedaling stores enough power to run the TV set for one hour.

Gregory L. Sutherland, for Pedal Vision Inc., Scotts Valley, Calif.

ACT TV TIME CHART

Involve your child and the whole family by playing this game. Here's how. Help your child darken the TV screen for every hour of TV viewed by your child during one week.

For one half hour of TV viewing, have your child darken only half the screen (Example A) ...the rest of the screen should be filled in when your child watches another half hour of TV (Example B).

If the week is completed with 20 to 30 hours of viewing on the scorecard, you need to recommend a TV diet for your child.

If the score is 10 to 20 hours a week, turn off the set more often and read a book, talk, play, take a long walk.

If the chart shows a score of 0 to 10 hours you win! Hooray!

Keep track of your score for several weeks. Are you making progress?

 Example A   Example B

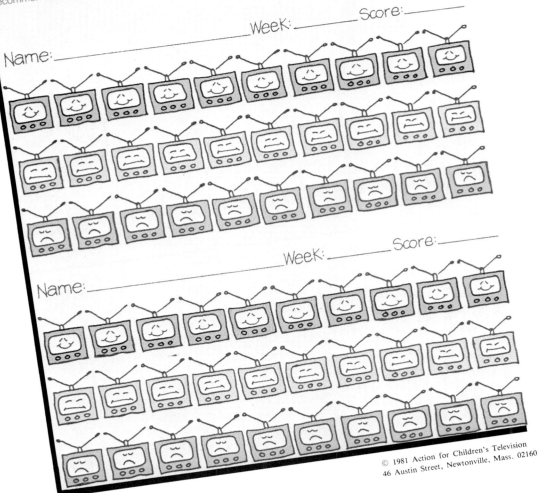

Week: _____ Score: _____

Name: _____

Week: _____ Score: _____

Name: _____

Would You Believe?

- The average American family watches more than six and a half hours of television a day.

- Children watch an average of 26 hours of TV each week or almost four hours each day.

- By the time they are 18, most children will have spent more time watching TV than in school.

- Advertisers spend over $800 million a year selling to children on television.

- Children see about 20,000 30-second commercials each year or about three hours of TV advertising each week.

- Most of the programs children watch were made for adults.

- Over a million young children are still watching TV at midnight.

Designing a TV Calendar

All too often program schedules change, or our own activities prevent us from watching a special we really want to see. Again, we suggest planning. By choosing special programs ahead of time and marking them on a TV calendar, you'll know when to watch. If you're all going to be watching a TV movie or entertainment special on Thursday, you may be inclined to find something to do away from the set on Wednesday. Networks sometimes take large newspaper ads to announce their scheduled specials. These are helpful for advance planning, but time slots often change. Watch for other advertisements and check local listings when you know your programs are coming up. Revise your calendar every week. This could prevent your being stuck, wondering ''if there's anything good on TV tonight'' —only to find that the movie about your favorite actress was on

last night! The same thing goes for after-school viewing. Those specials are worth planning for.

Thanksgiving Day: A Special Example

By working out a sensible viewing schedule, you can begin to help your family cope with the intrusive aspect of television. And all of us know how intrusive television can be. Take Thanksgiving Day, for example. Thanksgiving has always been a special day in the life of an American family. Today it is a special day in the lives of broadcasters and television fans. Before TV, Thanksgiving was a time when the clan would gather together; a time when aunts, uncles, and cousins would spend the day talking with each other, getting reacquainted. It was a day when groups of relatives would go off to a local football game, and afterwards, everyone would participate in preparing the family feast.

Today what happens? Instead of visiting with each other, instead of helping to shell the peas or stuff the turkey, the children are glued to the set early in the morning watching the parades that have become a new Thanksgiving tradition. Meanwhile the adults are grouped around the other TV sets watching the never-ending succession of football games that begin in some locales before most members of the family are even out of bed.

Because Thanksgiving Day is one of TV's two highest viewing days (Christmas is the other), the networks pack the evening hours with some of the best programming of the year. In fact, if there is one time when children and adults get more than enough choice in their TV fare, it is the four weeks between Thanksgiving and Christmas. How much better for everyone it would be if all those special television programs were spread out throughout the year. But Thanksgiving Day marks the launching of all commercial campaigns that have become so much a part of our holiday season. And what better way to feature these ads than with a barrage of super-deluxe specials on a day when there is such an enormous captive audience? As a result, Thanksgiving is turned into a TV-watching extravaganza rather than the family experience that many of us remember so fondly.

If you want to turn back the clock for this one special day a year, what can you do about the intrusion of television? First, if you have access to a video recorder, you could tape whatever shows or specials individual members of your family want to see and watch them later when the programs don't compete with the turkey and the family get-together. You can have two Thanksgivings: the real one and TV Thanksgiving. Or you can read up on the history of Thanksgiving and plan a real old-fashioned celebration with your whole family participating—without TV. You can remind your family that they can always go back to TV the following year if they really feel deprived without it. If everyone actually votes for TV over family and real life, you can give in. But in that case, you may wish to serve TV dinners and use the time saved from cooking to read up on the meaning of Christmas and Chanukah.

These suggestions may work for you; you may think of better ideas. Perhaps you can begin the day by taking a family vote on which one "special" everyone wants to watch. What is most important is that you remember that planning for any special day—Christmas, New Year's Day, or even a birthday—may no longer be successful without consciously deciding how to cope with television.

Where Not to Keep the TV Set

The television set is not simply a piece of furniture. The decision about where sets should be located is one that you should make carefully, knowing that where you put the set is going to influence your children's viewing habits.

Most American families now have more than one set. Some have begun to take a closer look at where each set is placed. Is it the predominant piece of furniture? Is it located in such a spot that the most natural thing for anyone entering the room is to turn it on? Is it centrally located in the room, so that everything

"Would you care to join us? We're having a family reunion in the dining room."

else that takes place there is subordinated to it? What kind of statement are you making to your children about the importance of TV by making the set itself the most significant piece of furniture in the house?

The most inappropriate place to put a TV set is in a child's bedroom, where you have the least control over what your child is watching and learning from TV. But if one of your children is sick, then certainly a set could be brought into the room. Some parents find that there are advantages to keeping a small portable set in a closet, taking it out to watch a particular program, and putting it back into the closet once the program is over. The fact that the set is small is also important. Some families use only small black-and-white sets because watching programs on them is less appealing than watching shows in color on large screens.

Many families have a TV set in the kitchen. If your children watch before dinner, you can watch with them while preparing a meal. However, if you eat in the kitchen, there is a temptation to keep the set on during mealtimes. And nothing kills a family dinner conversation more quickly than the noise of a television set. With some planning, however, it is possible to have TV contribute to an interesting dinner table. If, for example, you eat at a regular time like 6:30 P.M., you can watch a portion of the news, turn off the set, and use the news items as a stimulus for conversation.

TV as Reward and Punishment

Since television is so important to many children, parents often find it a convenient means of punishment or reward. Using TV in this way has its drawbacks. By depriving children of television when they are "bad," we create the assumption that "good" behavior merits additional hours in front of the set. There may be better ways to show your disapproval than by limiting television; the most effective rewards and punishments are usually the ones that are closely related to the behavior involved. An early bedtime has always been an effective response to a child who gets out of bed too late to get to school on time. And parents often make children pay for windows they've broken

out of their allowances. Withdrawing TV privileges for staying out past curfew or breaking a sibling's toy doesn't make the same kind of sense.

On the other hand, when television causes problems, television should be part of the solution. If the reason your daughter cannot get to school on time is that she watches television too late, curtailing her TV-watching is appropriate. If your son's homework doesn't get done because he watches television instead of studying, denying TV is sensible.

Homework versus television is a big issue for some families. To help your children set appropriate priorities, your expectations should be made very clear, and you should react when those expectations are not met. This means that if homework is number one on your list, you need to be emphatic about its coming before television on your child's list. Of course, your rules about homework and television can be flexible enough to accommodate exceptions.

Limiting television is tricky. If you're going to set up restrictions, short- or long-term, make sure they're workable. If you say "No TV for you tonight!" to a child, but the TV set is on during dinner, you undermine your efforts. You can turn off the set during the meal, of course, but will that make the rest of the family feel that they're being punished, too? If the family usually gathers around the television set in the living room, will a "No TV for a week" order mean the child is excluded from relaxing with the family? You may not want the punishment to have that kind of impact. Being aware of these considerations, and others pertinent to your own life, may help you to set enforceable limits. The more specific you are about how television is used in your home, the smaller problem you'll have with TV's taking on added—and possibly unwanted—significance.

Seeing through Television

Demystifying television is a goal of many educators and child experts, who feel that one of the best ways to help children cope with the TV phenomenon is to help them understand how television works, and how to distinguish between TV "magic" and reality.

You can help your own children make the distinction between what is happening on the screen and what is happening in the studio. One of the best ways to understand this difference is to pay a visit to a TV station. Every TV station isn't willing to show you and your family around, but most stations have a public affairs department you could contact. By giving enough advance notice, you may be able to arrange a tour of the station's facilities, perhaps for a neighborhood or youth group. You may even get a chance to watch a show being produced. If you're fortunate enough to live in a city with a science or children's museum, contact them to find out if they have a video room for the use of children, or if they have an exhibit that shows how television works.

Children need to understand that many of the things they see on TV don't happen in real life. Real people don't fly, or disappear, or walk through walls, or get beat up and bounce back unscathed. Try to explain that it is all make-believe. You can point out that the fighting they see on television is performed by skilled actors and stunt men, experts at faking and taking punches. This make-believe mayhem is made possible by many props and sound effects. Your children will probably be fascinated to learn that the bottles that are continually broken over people's heads on TV are really made of spun sugar, so they will not hurt the actors; that the furniture used as weapons is prebroken, made to fall apart at contact; and that the windows through which so many TV characters are hurled are actually made of light plastic, so that the actors won't get hurt. Most important, of course, is the fact that children should understand that if people went through these antics in real life, very few would survive to try it again.

TV magic is sometimes accomplished by manipulating the TV cameras. When the camera is placed very high, the person or thing being photographed can be made to look very small. When the camera is lowered, the objects look bigger. And by using special zoom lenses, camera operators can create all kinds of special effects.

You can explain to your children that almost every TV show is on film (or tape), that it is not happening at the time it is being watched. That is how a program can be shown over and over. The most common special effects are achieved through editing. A TV editor can cut out or rearrange certain portions of the film or tape to make people disappear. At the end of this chapter we've listed a few books that go into more detail about TV production. The more children learn about how TV works, the better they will be able to make distinctions between TV fantasy and what is real.

Saturday Morning Mania

Anyone old enough to have read best-seller lists from years past will remember the longest title in the nonfiction category, *Where Did You Go? Out! What Did You Do? Nothing!* The "nothing" that children did in those days, an

Would You Believe?

Soupy Sales, zany host of a popular children's Saturday morning show, once asked his young viewers to "go into mommy and daddy's wallet and get all the dirty wrinkled green pieces of paper and send them to Soupy."

What happened? Soupy received hundreds of dollars from his innocent audience. What else happened? Soupy got suspended and the money went to charity.

important part of the process of growing up, has all but disappeared from American childhood. With a TV set to turn to, a child need never again have nothing to do.

This depressing fact of life is most obvious on Saturday morning. In country mansions and city tenements, suburban split-levels and high-rise apartments, parents do not wonder where their children are on Saturday morning. They know! Over 9 million of them are watching TV. They are watching an animated world of meanness and mayhem, interrupted by invitations to jeopardize their own health and the financial well-being of their families.

The Face of Saturday Morning

If your children are cartoon maniacs, join them one morning for a fact-finding session. You may enjoy the experience. Or you may agree with Washington *Post* TV critic Tom Shales, ". . . that come Saturday morning it's largely the same old bash 'em–crash 'em ghetto."

Whatever your verdict, tell your child what you think about the shows, and remember to let the networks know, too. Here are some questions to keep in mind as you watch. They may help you to figure out how to judge a cartoon.

- *Does the animation provide a good art experience for your child?*

Very often financial limitations prompt animators to use shortcuts in their animation techniques. Look at the movements made by a cartoon character. When it talks, is its mouth the only thing moving? When a figure is shown running, is its body fluid, or is the body rigid while the arms and legs move back and forth? Notice also how certain shots of scenery or background are used over and over again.

If your child enjoys cartoons, make a point of watching an animated special such as "A Christmas Carol," based on the Cruikshank illustrations, or the theatrical features made by Ralph Bakshi or the Disney studio. Compare Saturday morning fare with these longer, more subtle dramas. Much of the weekend animation resembles comic-book art more closely than it does film art. Animation features at a local movie theater frequently provide an opportunity to enjoy prize-winning short features from around the world. You may also find that your children are as delighted by beautifully illustrated storybooks as they are by cartoons.

- *Is there a laugh track, and is it used to make children laugh at things that aren't funny?*

The laugh track is used as a gimmick to trivialize the use of slapstick violence in cartoons. No longer a simulation of the way a live audience might respond, the hysterical laughter increasingly serves to persuade children that the action taking place is funny, or to make them feel they ought to find it funny. It might be interesting to see whether the canned laughter is used more at certain times than at others: is it used following word plays or just to underscore physical jokes? What kind of "joke" is made funny: a villain being cleverly outwitted or an old woman slipping on a banana peel? Many cartoons still being aired were produced in the thirties and forties, when racist or sexist humor was tolerated. See what kind of humor is being popularized, and which cartoons you think are genuinely and appropriately funny.

- *Is violence used as the major means of keeping the story moving?*

Certainly violent action is appropriate to some stories. Good guys, after all, do not always triumph by wit alone. But many cartoons seem to be propelled on an unending stream of physical mishaps as the characters try to sock it to each other. In these cases, it may be that there's no story left once you remove the plummeting from cliffs, the dynamite blasts, and the wind-up punches. Some experts believe that stories full of such casual violence may be as damaging to a child as the violence in more realistic stories.

Sometimes violent action is replaced by ominous-sounding music that threatens impending danger or violence. This is an intentional ploy, designed to grab a child's attention without having to develop dramatic tension within the story.

- *Is there dialogue or just noise?*

One enlightening way to determine just how much conversation is in the script is to tune out the picture and leave the sound on. Most Saturday morning cartoons are filled with the sounds of crashes, screams, and hysterical laughter. Compare the sound track to a half-hour spent with PBS's Mr. Rogers or "The Spider's Web" on National Public Radio.

Television has given us some shining examples of cartoons using exceptional animation techniques. Shown here are scenes from "Simple Gifts: Six Episodes for Christmas," "Really Rosie," and "A Story—A Story."

- *Does the cartoon include characters from minority groups? What are their roles?*

While there are exceptions, there is no question that, relying as heavily as they do on broad slapstick humor, cartoons resort to broad ethnic and racial stereotyping. See whether ethnic characters are leaders or just one of the gang. Do they earn respect, or are they the butt of jokes? In ''Plastic Man,'' the hero's Hawaiian side-kick, Hula Hula, is not just fat or stupid—he's both fat *and* stupid. See whether there are characters of a distinct ethnic heritage who are both likable and respected.

- *How are females portrayed?*

In a cartoon series called ''Smurfs,'' there is only one female in the entire Smurf village. Smurfette is a little blond with long, fluttering eyelashes. And longtime favorite Olive Oyl is usually found standing around helplessly, although sometimes she seems to have more brains than Popeye and Bluto put together. It's important to note thoughtless negative stereotypes, but it is also useful to point out to your children the good things about any well-portrayed cartoon woman. In any case, you can be aware of the discrepancies between the messages you choose to convey in your home and those that some television cartoons put across.

- *Do elderly people receive respect or ridicule?*

Old people in cartoons are often portrayed as doddering fumble-bums; they are rarely valued for their contributions, past or present. In fact, there are not many elderly cartoon characters, although the series ''Blackstar'' features a group of gnomelike village elders who display varying amounts of brainpower. Actually, we are all so used to the original cartoon stereotype of the elderly that we may not even think twice about poor Mr. Magoo. Not only is he aged and befuddled, but his weak eyesight is the basis for much of the humor in the cartoons in which he's the title character. It is worth watching out for other cartoons that make fun of handicapping conditions, especially in the portrayal of elderly people.

- *How are professions portrayed?*

Many cartoon characters, of course, have no real-life occupations. But when they do, do you like the way people in various professions are characterized? Scientists serve as the best example of career stereotyping, for they are often shown in cartoons as crazed arch-villains trying to control or destroy the world. While this idea of what a scientist is like may not actually determine your child's relationship to science, it is worth discussing the good and exciting discoveries that can happen through science. Occasionally you'll find superheroes sensitive to environmental issues on Saturday morning cartoons. Their efforts to save the world can be a starting point for talking with your child about the role of science in everyday life, and about opportunities for both males and females to work in the science field.

Commercials

As parents we worry about the messages that our youngsters get from the programs they watch. We sometimes forget that the thousands of commercials that our children view every year contain messages as well. And because these ads are prepared with much more care than the programs, the messages are extremely persuasive.

Our children are bombarded with commercials. Believe it or not, the broadcasters' own code permits them to air more commercials during children's prime time viewing hours than during adult prime time. And with good reason. Children are the easiest target for manufacturers with toys and sugary foods to sell.

We suggest that you make a conscious effort to watch the children's ads that your youngsters see. You might even want to keep a record of what TV is selling to children, and if your children are old enough, let them help. Divide your list into categories: Commercials for Foods That Are Dangerous for Children;

Commercials That Take Advantage of Children's Inexperience in the Real World; Commercials That Exaggerate What a Product Can Do; Commercials That Pitch Inappropriate Products to Children (like Cosmetics); Commercials That Pitch Too Many Products in a Single Ad; Commercials for Toys That Are Too Expensive; Promotional Spots for Adult Programs That Are Likely to Confuse or Upset a Child.

Food Commercials

Almost all children's commercials are for food or for toys, and most of the food ads are for products that are highly sugared. This is not true of adult television. TV food ads actually present a better-balanced diet for adults than for children. Notice the foods advertised on Saturday morning children's shows. An ad that advocates ''Snickers between meals'' can provide the basis for a talk about how sticky sugar between meals causes cavities and reduces the appetite for a well balanced meal. Wouldn't it be better if the commercial said, ''Candy sometimes for dessert and be sure to brush your teeth afterward''? Note the names of certain products. Take Froot Loops: is there really fruit in the loops? (The answer is no.)

Check the disclaimers in the ads. Most cereal commercials aimed at children now contain a phrase like ''part of a balanced breakfast.'' Instead of responding to concern that children and parents would think that certain sugary cereals would supply all that was needed for a nutritional meal, the advertising agencies hide this disclaimer in phrases extolling the virtues of the cereal. The need was for a warning. Instead, the advertisements imply that in order to get a balanced breakfast, all we need is to down a bowl of Cookie Munchies.

You may find a good way to heighten your child's awareness of advertising techniques is to ''create'' a commercial. You may want to start with an ad for a healthy food that's missing from your menu. Or you can produce an ad that satirizes children's commercials. You can involve the neighborhood or your child's classmates in this one. Hold a contest and give prizes for the funniest spoof, the meanest satire, the weirdest skit (everybody wins).

There are other ways to counter the fact that children's TV ads provide some strange

Makeup for eight-year-olds? It's a multimillion dollar business. Part of the voice-over for this ad states, ''Your eyes look mysterious.'' At eight?

education about nutrition. Take your children on a trip to the supermarket. Check the labels. Did you know that the ingredients are listed according to amounts? If sugar is listed first, there is more sugar in the product than any other ingredient. Why are the cereals pitched to children on the lower shelves? So they can reach them, of course. Visit the fruit and vegetable counter. Talk about why these foods are not seen in children's advertisements. One reason is that the many small suppliers of farm and dairy products cannot afford to advertise. Another is that there is no brand name to sell to consumers.

Don't hesitate to "talk back" to your set when your children are around. It's particularly important in helping them deal with commercials. By verbally proclaiming, "How come they call it Froot Loops when there's no fruit in it?" you counter the misleading messages that your child is getting at the time when the messages are most persuasive.

Toy Commercials

If you are a parent, we hardly need to remind you that television sells toys in an incredibly effective way. This is particularly true in the period prior to Christmas and Chanukah, which seems to grow longer every year (holiday toy ads begin in September), giving manufacturers even more time to reach children with ads that tell them that they need expensive toys in order to be happy and have lots of friends. This advertising barrage infuriates most parents. TV personality Barbara Walters once became so fed up with constant preholiday advertising that she actually made a public vow never to buy any TV-advertised toy for her child.

It is difficult to issue a blanket rule prohibiting the purchase of any toy advertised on TV. It puts a strain on the parent-child relationship and may not be as helpful to your offspring as dealing with the requests in a way that gives them some opportunity to participate in the buying decision.

TV toys are expensive. Part of the expense, of course, is the cost of the advertising, which is passed on to the consumer. The cost of making

the commercial is high. In order to make these expensive thirty-second messages as effective (and thus as profitable) as possible, manufacturers often use deceptive advertising techniques. The apparent size of dolls is increased by low-angle camera shots; toy cars are shown whizzing around tracks at unrealistic speeds; fantasy and animation are used to make a product seem more exciting.

Statements like "Batteries not included," or "Some assembly required," are often printed in small letters at the bottom of the screen, just before the commercial ends. Most preschoolers can't read. And even if the statements are spoken, does "Some assembly required" make sense to the average five- or six-year-old? Some toy ads have progressed to the point of reminding the viewer that "You have to put it together." But don't let any of these "honest" statements at the end of the

Would You Believe?

The following remarks were made by the vice president of one of America's major advertising agencies:

"Children, like everyone else, must learn the marketplace. You learn by making judgments. Even if a child is deceived by an ad at age four, what harm is done? He will grow out of it." And if kids ask their parents for TV-advertised toys, "what harm is there in that? Even if, as many psychologists claim, a child perceives children in TV advertisements as friends, and not actors selling them something, where's the harm? All a parent has to say is 'shut up or I'll belt you.' "

commercials lull you into thinking that the hard sell to children has died away. Inside its refurbished velvet glove, the iron fist is as hard as ever.

One of the most serious of all the deceptive practices in commercials for children involves the practice of pitching a whole line of toys in a single message. In the 1980–1981 holiday season, the Tomy Company advertised a "super deluxe" dollhouse on national television. The commercial showed two happy children playing with a house filled with furniture. The dollhouse included, according to the ad, "a cozy bedroom with a rolltop desk that rolls." What parents and children could not tell from the commercial was that the "cozy bedroom" and all the other rooms of furniture were not included in the price of the dollhouse. They each had to be purchased separately. And the rolltop desk didn't even come with the bedroom! In order to get the dollhouse and furniture as shown in the ad, a parent would have had to pay over $145.00. How many families can afford that kind of money for a single toy? And even if they could, how many mothers and fathers are willing to spend that much for a dollhouse?

In addition, children believe (and why not?) that once they are given a dollhouse they will get everything they saw in the ad, including the little record player that actually goes around. If you buy an empty dollhouse, you can be sure that's not what the child meant by the plaintive "I want Tomy for Christmas." And if you buy the furniture for two of the rooms and not for the other six, you will have a lot of explaining to do.

> **"Fundamentally, we feel—and feel we can document—that advertising to children is a service to children. Hence, any cutback in time devoted to advertising to children is in no way beneficial to children."** Peter Allport, president, Association of National Advertisers

Another serious problem in TV-advertised toys involves safety. Millions of boxes of a particular toy can be sold before the product has a chance to get use-tested in the marketplace. Before television, when a manufacturer made a particular sled or a bicycle, there was time to "shake out" whatever problems there might be with a product before it went into homes all over America. That is not the case today. Once a toy ad appears on national television, millions of children all over the country will immediately begin badgering their parents for the product and the shelves will most likely be bare of the toy before December 1.

Manufacturers do not mean to hurt children. The Mattel Company, for example, did not know that children would eat the small missiles included in its "Battlestar Galactica" toy—or that one child would die and several would be seriously injured by inhaling these missiles. But the fact is that the incredible demand for the toy, created by the slick TV ads that promoted it, put it into the hands of hundreds of thousands of children before Mattel had the opportunity to field-test it properly.

Speaking of "Battlestar Galactica," toys of this kind present a problem of a different kind. Like "Charlie's Angels" dolls or "Dukes of Hazzard" cars, it is a toy based on an actual television series. "Charlie's Angels" (now in reruns) may be a program that you, as a parent, complain about. Broadcasters have a legitimate reply to this. "It's simple," they say. "Your children shouldn't be watching the program. It is an adult show and it's your responsibility as a parent to keep them from seeing it." Fine, but by allowing a doll based on characters of an adult series to be created and advertised on children's programs, broadcasters keep your child connected to the very programs they tell you not to let your child watch. It's a highly profitable practice for both the broadcaster and the toy manufacturer. The toy maker knows that the program is a sales pitch for its product and the network knows that the product is a sales pitch for its program. Also, when children play with toys like the "Dukes of Hazzard" car, they model their play not on imagination but on the way the products are depicted in the TV episodes. The fantasies they enact are not their own, but spring from the TV scripts themselves.

There are several things you can do to help older children cope with these problems. During the preholiday season ask your children to keep a list of the TV toys that they want. Add up how many weeks it would take to buy a particular toy if the child were paying for it from a weekly allowance. If it won't add to your parenting problems, you might take them to a toy store and let them compare the actual toys with the commercials they have seen.

Price before you promise. And make sure you know what your child is asking for. If she's asking for the "Lone Ranger" doll, does she expect it to include Tonto, the tent, and the horses? They were all in the ad!

Don't hesitate to write to sponsors, manufacturers, networks, or local stations about the ads you feel are misleading. We've suggested this letter-writing strategy in several places already. That is because it's effective. You'll be surprised how much impact a letter can have.

And we have a suggestion that dates back to well before the days of television. Create your own substitutes for TV toys. Make a dollhouse out of an orange crate or a few big boxes from the supermarket. A shoe box can be turned into a very nice environment for tiny toy people. Children will probably get a bigger kick

One of the most lucrative facets of today's toy market is the toy based on a television series or motion picture. The irony is that most of these toys are based on characters in shows made for adults, not youngsters.

out of making their own toys, with your help, than in receiving expensive playthings that they ignore (or break) all too soon. More than one toy executive has admitted that when new toys are tested on groups of children, many children wind up playing games with the empty boxes and ignoring the complicated toys.

Special Problems of the Only Child

An only child often spends a great deal of time alone in front of the television set. If this is a problem in your family, you might want to think of ways that TV-watching could be a social time. Set up a Saturday morning club with three or four of your child's friends. When several children watch TV together, they talk, laugh, and may even find that playing together is more fun than television. When your turn comes to host the playgroup, you may discover that Saturday morning has developed into a Saturday mayhem that's equally hard to handle. But be comforted by the knowledge that even uncooperative play is more productive for your child than a steady diet of solitary TV viewing.

If your very young child is watching alone, it's a good idea to keep crayons and coloring books, toys, and picture books nearby to attract her interest to something other than a full morning of TV. If you can't be in the room, at least you're making it easy for your child to spend time doing something else.

The school-age child who comes home to an empty house day after day has a special problem—loneliness. This is one time when restricting television can be counterproductive. It may be as noted child psychiatrist Robert Coles has said, that for this "latch-key" child, "The television screen, with its banalities and flights of preposterous or mean-spirited fancy, ends up being one of the more reassuring elements in a particular set of circumstances: something there, and relatively reliable, lively, giving."

Bedtime vs. Specials

A common question that parents ask is "What do I do when 'The Cat in the Hat' is being shown after bedtime?" The dilemma for you as a parent is: should you let your four-year-old watch a network special from 8:30 to 9:00 P.M., knowing that the next day he won't be able to get up for nursery school or that he will be tired and fussy all day?

There are some solutions. You can ask your school or library to tape the program on a video recorder and then set up a late-afternoon or weekend community showing. Also, since many specials are based on books, you could get the book from the library and read it aloud. You might find that your rendition is better than the television production. And remember that the special program is bound to be repeated next year (and the year after) and your child may get more out of it (or enjoy it more) when he is older.

The Baby-Sitter

In many communities today, in order to get baby-sitters, not only do you have to assure them that your color TV set is in good working order; you may even have to give a status report on the size of the screen, what channels you receive clearly, and whether you subscribe to cable. When tending your child in the daytime or in the evening, baby-sitters expect to be able to watch television. And this presents problems. If you're determined to make TV-viewing rules for your children, there have to be rules for the baby-sitter while your youngsters are awake.

We suggest that you put together a baby-sitter's guide. Along with providing such information as emergency numbers, where you will be that evening, where the fusebox is, and what the children can and cannot eat, there should be some very clear guidelines about TV-viewing. If it's daytime and you don't want your child

Baby-sitter Guide

Phone Numbers

We can be reached at:

Doctor:

Neighbor:

Police:

Fire:

Mealtime Advice

What:

When:

How to Handle TV

Amount of time:

Set must be off by:

OK for viewing:

Not OK:

Bedtime Strategies

When:

How:

If they wake:

watching "The Young and the Restless" or "One Life to Live," you may have to get involved in a form of teenage education, explaining to your sitter why something that may be all right for her to watch is not, in your opinion, all right for your child. And it's just as important that you explain to adult baby-sitters not only what the rules are but why they are necessary.

Your baby-sitter's guide should include which programs your child can watch and which are forbidden. You may want to make a simple blanket rule: no television until the child is in bed. If you have a sitter who will read to your youngster or play games, you can make this rule with no problem. If you're concerned that you'll lose your sitter if you ban TV completely, then check the program schedule and leave a list of your suggestions. If your sitter can't live with this arrangement, then you may only have one choice. Difficult as it is, you may have to find another sitter.

On Minorities

You know your children imitate the people they see on TV. They walk like the Fonz, talk "Orkian" like Mork, and pretend to be Superman. Do you remember having to cope with your daughter wanting to have Farah Fawcett-Major's hair? And lately you've been worried about the influence of Luke and Bo Duke's driving habits on your teenagers.

Have you noticed one thing that all these hero figures have in common? They are *all* white. And so are most of the other people that your children see on television. Yes, there is Gary Coleman, and J.J., jive-talking his way through the syndicated reruns of "Good Times." But can you think of many more black characters your children see regularly on TV? And how often do they see Hispanics, Asians, or native Americans? If your children are non-white or non-Anglo, you are only too conscious of the lack of role models and hero figures. If

you are white and English-speaking, then perhaps you haven't thought about this problem. Maybe you should, because the lack of minority characters on television, especially on children's television, hurts everyone's children.

Here are the facts. According to the latest census, blacks make up at least 12 percent of the U.S. population and Hispanics constitute *at least* another 6 percent (and probably much more). Other members of minority groups, such as native Americans, Eskimos, or Asian-Americans, represent another 5 percent or more of our population. So, at a minimum, 23 percent of the United States population are members of minority groups. Are 23 percent of the characters on television minorities? TV doesn't even come close. Not only are there fewer minority characters on TV than there are in the population—but the number is actually decreasing. A comparative study conducted in 1981 showed that black males had 9.0 percent of the major roles in 1980. In 1980, black females had only 2.4 percent of major female roles, a severe drop from 1975. And other minority groups are underrepresented too. On the cartoons and sit-coms targeted to children, Hispanics represented only 3.1 percent of the total characters in 1981.

Dr. Alvin F. Poussaint, associate professor of psychiatry at Harvard Medical Center and Boston's Children's Hospital Medical Center, is worried about the effect that TV's lily-whiteness is having on all children. "It's important to have a range of people from groups other than white—Hispanic, Asian, American, black—talking to children in the role of teacher," he says. He is also concerned about the way that minority children react to the few, stereotyped role models that they do see. "Black children begin to see themselves in television role models. When these models are stereotyped, the children are embarrassed. They worry inside that white kids will identify them with the images of blacks on TV; 'Hey, you remind me of Gary Coleman!' "

White children suffer, too, especially those who have no contact with minorities in their everyday lives. Children who see only a few stereotyped images of blacks, Hispanics, or

Minority youngsters find few role models on television. In the words of James Baldwin, "It is a great shock at the age of five or six to find that in a world of Gary Coopers you are the Indian."

Asians on television will grow up believing in those stereotypes—believing that all blacks play basketball, that Hispanics spend their lives sleeping in the sun, that Asians are all karate experts or launderers. These are racist images. Whether we know it or not, TV is bringing up our white children to feel prejudiced and our minority children to feel invisible.

What can you, as a parent, do? First, and most obviously, you can look for television programs that have positive minority role models. PBS is the best place to find these programs (like "Carrascolendas," "Up & Coming," or "The Righteous Apples") but there are some on commercial television as well. Your young teenager might enjoy ABC's "Afterschool Specials," or "Livewire" on Nickelodeon. Second, you can find your child *other* nonwhite characters to identify with, in books. (Try *Nobody's Family Is Going to Change* by Louise Fitzhugh or the *Ludell* books by Brenda Wilkinson or *The Snowy Day* and other books by Ezra Jack Keats.) Third, you can make your children aware of the problems of racial stereotyping. Point out to them that the programming they see is full of whites; make sure they realize when a program shows a minority character in a racist way. Don't let TV's racism undermine what you are trying to teach your family.

Stereotyping is a serious problem in cartoons. Is this, for example, the image we want to give our youngsters of how Mexican or Chinese people look and behave? And what about the nearsighted Mr. Magoo? What do his bumblings and misadventures say to youngsters about people with handicaps?

Children with Special Needs

While television can never be a replacement for a supportive caring parent for children with special needs, it can provide role models through which they can learn to understand and accept their feelings about disabilities. Programs that include children with handicaps in both leading and supporting roles offer an important boost to children with similar disabilities. Programs that portray handicapped children in positive exchanges with other children can also provide a learning experience for the apparently able child.

If your special child is watching TV, be on the lookout for programs that deal openly and honestly with disabilities. Watch for segments that show blind or deaf children as they perform their daily activities in a family or classroom situation. Watch for programs that

TV has the potential for helping change the public's attitudes about the handicapped. Programs like "Blind Sunday" and "Feeling Free" have helped break down stereotypes about the disabled.

"Blind Sunday," Daniel Wilson Productions, ABC Afterschool specials.

Alan J. Brightman/from *Feeling Free*

Alan J. Brightman/from *Feeling Free*

depict retarded children in situations of competence and mastery. Watch for magazine-format shows like "Thirty Minutes" that show disabled people in a full range of occupations—not all deaf people are servants or craftsmen. PBS's "Feeling Free" featured a group of children with handicaps in a surprisingly upbeat delightful series of fun and friendship. Use these programs as jumping-off points for family discussions to uncover your children's curiosity, questions, and hidden fears about disabilities.

In 1981, the International Year of the Disabled, the Public Broadcasting Service began a special series of programs for and about handicapped children. One of the programs in the series, "Kahn Du," is about four teenagers learning to deal with the problems of adolescence in addition to their disabilities.

"Sesame Street" features as regular guests on the program children with physical and mental handicaps interacting with other children. These segments are valuable in dispelling myths about disabilities and in improving social attitudes toward the disabled.

Several ABC "Afterschool Specials" have featured young people and how they cope. "Run, Don't Walk," produced by Henry Winkler, is the story of an eighteen-year-old girl recently paralyzed in an accident, who refuses to admit to herself that she will always be in a wheelchair. Once she is emotionally prepared to accept her disability, she learns that others accept her too.

"Blind Sunday" is about the relationship between a young blind girl and a sighted boy. The drama focuses on Tony's awkwardness in figuring out how to treat his blind friend. He spends a day wearing a blindfold to experience the world of the sightless.

Check your program guide for shows that are close-captioned for the deaf and hearing-impaired. More and more series, specials, and movies are being close-captioned for the country's 14 million hearing-impaired citizens. Captioned programs for children and their families include "Sesame Street," "3-2-1 Contact," "Up & Coming," "Once Upon a Classic," "ABC Afterschool Specials," "Little House on the Prairie," "Laverne and Shirley," "The Flintstones," and "Here's Boomer." New programs are captioned each season.

Turn-Off-TV Week

One way to sense how television dominates your family's life is to conduct a Turn-Off-TV Week in your home. If your family is like most families in this country, it won't be an easy thing to do. One week sounds like a short period of time. But nothing better points out how addicted we have become to television than deliberately unplugging the sets for a week. And, just as important, after an initial period of TV withdrawal shock, you may find that members of your family start doing all kinds of constructive things together or individually that they never find time for when they're glued to the set.

Don't enter into this activity on the spur of the moment. We suggest that once you decide to do it you spend a week keeping a TV diary of what programs each member of your family watches, and what else they do when they're not in front of the set. Once you unplug the sets and start your Turn-Off-TV Week, keep another detailed diary, recording what family members now do during the times that they watched television the week before. Obviously, the purpose of the two diaries is for you to see how your family's way of life changes without television. Are people talking to each other more? Are they finding activities to do together? Has your family rediscovered reading or playing a musical instrument or listening to the radio while playing a board game?

As we said, it won't be easy. In the beginning your children may use the newly created free time to argue with each other. But at least they'll recognize that other people in the family exist.

There is a variation of Turn-Off-TV Week with which many families are familiar. It's the old Let's-Keep-the-Set-in-the-Repair-Shop caper. Many people discover that when their set is out for repairs they not only survive but begin to enjoy life more. Lots of parents "forget" to reclaim their sets for weeks in order to enjoy the opportunity of getting to know the family once again.

The Wheeler School TV Challenge

Peter Hufstader, chairman of the English department at the 540-student Wheeler School in Providence, Rhode Island, is concerned about the development of reading skills, and the competence, imagination, and critical thinking that reading encourages. Hufstader supports those studies that show a correlation between extensive TV-watching and poor learning skills. He maintains that "Children who watch more than one hour of television a day are straying into a pattern that will certainly jeopardize their becoming good readers. We consider children who watch four hours of television a day 'heavy' users, and we consider them 'at risk' readers."

Attempting to give his students a new perspective on the place of television in their lives, Hufstader invited Wheeler School families to take part in a month-long "Television Challenge." The challenge rules stipulated that for the entire month of November of that year, TV was not to be watched by any member of the family at any time or for any reason. The only exception was that, by unanimous vote, the family could elect to watch one program or event per week, and everyone in the family (except very young children) had to watch this show. To emphasize total and active participation, each member of the family had to sign a statement of intent.

Over one hundred people, representing about half of the fifty-two families that accepted the challenge, attended a "sharing session" after the month-long TV fast. They discussed the ways in which their lives were affected by the exile of TV. The mood at this meeting was very positive. Although television was missed, most families felt that they had benefited from the challenge. The loss of TV was felt most keenly on Saturdays—no football games!—but the result was that both children and parents sought active things to do. And, generally, everybody did more reading. Seventh- and eighth-grade youngsters had the most difficulty adjusting to life without TV; younger and older children adapted more easily. Parents who were at home on weekdays missed the accustomed companionship of TV.

Hufstader reported one unanticipated result of the TV turnoff: several parents reported that, in a radical departure from previous years, their children never mentioned Christmas during the entire month of November!

Turn-On-Special-Programs Week

As a variation to a Turn-Off-TV Week, you could have a particular week in your house when you turn on only special programs. This serves several purposes. It allows you to begin to use program guides in a creative way. It creates a situation in which you and your family actually search for different kinds of programs to watch. By spending a week seeking new shows, you may discover something really good and, more important, you may break the deadening pattern of watching the same programs with the same messages and techniques over and over again. This, by the way, is one of the

The Wheeler School

Bradford F. Herzog, Milton, Mass.

"The Late Great Me," Daniel Wilson Productions, ABC Afterschool specials.

"Dinky Hocker," Asselin Productions, ABC Afterschool specials.

Highgate Pictures/Learning Corporation of America, ABC Afterschool specials.

"A Matter of Time," Martin Tahse Productions, ABC Afterschool specials.

Through its late-afternoon specials, TV has presented programs for young people that deal with some of the most serious problems of our day. Subjects of these programs include alcoholism, drug addiction, race relations, and death and dying.

most potent problems with programs made especially for children. More than half of the Saturday morning shows are created and produced by a single production company, Hanna Barbera. The animated characters look alike, make the same gestures, and speak with the same voices.

Again, you will need to dig into program guides and local listings in order to find shows you think will be better for your family than those on their current TV diet. Remember, you are the best judge of what fits your children's needs. All of the programs don't have to be "four-star specials." It may be that you want to try watching a different mix of situation comedies. At least you'll be breaking your usual viewing pattern and you may find that you discover a show that is better for your children than what they ordinarily watch at that time.

Letters Make a Difference

If during your Turn-On-Special-Programs Week you discover some programs that you didn't know existed and that you feel are particularly good, let the sponsors and the networks or the stations airing the show hear from you. Too often we complain when we don't like something and forget to praise when we come into contact with something we like. You'll be amazed at how seriously your letter is taken by people in influential positions. The most common broadcaster response to questions from concerned parents is "You must be the only people who feel like this, because we never hear from the public." Believe it or not, your comments can make a difference.

And the comments of your children are important as well. If they particularly enjoy a program or a series, encourage them to write to the network or the local station responsible for the show (perhaps with copies to your local newspaper). If there are programs that they think are silly or too violent or objectionable for whatever reason, they should let these feelings be known as well. And they should tell broadcasters about ideas or stories they would like to see dramatized on TV. In addition to informing the producers of these shows that young people actually care about what they watch, this practice of letter writing will help your children confront their feelings about the shows they watch.

Occasionally, news stories provide an interesting opportunity for children to respond to TV. In 1978, the Federal Communications Commission asked for comments from the public as part of its children's television proceedings. A few journalists suggested that children be encouraged to write to the commission. Tom Shales, TV critic of the Washington *Post,* said, in a widely reprinted column, "The TV lobby and the food lobby have all had plenty of opportunity to throw their weight around. Now parents and the rest of the public—children as well—have a chance to sound off."

More than ten thousand comments from children were received by the agency. These letters became part of the public record. Here's a tiny sample ▶

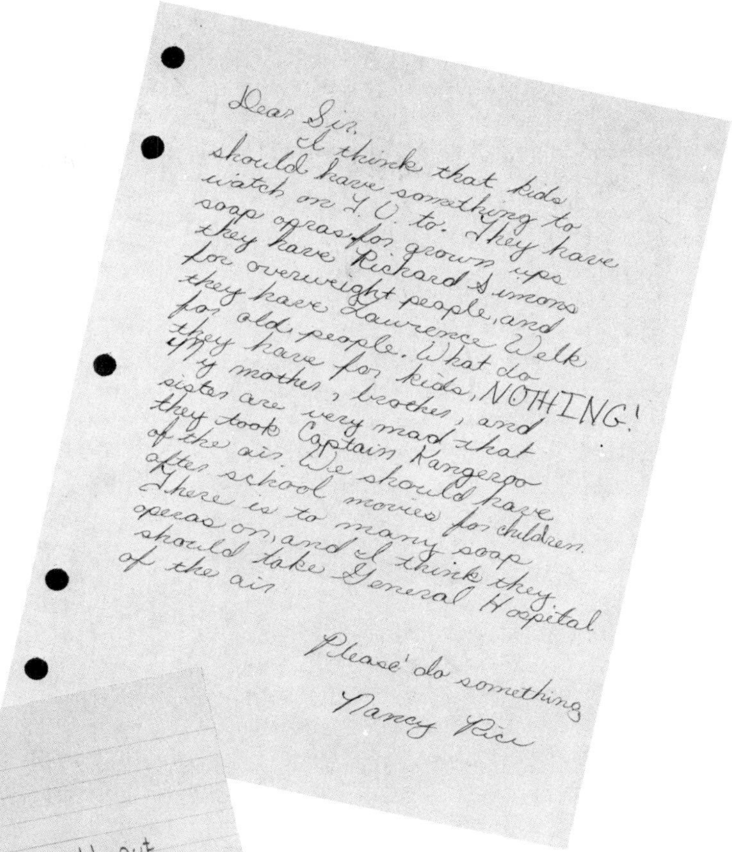

Dear Sir,
I think that kids should have something to watch on T.U. to. They have soap oprasfor grown-ups, they have Richard Simons for overwright people, and they have Lawrence Welk for old people. What do they have for kids, NOTHING! My mother, brother, and sister are very mad that they took Captain Kangeroo of the air. We should have after school movies for children. There is to many soap opras on, and I think they should take General Hospital of the air.

Please do something

Nancy Rice

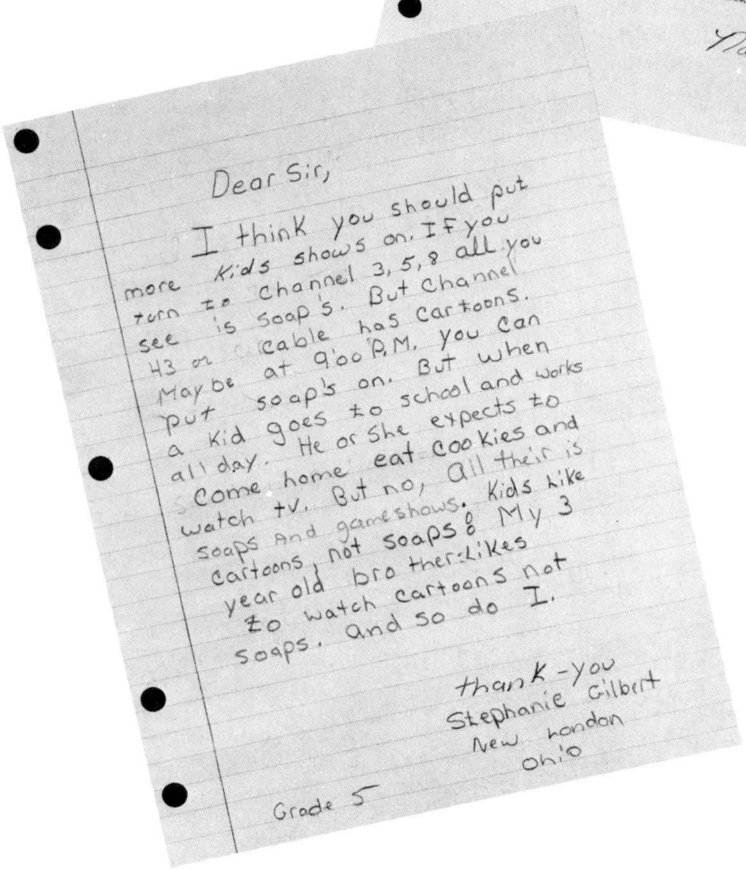

Dear Sir,

I think you should put more Kids shows on. IF you turn to Channel 3, 5, 8 all you see is soap's. But Channel 43 or Cable has Cartoons. Maybe at 9:00 P.M. you can put soap's on. But when a Kid goes to school and works all day. He or she expects to Come home eat Cookies and watch tv. But no, All their is soaps and gameshows. Kids Like cartoons, not soaps! My 3 year old brother likes to watch cartoons not soaps. and so do I.

thank-you
Stephanie Gilbert
New London
Ohio

Grade 5

Accentuating the Positive

In terms of the way we learn, it's always a good idea to accentuate the positive. This strategy is a good one to use with children and it can be applied to television in several ways. Increasingly, broadcasters insert public service announcements (PSAs) into the daily schedule. It's easy to differentiate them from commercials because they don't attempt to sell a product.

We've all seen them. There are fire safety tips, health hints, even messages that show how TV stunts are performed. In an actual case two youngsters, after seeing the Heimlich maneuver demonstrated in one of the public service announcements, saved a classmate from choking by employing what they had learned on television. There are messages that encourage healthy snacking, energy conservation, or exercise. An important point about these announcements is that children get a chance to see some of their heroes giving them helpful hints rather than trying to sell deodorants or beer. Brooke Shields has not only graced the inside of a pair of designer jeans—she has also done some effective antismoking spots aimed at young teenagers.

It could be useful to have your children develop a list of public service messages. By compiling a list, youngsters may begin to look more closely at what these messages are saying. This also creates a good excuse for you as a parent to talk with your children about such things as smoking and proper eating habits. And you'll get their attention because most young people will talk about anything as long as they've seen it on television.

Children might also have fun making up their own public service announcements. They could pick an issue that is of special concern to them. A younger sister could easily be inspired to design a PSA aimed at bossy older sisters. Or your children might enjoy putting together a message for you about children's rights around the house. They could write a brief script and act out their PSA.

PSAs represent a direct way in which television can serve the public interest. PSAs such as those shown here serve to counteract some of the other kinds of messages that children get from TV.

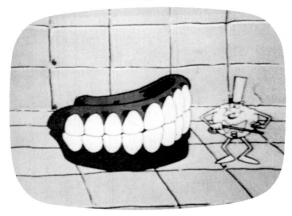

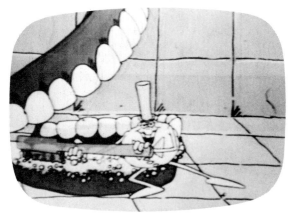

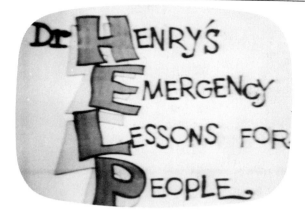

EAT FRUIT, SNACK SMART.

"SPIDERMAN AND THE MONSTER/BANANAS" :30

CLIENT: USDA   CODE NO.: NB-3144

(SFX: MONSTER)

SPIDERMAN: What's that escapee from a horror movie up to?

I'll head him off at the park.

(SFX: SPIDER WEB SPRINGING OUT)

We need a new cage, extra large.

MAYOR: ...and for saving our city, I'm giving you this medal and a cash award of four hundred trillion...

SPIDERMAN: Uh, pardon me.
MAYOR: Yes, Spiderman?
SPIDERMAN: Frankly, I'd rather have...

...a banana.

(SFX: ROARS OF ADORING PUBLIC)
ANNCR: (VO) Spiderman loves bananas. Eat fruit, snack smart.

How to Say No

What do you do about the programs that you don't want your children to watch, but that are shown during the hours they're up and about? This will become a bigger problem as cable and pay television develop, providing many additional channels. With these channels comes the possibility that distinctly adult fare will be shown throughout the day and night. If you dislike some of the messages your children get from commercial or cable TV, it's up to you to keep an eye on what they're watching. Then *turn off the television* if you don't like what you see. This is more reasonable and easier than trying to get certain programs off the air or trying to make everything on television suitable for children. And remember to tell the baby-sitter about the TV rules for your family.

There are many TV reform groups that want to eliminate what they consider violence, vulgarity, sex, and profanity from television. Most of them seem to take their rhetoric from television's soap commercials; they are obsessed with cleaning up, eliminating, removing, and controlling the content of TV programs. They seem bent on setting themselves up as television's quality control inspectors and they want to impose their definition of "quality," which can only mean censorship. No matter how noble their intentions, the inevitable result is a narrowing of viewing options. Are there alternatives to saying "Take that off the air because I don't like it"? Many families do not necessarily want R- and X-rated films and softcore pornography that cable is already bringing into living rooms across the country.

In addition to saying no to your children, you may be interested in a mechanical solution to this problem, at least with cable. Your cable company can provide a lock-out device, an electronic box that can be programmed to turn the television set on or off, change channels, or completely black out undesired programs. As TV critic Jeff Greenfield has said, "Right now in New York if a parent is out on a Friday or a Saturday night at eleven thirty or midnight, a twelve-year-old child can turn on the cable set and watch 'Ugly George' or 'Midnight Blue.' . . . [A cable system] should provide a lock box and I would like to see Congress mandate this before regulatory authority disappears entirely. . . . A lock box is the only proper answer because I believe that the First Amendment also includes the right to publish terrible things."

Lock box or not, the final control over what your child watches has to rest with you. Many parents who occasionally read titillating literature do not keep this kind of material in the home while their children are young. The same strategy can be applied to television. Parents who would enjoy adult movies on cable TV can postpone subscribing to those pay channels until their children are older.

Making the Most of Good Programs

Considering all the programs we'd like to forget as soon as they're over, it's nice to follow through on some of the shows we or our children especially like. Whatever the subject of the program—whether it's an arts special on dance or pottery, a dramatic special, or a sports event—if it interested your child, it is probably worth exploring further. A trip to the library to find related books is one way to start. Or, if possible, arrange a family field trip to the real thing: visit an artist's studio, attend a school sports event or a dance recital. Many of the after-school specials are adapted from novels. Your child could read the original or others by the same author. You don't need to turn every program into a lesson—we all need plain fun-and-games. But there may be one or two ideas

A Plug Lock

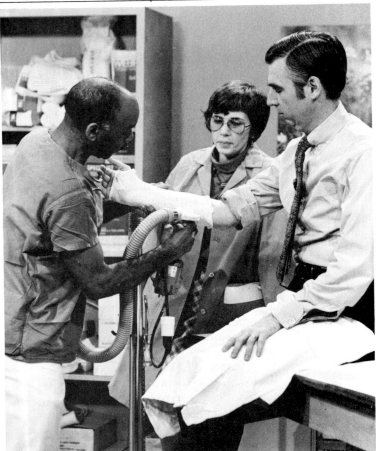

PBS's award-winning "Mr. Rogers' Neighborhood" has instructed and entertained millions of American youngsters. Informative award winners on commercial TV have included the series "In the News" and "30 Minutes."

Photo by Barry Myers/Courtesy of Family Communications, Inc.

your child gets from television that are worth pursuing. Then other programs on the same subject can be even more enjoyable than the first ones, and your child may have discovered a new skill or hobby. This approach works even if your offspring is turned on only by horror movies. Try to channel this interest into learning about the history of witches or the origin of ghosts, or reading *Frankenstein, Dracula,* or the stories of the Brothers Grimm or Edgar Allan Poe.

> "When 'Starsky & Hutch' was on the air, there was one scene when they got in the car and used their seat belts. . . . Within the next six days maybe 100,000 people bought seatbelts. When Fonz on 'Happy Days' went in and got a library card, something like 500,000 people went in and got library cards. Television is very powerful. I hope we can use it constructively." Norman Lear

Violence on TV

Actually it is not the issue of sex that most parents and child authorities feel is the most disturbing element on television. Psychologists, teachers, and pediatricians believe that it is the depiction of violence on TV that is the most harmful aspect of the medium as far as children are concerned. It's ironic. The American viewing public in general is vocal in its objections to the depiction of TV sex but when it comes to violence the majority not only seem to accept it, they actually expect it and look for it on their screens.

TV programming is filled with murders, beatings, shootings, rapes, and almost every form of mayhem imaginable. And television violence is not confined to physical aggression. Verbal abuse in the form of threats, sarcasm, and belittlement is a standard part of TV fare.

A 1982 report from the National Institute of Mental Health on the behavioral effects of television concluded that there is overwhelming evidence that excessive television violence leads to violent and aggressive behavior among children and teenagers. In dealing with TV violence review all of the strategies we have suggested so far. You can go through the recommendations of program guides to see if any of the shows appear to be violent in nature. If nothing else, this exercise will graphically point out to you the need for better, more detailed program guides, and for more diverse programming. If you're serious about controlling the amount of violence your youngsters are exposed to, then you will periodically need to watch at least part of these programs with them. You will need to apply the applauding and booing strategy here. Point out when someone is being verbally abused, and comment on physical violence, making comments such as "That's ridiculous, no one could survive a crash like that," or "What other ways do you think they could have solved that problem without having a fist fight over it?" or "Do you really think it's funny to insult a friend?" You can point out the disparities between violence on the screen and violence in the real world, helping them to understand that victims of real life aggression do not emerge unscathed, like cartoon heroes; that violence hurts.

Whoever is taking care of your children when you are not around should be informed as to your feelings about watching violence on TV. Your baby-sitter's guide could make clear your definition of too much violence and should list specific programs that your children are not permitted to see.

Remember, nobody understands your child better then you. If your youngster has nightmares about watching the Bionic Man misplace his arm or if you see no particular benefits in his watching the Guyana massacre reenacted for the fourth time, you don't need a lock box to solve these problems. You can employ one of the oldest and most effective devices a parent has ever used with a child—a simple "No."

Saturday Morning Mayhem

The effects on children of watching repeated acts of violence hour after hour, week after week, are a subject of deep and growing concern.

Children and Adult Commercials

Children who watch hour after hour of TV shows are also absorbing hours of commercials targeted to adults. The direct impact of these ads on young audiences is minimal. After all, how many nine-year-olds are going to hound their parents for a new Buick, a fancy-smelling deodorant spray, lemony-fresh oven cleaner, or better insurance coverage?

But the indirect impact of these commercials on children cannot be discounted. Commercials play on all our insecurities, convincing us that we have to own more to be happier. Commercials reduce men and women to sexist caricatures; they portrary children as nagging monsters who complain about mother's cooking or dad's ring-around-the-collar. Old people in commercials worry about arthritis, hemorrhoids, and dentures; teenagers worry about their hair and breath. All these clichéed images and materialistic messages cannot help but have an impact on children. The nine-year-old may not beg for a Buick, but he could decide that a big luxury car is better than his parents' Toyota. And although the statement that "Gentlemen prefer Hanes" won't send a little girl out shopping for pantyhose, she may remember the covert visual and spoken message in the ad about women competing for men's attention and dressing to please men. It is disturbing to think that manufacturers' distorted portrayals of everyday life are shaping the way children imagine the adult world. And the only evidence to counteract these commercial messages is the lives of their own parents. Does domestic reality have a chance in the face of Madison Avenue hype?

The best advice we can give you is to stay tuned to the hidden messages your children absorb from TV's hucksters. And while you try to counter the commercials for face paint and fast cars, remember that the best defense your children can have is the sense that they are loved, that you care. Mister Rogers sings a song that says it well: "I like you as you are!"

Cable and Children

Since so many communities in this country are either in the process of awarding a cable franchise or are already wired into a CATV system, we feel that it is important to include this special section on cable and children. Television today means much more than the programs that for the past four decades have come into our homes via the VHF and UHF bands. With an ever-increasing number of households hooked up to cable, there is now an opportunity for increased choice in children's programming.

Preschoolers, schoolchildren, and young adolescents are lively audiences, with interests in the arts, science, and social problems, and with a taste for good entertainment. They deserve to be taken seriously, and cable may provide the solution for families who can afford to sign up for its services.

Because cable television is paid for by subscribers on a regular basis, it can show commercial-free programs for children. Because cable provides so many channels, it can program for children of different ages and interests. And because it can provide a number of public access channels for programs made by members of the community, cable can give young people the chance to design, produce, direct, and star in their own programs. Already there are some shining examples of what cable can do for children. We've listed a few below so that you can get an idea of the potential of cable to enhance children's programming:

- Warner Amex's Nickelodeon is a national cable channel with thirteen hours of programming, seven days a week, all for young people. Some of the programs on the channel are for preschoolers, some for preteens, and some for teenagers. Any cable system in any part of the country can buy Nickelodeon for its subscribers.

- "KIDS 4" was the first local children's channel in the United States to be mandated by city ordinance. Serving Sun Prairie, Wisconsin, the channel was founded by citizens, with the support of their local cable company, and is now totally staffed by children aged eight to thirteen. They create their own programs and serve as writers, sound and camera technicians, lighting and stage designers, and directors. "KIDS 4" includes a weekly news magazine and programs on local heritage, culture, sports, school activities, and other items of interest to the young community. Recently "KIDS 4" producers staged a satellite-connected demonstration of an interconnect between American children and children in Australia.

- In Hurst, Texas, a guitar-playing ex-teacher has teamed up with a mime in a clown suit to produce a warm, funny, educational program called "Reach for the Sky." Local preschool children, with their families, appear on the show, which is produced in a local library by Blackhawk Cable Television.

- In Reston, Virginia, "You Gotta Have Art" teaches children about painting, pottery, puppet-making, and other art forms.

- "Mark Schictman's Kids News," on Manhattan Cable TV, is a news program produced and anchored by young people. Mark Schictman, the producer, originated the show in 1980, when he was thirteen. Local, national, and international news, movie and book reviews, and weather are all delivered with emphasis on children's interests.

- Continental Cablevision in Concord, New Hampshire, shows a series called "I Like Kids Creating," produced by the fifth- and sixth-grade students of the Melville School. Some programs deal with local subjects chosen by the children; others have dealt with such nationally important topics as the New Hampshire presidential primary.

These are all examples of cable serving the needs and interests of young people. Unfortunately, to date they are the exceptions rather than the rule. Most cable systems thus far consider a few hours of cartoons each day sufficient children's fare; others forget about the two- to fifteen-year-old audience completely. Still others think their commitment to young audiences begins and ends with educational programming that consists of a teacher with a blackboard and chalk diagramming sentences or explaining algebra problems.

That is why a national channel for children like Nickelodeon is such a good idea. In fact there should be more children's networks. It is also important to remember that there is room for service to young people on the other specialized cable channels. Minority networks like Black Entertainment Television could feature a series for black preschoolers. Twenty-four-hour news channels like Cable News Network could offer some news programming and interview segments aimed at young people. Arts channels like Bravo could include programs for children and teenagers. There is room for shows designed for young audiences on the Entertainment and Sports Programming Network, the National Spanish TV Network, and the Women's Channel as well.

And the same holds true for *local* news and sports on cable. Segments of it can be geared to young people on a regular basis.

Cable can encourage leisure reading, too. Programs from the local library can combine reading aloud, children's book reviews, story

Courtesy of Warner Amex
Satellite Entertainment Co.

Cable, with its multiple channels, has the potential of opening up a whole new world of children's television. Nickelodeon, the young people's cable channel, has already presented a variety of programming.

In some cities public access cable has
given youngsters the opportunity to
make TV shows for themselves.
(Shown here, "KIDS 4" in Sun Prairie, Wisconsin, and "Mark Schictman's Kids News" in Manhattan.)

Paul Whiting/US Cable of Viking

dramatizations, and segments of films to interest young people in different books.

Finally, young people learn more by making their own TV than by watching TV made by someone else. And the results can be surprisingly competent and interesting to watch, even for adults. Children can film anything from a high school play to a trip to the local museum or the newsworthy visit of a famous person. In fact, children's interviews with famous people often bring out interesting anecdotes, since children ask questions that few adults would dream of asking. "What was your favorite book when you were young?" "How do you go to the bathroom in the space shuttle?"

If cable and the other new technologies do represent a second chance for the American viewing public, then parents must take a real interest in how the cable franchise in their community is awarded and how it is maintained once it is in place. The final chapter of this book is devoted to providing you with concrete suggestions and examples as to what you can do to make television in your community better for yourself and your children.

7 Resources

Books for Parents

Moody, Kate. *Growing Up on Television: A Report to Parents.* New York: Times Books, 1980. A survey of research done on children's television, with suggestions for improving children's TV-viewing experience.

Singer, Dorothy; Singer, Jerome; and Zuckerman, Diane. *Teaching Television: How to Use TV to Your Child's Advantage.* New York: Dial Press, 1981. A home mini-course to encourage parents to use TV programs to stimulate their children to be more selective television consumers.

Stein, Aletha Huston, and Freidrick, Lynette Kohn. *Impact of Television on Children and Youth.* Chicago: University of Chicago Press, 1975. A good brief overview of research on children and TV violence, patterns of viewing, prosocial television, stereotypes, and other topics.

Films and Tapes for Parents

Kids for Sale. A 16-mm color film, 22 minutes. 1979. Action for Children's Television. A look at commercial television and how it shapes the values of American children, with excerpts from children's programming and commercials. Available from Mass Media Ministries, 2116 N. Charles Street, Baltimore, Md. 21218.

TV: The Anonymous Teacher. A 16-mm color film, 15 minutes. 1976. Advertising, violence, and sexual and racial stereotyping on television are examined, with commentary by noted researchers in the field of children's television. For high school and adult audiences. Available from Mass Media Ministries, 2116 N. Charles Street, Baltimore, Md. 21218.

TV or Not TV. "Bill Moyer's Journal," shown on PBS, studies the effect of TV withdrawal on the members of five family groups who were paid $500 each to suspend TV for a month in Minneapolis.

Books for Children

Angell, Judie, *A Word from Our Sponsor or My Friend Alfred.* Scarsdale, N.Y.: Bradbury Press, 1979. A fast-paced, funny, contemporary story of twelve-year-old Alfred's adventures in consumerism, for grades 5 to 7.

Burns, Marilyn. *I Am Not a Short Adult: Getting Good at Being a Kid.* Boston: Little, Brown, 1977. An illustrated guide to life for grades 5 up. Chapter 8, "The TV Picture," offers helpful advice on how to deal with television.

Byars, Betsy. *The TV Kid.* New York: Scholastic Book Services, 1978. An effective and humorous novel for grades 4 to 6 about Lennie, who plunges with all his imagination into the world of television until he's faced with a frighteningly real situation.

Fenten, Don, and Fenten, Barbara. *Behind the Television Scene.* Mankato, Minn.: Crestwood House, 1980. Clearly describes and illustrates with photographs the activities that take place during the production and presentation on TV programs, for grade 4 level.

Phelan, Terry Wolfe. *The Week Mom Unplugged the TVs.* New York: Scholastic Book Services, 1979. An imaginative story about three children's reactions to a week without TV, for grades 2 to 6.

Polk, Lee, and Le Shan, Eda. *The Incredible Television Machine.* New York: Macmillan, 1977. A discussion of the background, history, and influence of TV for grades 5 and up.

Rosen, Winifred. *Ralph Proves the Pudding.* New York: Doubleday, 1972. A winning story for younger children about TV commercials, illustrated by Lionel Kalish.

Television and Education

For most of us, the phrase "educational television" calls to mind daybreak lectures on igneous rocks, puppets reciting the alphabet, and the on-camera wanderings of Our Friend the Muskrat. Today, more than three decades since the first airing of "Kukla, Fran, and Ollie," we accept that television can be used to teach all of us certain facts or skills. "Sesame Street" teaches preschoolers the sounds of letters; Julia Child illustrates the perfect *daube de boeuf;* and network news informs us nightly of the world's choice events.

TV teaching is a much more widespread phenomenon than we think. TV can—and today, it does—teach mechanics how to repair particular makes of cars, help young people practice how to behave on a job interview, offer courses for college credit, and keep dentists up-to-date in their profession. Television's capacity for teaching academic and occupational skills is not limited to a few programs on PBS, either. Cable television's multiple channels draw many specialized audiences of pupils. Businesses, universities, government agencies, and even schools have libraries of educational videotapes, many of which they produce themselves.

But to think of television as educational only when it is most obviously teaching is to deny its power. Television, even at its most entertaining, imparts an enormous amount of information (and sometimes misinformation). Much of our knowledge of the early days of America's West is based on what we have seen on "Gunsmoke," "Bonanza," and "Little House on the Prairie." Our supposed familiarity with police routine or life at an army medical unit also has video roots. Even as it entertains and informs us, television also communicates ideas and values. This is obviously true of a "Mister Rogers' Neighborhood" segment on the importance of sharing. But it is equally true of "Lou Grant," "Fantasy Island," or "Love, Sidney."

This chapter looks at television as an educator and as an educational tool—inside the classroom, in the home, and at work; for preschoolers, young people, and adults. It is a useful chapter for teachers, but it is intended for all television-watchers, since we all learn from television, whether we want to or not.

TV Teaching in the Classroom

TV today is used in a variety of ways to teach a variety of subjects, including TV itself. TV programs are used to aid in the teaching of a specific subject or to explore an issue in a class. The programs are often videotapes or videodiscs shown in the class during school hours, or assigned viewing of regularly scheduled programs at home. PBS's reading series, "Electric Company," has been shown in thousands of elementary school classes around the country, and videotapes about everything from art history to sex education are available as teaching tools. Teachers have been using special commercial television programs such as "Eleanor and Franklin" for many years to supplement their lesson plans. At Memorial Junior High School in Minot, North Dakota, a videodisc performance of "Tom Sawyer" inspired an English class to devour the Mark Twain classic and biographies of the author as well. The same school uses videodiscs to supplement biology, physics, home economics, social studies, English, and even physical education classes.

Television programs can also teach more abstract skills like logical thinking, or values, or interracial harmony, or they can help spur students' discussions about social or political issues. The Agency for Instructional Television (AIT), a company that produces hundreds of programs for classroom use, offers a series called "Thinkabout" to teach ten- to twelve-year-olds problem-solving skills. Each program shows that value judgments are an important part of decision-making. One of the segments, grouped with a cluster of programs labeled "Finding Patterns," tells the story of a boy who recognizes that people's behavior follows certain patterns. When an older neighbor fails to follow his normal, everyday pattern of behavior, the boy is worried and decides to check up on him. In doing so, the boy helps save his older neighbor's life. Under the heading "Judging Information," another segment of "Thinkabout" tells how one boy is convinced that another has stolen his bicycle, until he gathers facts, examines the evidence, and comes to a different and more realistic conclusion.

Many schools have access, through the school audiovisual department, to video recorders and are using prerecorded programming from off the air or specially purchased tapes with encouraging results. And a growing number of schools are using videodisc machines.

> "... highly compressed TV learning modules, especially those of ten- to thirty-second commercials, are affecting attention span. Many teachers have commented on the fact that students of all ages 'turn off' when some lesson or lecture takes longer than, say, eight to ten minutes. TV conditioning leads to the expectation that there will be a new point of view or focus of interest or even subject matter every few minutes." Neil Postman, *Teaching as a Conserving Activity*

"*Miss Jones, may I go home and watch television?*"

Here are only a few examples of TV teaching:

- A fifth-grade teacher in Baltimore County, Maryland, found "Mork and Mindy" useful for stimulating discussions about how newcomers to a country, like Mork, can make mistakes in the English language. In math class, students translated the number of TV commercial minutes per hour into fractions.

- In Islip, New York, a junior high social studies teacher used Alex Haley's "Roots," both book and TV versions, to inspire the class to investigate their own family trees and compare their family histories to Haley's.

- A second-grade teacher in Jersey City rescheduled science as the first subject of the school day so she and her pupils could discuss what they had seen the night before on PBS's "3-2-1 Contact," a science series for eight- to twelve-year-olds produced by Children's Television Workshop.

- In Shelby, North Carolina, the high school librarian talked the principal into buying the school a videotape recorder, and then made tapes available to teachers on subjects ranging from astronomy to alcoholism. An English teacher who brought her class into the library to see the video version of a Hawthorne short story later reported to the librarian that, during a subsequent discussion of the program, students who had never before volunteered a remark in class spoke up eagerly. In fact students who saw the TV program gained so many new insights into the story from their discussions of the program that they asked the librarian to show it to the class a second time.

- In Spring Valley, Illinois, vocational education students and science club members at Hall Township High School built a satellite receiver behind the football field. As a result, the school was able to watch hours of NASA-transmitted pictures of Saturn, taken by Voyager II. The high school earth station, built for $4,100 (mainly from army surplus materials), picks up transmissions from five American and three Canadian satellites, each of which carries from twelve to twenty-four channels.

- C-SPAN (Cable Satellite Public Affairs Network), which shows telecasts of the House of Representatives debates to millions of cable subscribers, also offers high school students a series of public affairs programs that televise teenagers' interviews with congressmen and other Washington officials. Sponsored by the Close-Up Foundation, which brings thousands of teenagers to Washington each year from all over the country, the programs show live meetings between teenage visitors and politicians, and also use telephone hookups to allow young people in other cities to question members of the government.

Teaching with ITV

Until recently, instructional television, or ITV, meant broadcast television, usually on PBS. The public broadcasting stations carry about two thousand programs each year designed and developed specifically for use in the classroom. One of the most popular of these is "Electric Company." ITV also means the thousands of instructional tapes produced by organizations like the International Instructional Television Cooperative (ITV-CO-OP), the Agency for Instructional Television (AIT), and other production houses that develop their materials for in-classroom use.

The spread of cable television to so many communities in the United States takes ITV beyond its PBS beginnings. On cable, ITV becomes more readily available. Already there are several networks of instructional programming for different ages available through cable. In addition, local cable companies produce their own instructional shows to meet the special needs of students in their communities. In Woodbury, New York, the local cable system produces a program called "Extra Help" that brings teachers in front of the camera every school night to answer junior and senior high school students' phone-in questions about their homework assignments.

The videodisc as a source of ITV is still a newcomer on the scene. While three million videotape recorders can be found in homes, businesses, and schools around the country, fewer than half a million disc players have sold; the videodisc is still considered the technology of the future. But that future is rapidly on its way, and a few educators are preparing for it. One of the biggest educational videodisc projects in the works is the ABC/NEA SCHOOLDISC program. The National Education Association and the American Broadcasting Company are collaborating on a

Scott Schwarting for Hall High School, Spring Valley, Illinois

Scene from "What's Next," produced by the Agency for Instructional Television in Bloomington, Indiana

Scott Schwarting for Hall High School

Using old Army/Navy parts, students in Hall High School in Spring Valley, Illinois, built their own satellite receiver. They now augment their foreign language training by tuning in to programs from all over the world.

Courtesy of the Agency for Instructional Television

set of instructional materials for grades four through six. Five teachers, selected by the NEA for their skill at curriculum development, are working with ABC staff to design twenty one-hour videodisc programs. The hour program contains six ten-minute segments on language skills, social studies, science, the arts, and current events. Each program will be based on a theme, such as interdependence, pride, decision and consequences, or openness to change. The programs, which are only the first phase of the project, will be available on videotape as well as disc. According to one of the teachers involved in the project, television programs are something that children can identify with; their familiarity with the TV medium helps make video lessons like the SCHOOLDISCS really meaningful to them.

Recently teachers have begun to make television content a subject of study by itself. Accepting that television is an inevitable part of children's lives today, a number of teachers have decided to teach their pupils how to watch it critically, to understand how it works and how it is shaping their attitudes. Critical viewing also means paying more attention to the story elements—characters, setting, plot, theme—and to particular details. The purpose of critical viewing, say its supporters, is not to make everyone feel guilty about watching "Bosom Buddies" instead of "Washington Week in Review" but to help people get more out of what they watch. Horace Newcomb, an associate professor of English at the University of Texas at Austin, has gone so far as to say that "there is no television program that doesn't lend itself to close, extended analysis."

Educational materials on critical viewing are intended to teach more than just how to watch television. They were developed to encourage critical thinking about media in general, not just about TV. Children who can decipher the theme of a television program can carry the same skill to the theater, to a movie, and to their reading. Youngsters who learn to listen for a speaker's bias on a TV program or commercial can listen for the same qualities in any conversation or public address. Children who have thought about what makes a "good"

television show or a "bad" one can apply value judgments to other major influences in their lives. According to George Gerbner, dean of the Annenberg School of Communications at the University of Pennsylvania, "The development of . . . analytical critical skills and their application to television is the fresh approach to the liberal arts and a principal task of education today." The key product of learning to analyze the media is the ability to choose—a vitally important skill in our culture of overabundant information and stimuli.

Few teachers encourage children to perform an in-depth analysis of every Saturday morning cartoon show. But some do help their classes to be more critical of what they see on TV. A number of critical viewing classes make use of the curriculum materials developed in the late 1970s under a $1.6 million grant from the U.S. Department of Health, Education, and Welfare's Office of Education. Four different sets of materials were developed by organizations in different parts of the country for four age groups: grades K–5, grades 6–8, grades 9–12, and postsecondary students. These materials, which have the support of the NEA, have been introduced to teachers and librarians through state education association conferences. Teachers have also developed their own curricula materials to help children deal with TV. These school projects may ask children to keep a log of what they watch, to discuss their viewing in class, to take notes while watching, to create and act out their own commercials, and to vote on their favorite programs. Some of the projects get parents involved by encouraging students to watch with their families and discuss what they see.

The critical-viewing-skills workbooks funded by the USOE cover a wide range of subjects. The middle school workbook has chapters like "Who Puts a Television Program Together?," "How Does Television Persuade Us?," and "How Do You Analyze Television News?" Segments from the textbook for high

Ask Me Another

Here are some questions teachers use to get their students to think about television:

1. When do you watch television? Whom do you watch it with? Did you ever stop to think about why you watch it?

2. What are your favorite programs? Do you have a favorite kind of program? What is the general theme of these programs? For example, are they always about someone who gets into trouble? Or about someone who solves crimes? Do they seem to teach a particular lesson?

3. Think of one TV program you saw recently that you particularly liked. What was it about? Do you think it had a hidden message? In other words, if you look behind the program's story, is it teaching you something extra? What is the hidden message in "The Dukes of Hazzard" about cars and how to drive them? About Southerners? About women? About problem-solving? What is the message in "M*A*S*H" about war? About friendship?

4. Sometimes a program teaches you facts; sometimes it offers you different people's opinions, and sometimes it tells a made-up story. Can you think of an example for each type of program? It can be very difficult to tell when a TV program is fact and when it is fiction. Can you think of shows you have seen that blend reality and fantasy? Or fact and opinion?

5. Talk about the people who are involved in making a TV program: the script and score writers, directors, producers, set and costume designers, camerapeople, lighting technicians, special effects personnel, musicians, and others. What are their jobs? Do you ever find yourself forgetting that the heroes of your favorite programs are just men and women doing a job?

6. What are special effects? How are special camera effects used to make you think something impossible is happening on TV? For example, explain how David Banner turns into the Hulk. How are special effects or trick photography used to make products on commercials look better than they are? What kinds of tricks can be achieved with makeup and costuming? By using stuntmen and women?

7. Do you think the background sounds in a program are important? How can music influence the way you feel about the program? What about the laugh track? Describe the sound track of a Saturday morning cartoon.

8. What is the purpose of commercials? How much information do they provide about the product? What kinds of persuasive techniques do commercials use to make you want something?

9. Does television influence the way you feel about yourself? About other people? About the United States? About other countries? Does television teach you things? What do you feel TV has taught you?

10. How much TV do you watch? How much does the rest of your family see? Do you think it is too much? How do you choose the programs you are going to watch? Do you think you are a selective TV-viewer? What would you be doing if you weren't watching TV? If you think you watch too much TV, what can you do to watch less?

school students, *Inside Television,* range from explanations of how the Nielsen ratings work to statistics about minorities on TV.

What is missing from these materials, according to many media critics, is any information about how young viewers can try to change TV. The critical-viewing-skills curricula teach children how to watch TV as it is today; in doing so, say consumer advocates, the materials apparently condone the TV status quo. The USOE workbooks teach children to notice how commercials persuade, but do not encourage them to question a TV system that is dependent on commercials. The workbooks explain that broadcasters are licensed to operate in the public interest, but do not point out that broadcasters' programs fall far short of most viewers' concepts of public service. To many people, the critical-viewing-skills materials being used in classrooms today just aren't critical enough.

One thing that almost all critical-viewing-skills curricula do is explain how television is made. But few explanations work as well as do-it-yourself. That is why some teachers are putting video cameras in their students' hands and letting them learn critical viewing through the camera viewfinder.

Do-It-Yourself TV

Since 1975, students from the DuFief Elementary School in Gaithersburg, Maryland, have been producing in-school programs on WDUF, the school's closed circuit TV system. WDUF's twice-a-week newscasts are produced by a staff who range in age from eight to twelve. Segments on the school cafeteria menu, the faculty-student softball game, Shakespeare rehearsals, and the habits of tarantulas are supplemented by movie reviews, weather reports, and even news segments on events in nearby Washington, D.C. Cameras in classrooms cover "live" events like the fourth-grade show-and-tell, and an anchorperson in the studio pulls it all together on-air. At DuFief, jobs among the WDUF staffers are rotated, so that everyone has a chance to be producer, cameraperson, reporter, and lighting technician. Staff

trainees are recruits from the third and fourth grades, who sign up each semester for WDUF internships.

In March, 1980, CBS aired "Too Late for Me," a film on gang violence produced by the students of Clemente High School in Chicago. In the neighborhood around the school, gang fights are common, and a number of gang members attend the school. The high school provided space, equipment, and adult producers to help with the film, and local businesses supplied much of the funding and supplies. The bulk of the work on the film was done by students. Since "Too Late for Me" was aired, Clemente students have produced another program, on venereal disease, at the request of CBS's network staff.

Irvine, California, has connected twenty-four of its schools, its colleges, science center, city hall, and school district office by two-way cable television. Now education graduate students at the college can watch an elementary school teacher in action with a class and ask questions when the class is over—via TV. Third-grade students in one school can make friends with students at another school over the TV screen; the two classes can show their drawings to each other, share book reports, and talk to each other's teachers. High school students offer TV classes to younger children on the other

The yearly district "Authorfest" in Irvine, California, invites authors of children's literature to share the creative process with students all over the district, through multiple school hook-ups via interactive cable.

M. Kishina for the Cable TV Network, Irvine, Calif.

side of town. In addition, the TV system allows one instructor to teach English to non–English-speaking young people located in schools all over Irvine. The school superintendent holds meetings with teachers over TV, and school personnel can take college refresher courses by watching a screen rather than attending classes in person.

The basic equipment that makes all of this possible is a mobile video unit with one camera and two TV sets. With this equipment, a fifth-grader delivering a report to his classmates and to another fifth grade across town will see himself on one TV set as he is filmed by a member of his own class; on the second TV set he can see his listeners at the other school, who are being filmed simultaneously by one of *their* classmates. The listeners have their own mobile classroom unit and can see both the reporter and themselves on their two screens.

Making TV: What Does It Teach?

A young person who has helped design, script, produce, direct, film, and finally show a TV program has learned a great deal. Take the example of a junior high school student who does a TV segment on the unveiling of a park statue of her town's founder. Here are some of the things she will learn and some of the responsibilities she will have to handle:

- *Designing the Program:* This requires the same kind of critical thinking as a written school assignment. The student has to decide what she thinks is important about the story. Does she want to interview the artist? Talk to descendants of the person being honored? Can she get any shots of the statue being made? Does she want to film the unveiling? Should she include the mayor's speech? How should she structure the film? Should all of it lead up to the moment of the unveiling or should the unveiling be followed by interviews?

- *Writing the Script:* In writing the script, the young filmmaker has to put her narrative writing skills to good work. She also has to try to decide how much of the film's

story she should tell as a narrator, how much of the story should be told just by pictures, and how much should be based on interviews or the words of the story's protagonists—the artist, the mayor, the descendants, perhaps the person who decided to have the statue made.

Both designing the film and writing the script will require the student to use research skills. She will probably have to go to the library and read up on the town's history to find out why the subject of the statue has been chosen to be honored. If she interviews the artist or films him at work, she will learn something about sculpture as well as history.

- *Producing the Program:* Few classroom activities can teach organization skills as well as TV production does. As a producer, the student has to make sure she has the right equipment and supplies. She has to set up the interviews she needs, arrange transportation to the sites she wants to film, decide what kinds of help she is going to require, and request it. If she is not going to be her own cameraperson, she has to "hire" another student or someone else to do the filming.

- *Directing and Filming:* To be a good director, the student has to have good planning and visual skills. The director decides how the program will be filmed, sometimes after much planning and sometimes on the spur of the moment, when an excellent shot presents itself. She must also decide how to use the sound—the interviews, the mayor's speech, the noise of the sculptor's hammer, the murmur of the crowd gathered to see the unveiling, her own voice narrating. If she is doing her own camera work, then she does not have to explain all her decisions to someone else. But if she has an assistant to handle the camera, then she has to practice some management skills as well. She has to communicate her ideas

"I Like Kids Creating"

The fourteen sixth-graders at Millville School are more blasé about being in front of a camera—or behind one—than most adults. For the past five years, being in the sixth grade at Millville has meant a chance to produce "I Like Kids Creating," a cable television series shown monthly by Continental Cablevision of New Hampshire.

The democratic nature of the production process would make a network producer wring his hands, but it works for Greg Uhrin, program director of Continental Cablevision's Channel 12 and adult adviser to "I Like Kids Creating." "Each fall the kids vote on the format that the program will take during *their* production year," explains Uhrin. "One year the program was a set of monthly specials, each on a particular subject. This year the program has a kind of magazine format that repeats certain types of segments each month. Every program contains an interview with an interesting senior citizen, a profile of a Millville student, a calendar segment on interesting things for kids to do that month, a visit to another school in the area, and a minifeature on a special subject. So far, it's working very well."

Students not only change the format of the program each year; they also switch production assignments for each segment. By the end of the school year, all the students in the sixth grade class will have had a chance to be interviewers, camerapeople, directors, editors, and writers for the show.

Students who have been in the Millville School since the first grade are old hands at TV production. They start doing simple animated films and still photography in the first grade; by the third grade they are handling a camera off a tripod and designing documentaries and film dramas; by the fifth grade they have learned to videotape programs. When they reach the sixth grade, they are ready and eager to construct their own TV shows.

"These kids are pros," laughs Greg. "By the time they are eleven they have been around TV cameras for six years. Most of them have been subjects of program segments; they have more savvy about how to talk into a camera than half the adults they interview."

The quality of "I Like Kids Creating" proves that the student production staff—and their grown-up adviser—know what they are doing. The program won a 1980 Action for Children's Television award and was awarded a citation by the governor of New Hampshire.

"I Like Kids Creating," Continental Cablevision of New Hampshire.

to the camera operator clearly and calmly, so that he or she doesn't get flustered during the filming. And the student director also has to be willing to listen to the camera-operator's suggestions and opinions and must sometimes change her plans to suit these new ideas.

- *Showing the Program:* When the TV program is finally ready to the filmmaker's satisfaction, she will probably have to show it to her schoolmates and teachers. This means she has to be prepared to answer questions about how and why she put the program together as she did. It also may mean listening and responding to criticism without getting upset. Taking criticism is not easy, but it is something important that a filmmaker who shows work to the public has to learn, and it is a good lesson for any student.

Of course, few junior high school students could do all of this work singlehandedly, and few if any of them are going to produce a videotape that can compare to the work of an adult professional. But by being part of this TV-making process, the girl covering the unveiling of the statue will apply her knowledge of history, art, and writing, and will use critical thinking, organization, and planning skills that few classroom experiences offer. To top it off, she will probably enjoy herself immensely and produce a piece of work she is proud of. Teachers have found that young people love to make and be in television programs; as much as TV has become part of their lives, it still hasn't lost its glamour. And glamour is not something school can offer children very often.

As young people become familiar with the TV-making process, much of the glamour fades away. And with it fades much of the mystique. A young person who has helped to make TV will never again look at TV programming with quite the same passive, uncritical eye. This is not to say that the average student producer will be able to watch "Magnum P.I." with an interest in the camera shots rather than the story. But a person who has experienced how a program is made doesn't take TV for granted.

The student TV producer becomes a more critical viewer, sensitive to what is bad and what is good, because the student understands that TV-making is a craft (and only occasionally an art) that requires a great deal of work by a great many people. TV is no longer a kind of mystical emanation from an unseen authority. This "humanization" of television is probably the most important product of learning to make TV programs. Few children are going to take their elementary school experience with television production on to adult jobs at CBS. But most children who gain some hands-on video experience in school will take away with them the ability to make better judgments about the TV programs they see and, as a result, to make better TV-viewing choices. And that lesson *will* be useful well into adulthood.

A Word of Warning

The National Education Association (NEA) is an enthusiastic supporter of teaching with television, because the NEA staff believes that television can be useful and because they think that teachers who ignore television are ignoring a major influence in children's lives. NEA executive director Terry Herndon has said, "The public schools, which are decentralized by law, are about the only institutionalized safety valve capable of preventing television programming from intellectually dominating the public."

But not all teachers or all parents are reconciled to TV in the classroom. To many of them, watching TV in class sounds like a waste of learning time. And many are reluctant to do anything that might encourage TV-watching, when it already fills so many hours of most children's days. Teachers argue that TV shortens students' attention spans and makes them unwilling to concentrate on a project that doesn't bring instant gratification. TV, teachers say, has made their students passive; TV-bred young people sit back and wait to be entertained instead of reaching out for information. Young children today seem to have trouble playing, and their imaginations seem duller, according to teachers who have been observing particular

Children making TV. What better way
to learn about the medium?

Photos: Paul Whiting/US Cable of Viking

age groups for years. Educators who believe that television has a negative effect on children are reluctant to bring it into their classrooms. Professor James M. Larkin, chairman of the University of Pennsylvania Elementary Education Department, believes that children should be forbidden to watch any television and that TV shouldn't even be mentioned in the classroom. To do so, he claims, is equivalent to condoning cigarette-smoking or drinking by children, because television drugs children into passivity and keeps them from reading.

New York University Professor of Education Neil Postman goes even further. He believes that "television is causing the rapid decline of our concept of childhood." He writes that, largely because of TV, "the behavior, attitude, desires, and even physical appearance of adults and children are becoming increasingly indistinguishable." Postman considers this a tragedy for many reasons, but as an educator he is most conscious that it is "disastrous because it makes problematic the future of school, which is one of the few institutions still based on the assumption that there are significant differences between children and adults and that adults, therefore, have something of value to teach children." TV, Postman feels, has very little of value to teach children.

Prime Time School Television, a national nonprofit organization that works to encourage parents and teachers to make better use of TV as a learning tool, produces study guides on TV series and specials. Public Broadcasting distributes valuable teaching aids and transcripts. Cynics among parents and teachers argue that the only real benefactor from TV in the classroom is the TV industry. And it is true that the commercial television networks are tremendously supportive of the trend toward TV education. Even the most dedicated user of these network-funded materials would not argue that the TV industry's motive is pure altruism. An NEA study shows that about half a million secondary school teachers used ABC's "Roots" in their classes; their attention to the program

meant a boost for ratings. It is therefore not surprising that ABC spent $37,000 on "Roots" study guides.

Perhaps the most controversial use of television in the classroom involves instruction in critical viewing skills. Those in favor of these lessons in how to watch television argue that children who have acquired critical viewing skills will use their time in front of the TV more constructively. The many opponents of critical viewing skills consider them, at best, a waste of time and, at worst, an inducement to children to watch more TV. The fact that some of the critical-viewing-skills projects are funded by broadcasters adds credence to the latter argument. The argument may be moot because, with sharply reduced education budgets, few schools can afford the critical skills curriculum materials.

TV Teaching at Home

The TV education experience that everyone is probably most familiar with is "Sesame Street." It is made for preschoolers and is therefore generally seen outside the schoolroom, although in fact many day care centers, nurseries, kindergartens, and even primary schools use the program as part of their curricula. "Sesame Street" is designed to teach letters, numbers, and the meaning of words like "up," "down," "around," "through," and "between." It also tries to encourage logical thinking and to teach concepts like friendship and behaviors like sharing and helping. Many of these lessons have proved effective. For example, a study done at McGill University showed that young white children who had seen segments of "Sesame Street" in which children of different races play together were more likely to choose nonwhite children for their playmates than were white children who had not seen the TV segments.

"Sesame Street" has been going strong since 1969; it is watched in approximately nine million American households with preschool children. A part of the American folk culture, "Sesame Street" has also grown beyond its native roots and established itself as an international institution. "Barrio Sesamo" or "1, Rue Sesame" or "Sesamstraat"—the street is a global address visited by millions of children every day. The program, originally funded by PBS and foundation subsidies, has also become self-supporting, thanks to royalties from its spinoff books and toys and sales of foreign rights. Successful as it is, "Sesame Street" has aroused criticism from educators, particularly for its fast-cut pace, its emphasis on cognitive rather than affective learning, and even for Cookie Monster's grammar.

A PBS program that reverses these "Sesame Street" tendencies is "Mister Rogers' Neighborhood." Adults who watch Fred Rogers take five on-air minutes just to change his shoes or ten minutes to fill his fish tank are stricken with fidgets, and the extreme gentleness, patience, and depth of feeling with which Mr. Rogers tells his young audience about the death of the show's goldfish make some people squirm with embarrassment. But it would be hard to find another TV show that does such a good job of dealing with the human emotions

and fears of young children. Fred Rogers meets some important needs for the six million preschoolers who watch his program.

In addition to nationally broadcast preschool programs, instructional TV series are usually available on public broadcasting channels during weekdays. Many parents have discovered that these shows appeal to children who miss school because they are home sick.

"Kidisc": The Videodisc Revolution

Using television to encourage active rather than passive behavior sounds like a contradiction in terms. But that is exactly what a new program called "The First National Kidisc" does. "Kidisc" is designed to take advantage of the laser videodisc machines, which allow users to stop the program, watch it frame by frame at whatever speed they like, play it in reverse, or slow motion, or with only one of the two sound tracks. "Kidisc" comes on one side of a videodisc and is filmed "speeded up," so that it takes only twenty-seven minutes to play from beginning to end. But it is designed to be played, not nonstop, but in slow motion and even frame by frame, so that its games, jokes, projects, and lessons can provide children aged five to ten with hours of fun and learning.

One "chapter" of the disc teaches the sign language alphabet; children can stop the disc as each sign is shown to practice it until they have it right. Another segment shows viewers how to make a xylophone out of glasses of water and then gives them twenty-five play-by-number tunes to perform at their own pace. Other "Kidisc" segments teach children how to tie knots, fold origami, do magic tricks, make paper airplanes, and dance an Irish jig. The disc also provides the fun of visiting the San Diego Zoo and Universal Studios, and it has sections of riddles and puzzles that can be solved by moving the disc from frame to frame. One of the chapters even explains how animation

> "Indeed, perhaps the lesson of *'Zoom'*, and similar programs, is that when children are at least allowed to commune with each other across the airwaves, instead of having to watch middle-aged men hit each other with plates of pizza (as occurred midway through 'Bozo's Circus' the other day), they find all kinds of things they want to say to one another—as they always have. Our TV system could probably permit children to speak more often to other children without the foundations of the Republic crumbling. And when it's necessary for adults to speak to children—whether to tell stories or to make jokes or to instruct or to pass the time of day—at least let them speak in a language they believe in, and not in kidvid."

Michael Arlen, *The View from Highway 1*

works and shows the viewer how to make a flip-book of "moving" pictures. "Kidisc" lets children make use of television in a way they have never done before; it entertains them by showing them how to entertain themselves. Optical Programming Associates (OPA) also makes discs for adults that require "active" TV-watching. One of these is Craig Claiborne's cooking course; another, an exercise class. If the price of the laser recorders becomes competitive, this technology will make a significant contribution to education—and entertainment—in the home.

TV and Adult Education: Video Colleges

Although television can be tremendously useful in the education of children and young teenagers, it is hard to imagine that TV programs could ever replace schoolteachers. Teachers answer questions, offer guidance, and personalize the learning experience for their students. Television cannot provide that kind of attention. But college classes are less personal; a televised lecture by a professor is not very different from a flesh-and-blood performance. For many would-be undergraduates and graduate students, therefore, a TV degree is a very practical option.

One of the best-known TV degree programs is Britain's Open University, which has been under way since 1971. In Britain, where the opportunity to attend a university is

Scene from "The First National Kidisc"

© 1981 Optical Programming Associates

limited to relatively few, TV education, supplemented by correspondence courses and reading, has been extremely popular. Although the United States has no shortage of colleges, there are still a number of TV classes-for-credit offered in the States. One of the oldest American programs is New York University's "Sunrise Semester," aired nationally by CBS stations; it has been on the air since 1957 and offers its TV students two undergraduate courses per semester for college credit. Another sponsor of TV education is the National University Consortium, a group of seven colleges and universities that offers a six-year degree program via satellite. Students all over the country participate; courses are available on either cable or public broadcasting, and the program includes printed course materials, reading assignments, and phone-in help from tutors.

A second consortium of schools offering college via TV is the University of Mid America in the Midwest. Most of its courses have been available on public television, but Mid America is eager to sell its program package to cable operators. Sixty-five cable companies already carry educational programming produced by Appalachian Community Services Network (ACSN). This nonprofit production service charges cable operators who carry the ACSN educational channel one penny per month per subscriber. The channel, which is available on the Satcom I satellite, provides undergraduate and graduate courses and programs for engineers, lawyers, and other professionals. More college-via-TV facilities are available in New Jersey, where seventeen community colleges produce or purchase educational programs for local students; the accredited courses are distributed throughout the state on fifty-seven cable systems. One educational service is available from 8:30 A.M. until 10:30 P.M. seven days a week, with at least two dozen courses offered per semester.

Many of the TV education programs are still in their infancy, and many depend for their survival on cable systems' continuing to find it

profitable to carry their courses. At least two important communications organizations, the Corporation for Public Broadcasting (CPB) and the Annenberg School of Communications (ASC), think that TV degree programs are not a fly-by-night phenomenon, and they are betting $10 million on their success. In 1981 CPB and ASC created a project that has solicited proposals from individuals and institutions that wish to develop college-level TV education materials for a target audience unable to attend regular college. The project will use its $10 million to fund or help a number of undergraduate-level course-development programs and other services that "demonstrate the use of telecommunications systems for addressing unique higher education problems." It is difficult to imagine how the CPB/ASC-funded projects will differ greatly from the other TV education programs already available from PBS stations, cable systems, and satellites. Ideally, the project is a multimillion-dollar investment in the education of a great many people for whom jobs, family responsibilities, physical disabilities, lack of English, or other barriers have so far made college an impossible dream. But it will be several years before anyone will be able to measure the CPB/ASC project's success.

Medical Education via TV: Beyond "General Hospital"

Video is widely used in hospitals and clinics across the country for teaching patients and staff, for community health education, for producing health-related publis service announcements, and even for treatment. For years medical schools have been using video cameras to show students closeup views of complicated surgery, and videotapes of interesting treatments are presented as case studies for student discussion. Prerecorded videotapes are also helpful in teaching particular skills in "live" situations where it might be intrusive or inappropriate for the trainee to stop and ask questions—in learning crisis intervention techniques, for example, or interviewing skills. Simulating life-threatening emergencies (such as a hospital fire) for the camera gives students valuable experience in how to handle the situations without risking lives. And in some mental health clinics, video is used as a tool to assist the clinician in doing therapy. Skillfully adapted to the treatment situation, video can provide visual feedback to clients for self-confrontation and observation of discrepancies between their verbal and nonverbal behavior.

One of the most interesting forms of "telemedicine" being practiced today is not aimed at doctors, however, but at patients. Hospitals like the Virginia Mason Medical Center in Seattle have patient education centers that use videotapes to prepare people for surgery, provide them with background information about their disease, or teach them how to care for themselves at home. At Mason Medical Center,

volunteers have operated the patient information center for the past five years; its services are free to hospital patients and their families upon referral by doctors, nurses, and physical therapists. A trained volunteer shows the tape that the patient's doctor has recommended and then answers questions and clarifies anything the patient doesn't understand. Most of the tapes deal with preventive medicine, such as "Why Risk a Heart Attack?" or "Hypertension." One tape helps prepare patients for

A youngster learns what it will be like to have his cast removed by watching a demonstration on "Mr. Rogers' Neighborhood."

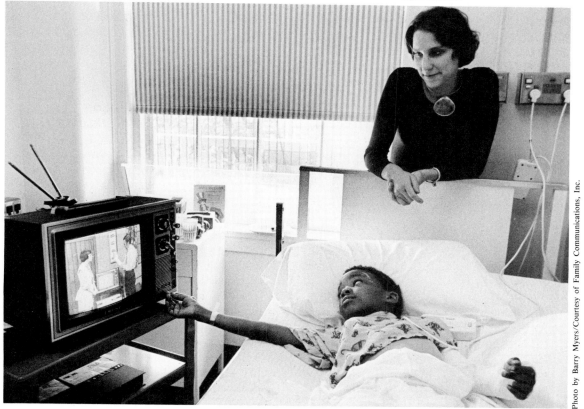

Photo by Barry Myers/Courtesy of Family Communications, Inc.

chemotherapy; another is directed to families with an epileptic child; another prepares expectant mothers for the demands of breast-feeding. One or two of the tapes are even followed by a short written test to make sure patients have absorbed important information about their bodies and techniques of self-care.

Some surgeons actually videotape their operating table performances. For the doctor, this variation on the home movie can be both a protection against malpractice claims and a method of self-critique; to the patient, the tape offers an opportunity to understand a complicated treatment.

Dr. Kenneth Bird, who for more than a decade has been using telemedicine at Massachusetts General Hospital as a method of long-distance emergency care, is excited about the prospect of cable channels' offering medical information. According to Dr. Bird, doctors on television "could blast out to all the diabetics on Channel 149 and tell them how to take better care of their feet. We could cover the whole Eastern Seaboard and talk to all the people with hardening of the arteries." He is also enthusiastic about the continuing education and expert advice that telemedicine could give medical professionals all over the country. Doctors who are not sure about the best way to deal with special problems can put their patients in front of a television camera and discuss diagnoses over two-way TV with experts in big teaching hospitals. But Bird's enthusiasm is not always contagious; most doctors thus far have been reluctant to participate in telemedicine. He explains that "A lot of doctors are unable to ask for help in treatment of a patient," because it threatens the superhero self-image they wear in our society. Many fear that telemedicine will downgrade rather than enhance their skills. So it will probably be some time before most of us are saying "Ahhhh" to a video camera.

Video Therapy:
The Shrink Meets the Screen

Surprisingly enough, psychiatrists have conducted therapy sessions with patients over television and have found these long-distance treatments effective, particularly with people who are uncomfortable talking to a doctor face-to-face. A more common use of video therapy is to show patients what they look and sound like during their sessions. In family therapy, the tape lets each member of the family see how he or she interacts with the others. Does the husband smile scornfully while his wife talks? Does he try to appear totally unconcerned? Does he sit near his children or apart? Videotape demonstrates all the nonverbal ways that people communicate with each other, often unconsciously. Video therapy also shows patients how they look to others; sometimes self-critical people are astonished to see how attractive they are on the TV screen. By taping sessions over a several-year period and then playing back the tapes, a therapist can help the patient discuss how he has changed. According to one patient, "In a mirror you can put on your best face, but with video therapy you're forced to face the truth about yourself and your relationship with others."

Video also helps people face the truth about their weight. Doctors in England have found that women with pathological eating habits are more likely to recognize the seriousness of their problems when they see themselves on television. Not only does viewing themselves on TV help obese women to diet; it also helps anorexic women (who deny that they are dangerously thin) to realize their emaciated condition.

TV creates self-awareness in other ways, too. Some therapists have found that people can use soap operas as a vehicle for talking about their feelings and learning more about themselves. In telling a therapist which soap opera characters they like and dislike most, and what they expect or want those characters to do, patients reveal a great deal about themselves. One psychiatric social worker who has used soap opera therapy says that her patients, who had difficulty talking about themselves, "would talk about the programs, and then after a while they'd pick up themes that were problems in their own lives. They related to characters like themselves who had similar kinds of problems."

Professional Education: Information or Infomercials

Another experiment in TV education was launched in September, 1981, by the American Educational Television Network, a commercial educational network aimed at the nation's thirty million doctors, nurses, dentists, real estate brokers, stockbrokers, accountants, lawyers, and other professionals who want to keep up to date in their fields. AETN made its satellite debut with a series on law enforcement, developed in conjunction with the International Association of Chiefs of Police; the programs were carried by more than two hundred cable systems that reach approximately two and a half million subscribers. The network hopes to offer educational programming on a daily basis that will be accredited by the various professional associations.

AETN supports itself only in part through course fees; its other revenues come from "infomercials," commercial messages disguised as educational material. A drug company that buys a spot on one of the AETN refresher courses for doctors, for example, can get a six-minute block of time to deliver an instructional message that may also recommend the use of that company's products. The similarity in tone and content between the actual program and the "infomercial" can make it difficult to distinguish between the two. This form of educating by advertising may prove particularly deceptive to viewers. But *caveat emptor* is the mood of today's TV marketplace. Cable television, with its capacity to "narrowcast" programming to specific audiences, has spawned its own special kind of commercial, and the infamous infomercials seem to be here to stay. Perhaps the professional audiences will demand

the protection of the disclosure, "This is an advertisement," to air during those messages. The public deserves to know when it is being addressed by a vested interest.

TV and the Corporate Community

TV has invaded the day care center, the classroom, the doctor's examining room, even the sanctum of the psychiatrist's office. It is not surprising that it has also found a home in corporate training offices. Large industries, government agencies, department stores, insurance companies, and other businesses use video for training, interoffice communication, and marketing. Most companies that use video extensively have their own studios; the General Telephone Company of Florida, for example, produces about a hundred and twenty programs a year. Videotapes are used to show machine operators how to use equipment; Tapes are sent out to distributors to illustrate and explain a complicated new product. Texas Instruments sends programming to a network of over five hundred locations; their annual stockholders' meeting was distributed internationally with the help of two satellites. Piedmont Hospital in Atlanta, Georgia, produces a monthly video "newsletter" for patients and staff; American Motors Corporation produces a daily program for the employees in their main auto plant. At a paper company, where dangerous machinery and frequent lifting of heavy equipment and supplies create safety hazards, employees are videotaped on the job and then shown the tape, so each person can identify his or her accident-prone behavior. In order to help prepare rookies for a real emergency, a police academy videotaped a mock shoot-out between police and burglars and then played the tape, complete with instant replays and critical asides from the TV cops, for a class of trainees to discuss.

One of the most common uses for corporate video is sales training; salespersons practice delivering their sales pitch into the camera, role-play difficult customer-sales con-

Corporate Video. The uses of television in business increase almost daily. Executives can now telecast their messages to employees around the world. Workers at every level can receive instruction of the most intricate nature by means of video cassette.

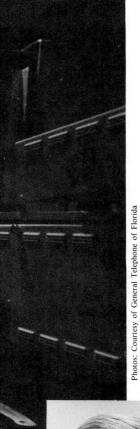

Photos: Courtesy of General Telephone of Florida

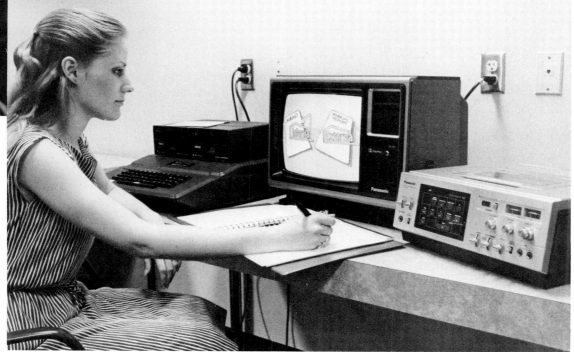

frontations, and criticize tapes of themselves in real-life sales situations.

Video has also created a new piece of corporate jargon: the teleconference. Sometimes a teleconference is a two-way meeting between executives, but this use of the technology is rare, because it is so expensive. More often the teleconference involves a one-way-only picture with two-way audio. A manager presenting a new product to a sales force in the field can be seen and heard by the salespersons over TV; they, in turn, can ask specific questions over a two-way audio system about the product's special features or its relevance to their customers.

Satellite Conferencing

Companies can now set up satellite video conferences by leasing time directly from satellite owners. In 1980 and 1981, Texas Instruments broadcast, via Westar, the annual stockholders' meeting from the Dallas headquarters to twenty- two company sites equipped with receiving antennas.

Not only job performance but job-hunting has come under the video sphere of influence. At CETA (Comprehensive Employment and Job Training Act) Career Placement Units, unemployed individuals who have been through a job skills training period complete their training with courses in how to get a job. Trainees are videotaped in mock job interviews; afterward the tape is played back and they criticize their performance with the help of a CETA job counselor. Did they project confidence to the prospective employer? Answer the employer's questions without evasion? Express an interest in the job? The videotaped session helps them perfect their interviewing style and also serves to reduce their anxiety about the interview.

Video in Education: What Is the Verdict?

Although television has been on the scene for over four decades, it is still not a common feature in schools, offices, or hospitals. This chapter has stressed the interesting ways that television can be used to teach and has offered examples to prove that TV education is not confined to schools in wealthy California suburbs and businesses the size of IBM. But, with the exception of the ''Sesame Street'' phenomenon, TV still has not become a commonplace teaching tool, as familiar in classrooms as the blackboard. Nor have critical TV viewing and TV production skills become commonplace school subjects.

Why? One reason, of course, is money—TV equipment that goes beyond the simple TV set is expensive. A second reason is that TV education requires teachers to rethink their lesson plans, to experiment with new ways of explaining concepts visually, to learn something about technology—in short, to change. Changing is not easy for most people and, in these days when teachers feel so beseiged by criticism, they are not likely to look forward to the challenge of teaching with television.

But there is a more profound reason that TV has not made more headway in education, especially for children, and that is our deep distrust of it. We are a nation that lets TV manipulate us, titillate us, brainwash us, and in the process, entertain us. Although we enjoy television, we feel that it is using us, and we resent it. Thus, teachers fear that television in the classroom will replace them or will ''rot'' their students' minds; doctors afraid to ask for telemedical advice fear that they will give away their lack of knowledge in a particular area of medicine; and businessmen are wary of slick new video training packages that could automate the workplace and reduce job opportunities.

There is no doubt that television manipulates and can even deceive us. But TV is programmed by men and women, not by a special breed of videographers. TV is simply a communications tool—a hugely elaborate workbook, a magnificent pencil-and-paper. When and if teachers learn to let TV complement rather than dominate their own communications skills, then perhaps TV education will take hold. Cables and videodisc players, satellites and two-way TV equipment can change our relationship with television, but only we the viewers can change the way we use TV.

8 Resources

Books

Blakely, Robert J. *To Serve the Public Interest: Educational Broadcasting in the United States.* Syracuse, N.Y.: Syracuse University Press, 1979. A comprehensive account of the origins, philosophy, technologies, funding, and sheer persistence that has sustained educational broadcasting.

Critical Television Viewing Skills Project. Four projects funded by the U.S. Office of Education to develop a coordinated curriculum designed to teach students and adults how to become active and discriminating television viewers. Each project has its own newsletter or brochure explaining the focus of its publications and products.

Critical TV Viewing Skills Curriculum
    (Elementary) Southwest Educational
    Development Laboratory
    211 East 7th Street
    Austin, Texas 78701
    512-476-6861

Critical TV Viewing Skills Curriculum
    (Middle School)
    WNET
    356 West 58th Street
    New York, N.Y. 10019
    212-664-7124

Critical TV Viewing Skills Curriculum
    (Secondary)
    Far West Laboratory for Educational Research and Development
    1855 Folsom Street
    San Francisco, Calif. 94103
    415-565-3100

Critical TV Viewing Skills Curriculum
(Post-secondary/Adult)
School of Public Communication, Boston
University
640 Commonwealth Avenue
Boston, Mass. 02215
617-353-3364

Doing the Media: A Portfolio of Activities, Ideas and Resources. New revised edition. New York: Center for Understanding Media, 1978. Video section discusses the ways in which using video equipment can help students become more critical viewers.

Educational Media Yearbook. Littleton, Colo.: Libraries Unlimited. Published annually. An authoritative source of up-to-date information about the field of educational media, including articles on the profession of educational technology, status reports, a guide to organizations and associations, doctoral and master's programs, directory of funding sources, and a listing of periodicals, books, and nonprint resources.

LeBaron, John. *Making Television: A Video Production Guide for Teachers.* Totowa, N.J.: Teachers College Press, 1981. An illustrated handbook to help teachers develop video skills and integrate video production with activities in upper elementary, junior high, and high school classrooms.

Postman, Neil. *Teaching as a Conserving Activity.* New York: Delacorte Press, 1979. According to Postman, the media are educating children more powerfully than the schools ever could and schools must now function as a countervailing force to television, the "first curriculum."

Price, Jonathan. *Video-Visions: A Medium Discovers Itself.* New York: New American Library, 1977. A discussion of do-it-yourself television in business, education, medicine, therapy, community affairs, security, and private communication.

Schramm, Wilbur. *Big Media, Little Media: Tools and Technologies for Instruction.* Beverly Hills, Calif.: Sage Publications, 1977. A helpful guide to selecting and using educational media, based on projects done in developing nations.

Periodicals

Agency for Instructional Television Newsletter. Agency for Instructional Television, Box A, Bloomington, Ind. 47402. Quarterly. Describes the series produced by Agency for Instructional Television and offers suggestions for teachers on how to use them.

Media & Methods. American Society of Educators, 1511 Walnut Street, Philadelphia, Penn. 19102. 9 issues a year. Covers all media, with ideas on how to use TV, radio, and film in creative ways in the classroom.

Prime Time School Television. Suite 810, 120 S. LaSalle Street, Chicago, Ill. 60603. Monthly. A source of information for high school teachers about prime-time programs and their uses as educational resources.

Teacher Guide to Television. 699 Madison Avenue, New York, N.Y. 10021. Semi-annual; Teacher's guide to upcoming TV specials and programs of interest.

Films and Tapes

Seeing Through Commercials: A Children's Guide to TV Advertising. A 16-mm color film, 15 minutes. 1976. Demystifies TV commercials by illustrating and discussing advertising techniques. For grades 3 through 8. Available from Vision Films, P.O. Box 48896, Los Angeles, Calif. 90048.

Six Billion $$$ Sell: A Child's Guide to TV Commercials. A 16-mm color film, 15 minutes. 1976. Uses clips from TV commercials, animation, and an original pop theme song to teach children about the techniques used by advertisers. For grades 3 through 8. Available from Consumer Reports Films, Box XA–35, 256 Washington Street, Mount Vernon, N.Y. 10550.

Soopergoop. A 16-mm color film, 13 minutes. 1975. A fast, animated story in which two irreverent characters concoct a TV commercial for a sweet cereal. Reveals selling techniques and commercialism behind the fun. Winner of American Film Festival and Columbus Film Festival awards. For grades 3 through 6. Available from Churchill Films, 662 North Robertson Boulevard, Los Angeles, Calif. 90069.

TV: Behind the Screen. A 16-mm color film, 15½ minutes. 1978. Shows children how TV shows are created by writers, editors, and film crews, reveals how special effects and dramatic productions are done, and introduces various television jobs. For grades 3 through 8. Available from Churchill Films, 662 North Robertson Boulevard, Los Angeles, Calif. 90069.

A TV Guide: Thinking About What We Watch. A 16-mm color film, 17 minutes. 1978. A police show, a commercial, and other vignettes lead children through an investigation of "reality" and values on television. Racial and sexual stereotypes, job depictions, and easy solutions to problems are examined. Winner of American Film Festival and Columbus Film Festival awards. For grades 5 through 9. Available from Churchill Films, 662 North Robertson Boulevard, Los Angeles, Calif. 90069.

Television and the Community

Previous chapters dealt with practical steps you can take to make the television experience a more sensible and rewarding one for yourself and the other members of your family. This chapter shows how the community can get involved in this process. One of the chief criticisms of television is that it has tended to break down our sense of community. Yet it is at the community level that we can work together to take advantage of the second chance with television that we have been given. The proliferation of cable, for example, gives all of us the opportunity to have a meaningful voice in what kind of communications system is established in our city or town, how it is maintained, and whether or not it serves the needs of all segments of the community. Groups within a community can use both over-the-air TV and the new technologies to serve their own purposes. And all of us can learn from the experiences of public action organizations and actively participate in these group efforts to make television better.

Community Action Groups: Working to Change TV

In an earlier chapter we talked about the various players in the game of television—the networks, the local stations, the public broadcasters, the FCC, the FTC, the Congress. Another vital group of players will probably in the long run have more to say than any other group about whether or not television operates in the public interest. We are talking about community organizations. Citizen action groups dedicated to reform in television are, like TV itself, a relatively recent phenomenon. In fact it was

not until 1966 that citizen organizations were even regarded by the FCC as "parties in interest" in matters concerning television.

It took a landmark case to change all that and to give citizen groups some standing in cases involving the way television operates. In 1964 the Office of Communication of the United Church of Christ filed a petition to deny the license of renewal of television station WLBT in Jackson, Mississippi. The Office of Communication, along with various private citizens, charged that the station was guilty of racial and religious discrimination. As it had done in the past, the FCC ruled that the organization was not a "party in interest" and could not challenge WLBT's broadcasting license. Two years later, in a historic ruling, the United States Court of Appeals in the District of Columbia overruled the FCC and ordered that the United Church of Christ Office of Communication be allowed to participate in public hearings on the license renewal issue. The opinion of the court was written by Judge Warren E. Burger, who later was to become the Chief Justice of the Supreme Court. Said Judge Burger, "We cannot believe that the congressional mandate of public participation . . . was meant to be limited to writing letters to the commission, to inspection of records, to the commission's grace in considering listener claims, or to mere nonparticipating appearance at hearings. . . . In order to safeguard the public interest in broadcasting, therefore, we hold that some 'audience participation' must be allowed in license renewal proceedings...such community organizations as civic associations, professional societies, unions, churches, and educational institutions or associations might well be helpful to the commission. These groups are found in every community; they usually concern themselves with a wide range of community problems and tend to be representative of broad as distinguished from narrow interests, public as distinguished from private or commercial interests.''

By ruling as it did, the court paved the way for effective participation of community action groups in broadcasting. Today there are many organizations that play an important, active role in television reform and serve as whistle-blowers on the industry. Among the most prominent of these organizations are Action for Children's Television, AIM (Accuracy In Media), the National Black Media Coalition, and the National Citizens Committee for Broadcasting. Certain national religious organizations, such as the Office of Communication of the United Church of Christ, the National Conference of Catholic Bishops, the Unitarian-Universalist Association, and the National Council of the Churches of Christ in the U.S.A. have also been active in broadcast reform. In addition, subdivisions of national organizations such as the Gray Panthers, the National Organization for Women, and the National Gay Task Force have acted as an impetus for change. These are only a few of the national and local groups that continue to work for the public interest in the communications field. At the end of this chapter you will find a detailed list of names and addresses of organizations throughout the country dedicated to changing television.

Although the odds against them have often been considerable, citizen groups have had a significant impact on the television industry. Not only did the WLBT case result in the court's historic decision about "parties in interest" but these "parties in interest" were successful in convincing the FCC to deny license renewal to WLBT because of the station's discrimination in programming and hiring practices. Similarly, in 1974 the license of the agency that operated the public education stations in Alabama was revoked as a result of a citizen action petition. Once again the issue was discrimination in hiring and programming.

Other petitions to deny, filed by diverse citizen action groups, have resulted in compromises that have prevented large corporations from transferring licenses or purchasing new stations in order to increase their control over the media in a particular area.

Petitioning to deny a station's license is a drastic action; it is also a costly and time-consuming process. There are many other activities that citizen action groups can undertake to bring about needed changes in the broadcast industry. They can write letters of complaint to

Hints for Improving Your Group's Public Relations

- Give interviews to local press about your group.

- Publish a newsletter and build a mailing list.

- Create brochures with detailed facts.

- Produce public service announcements for radio and TV.

- Send speakers from your group to local meetings.

- Organize conferences and seminars.

- Write articles for journals, newspapers, magazines.

- Get on local radio and TV shows.

How to File Comments in an FCC Rulemaking

The following guidelines are provided to assist you in filing comments with the FCC:

Your Experience

The FCC is interested in any experiences, judgments or insights you might have that would shed light on issues and questions raised in an inquiry or rulemaking.

Public Documents

You can obtain copies of a Notice of Inquiry or a Notice of Proposed Rulemaking by contacting the Public Information Officer, FCC, 1919 M St., N.W., Washington, D.C. 20554. (202) 632-7260.

All Notices of Inquiry and Proposed Rulemaking are printed in the Federal Register soon after they are released by the Commission. The Federal Register is available in most public libraries across the country.

Facts

Your comments should explain who you are and what your interest is. State the facts briefly, but fully. Clearly explain your experience and any additional evidence which supports your position.

Be Specific

Your comments should be explicit. If the details of the proposed rules or if only one of several provisions of the rule are objectionable to you, make this clear. If the rule would be acceptable with certain safeguards explain them and why they are needed.

Other Opinions

Your comments should include facts which might support a different position, discuss them and explain why the public interest requires that the matter be resolved as you propose.

Docket Number

Be sure to note the Docket Number or Rulemaking Number on your comments.

Filing Date

Arrange for your comments to reach the Commission on or before the comment or reply date included in the Notice of Inquiry or Notice of Proposed Rulemaking.

Filing Comments

Submit your written comments to: Secretary, Federal Communications Commission, 1919 M St., N.W., Washington, D.C. 20054

If you want your comments to be received as a formal filing, FCC rules require that you send an original and *six* copies of your comments; if you send an original and *eleven* copies, each Commissioner will get a copy, which is even more effective. The original is the copy that you sign.

Letting Your Voice Be Heard

When developments occur which are of concern to you, it's most effective if you react as soon as possible—both because you will be more motivated to do something "in the heat of the moment" and because the issue is also likely to still be a hot one for the legislator. Thus, if you read in your local paper that Congress has opened hearings on some aspect of television, sit down right then and write your representatives with your opinions on the subject. You can be sure the "other side"—the affected industries and broadcasters—are well organized and vocal. Don't worry that your message won't be as impressive or carry as much weight as the so-called big guns: Congress is as concerned about what the ordinary citizens, the homemakers, the local doctors, and the schoolteachers think as it is about the positions of big business, which is recognized as having the finances and resources to keep itself well-informed and

Sample Form for Submitting Formal Comments to the FCC

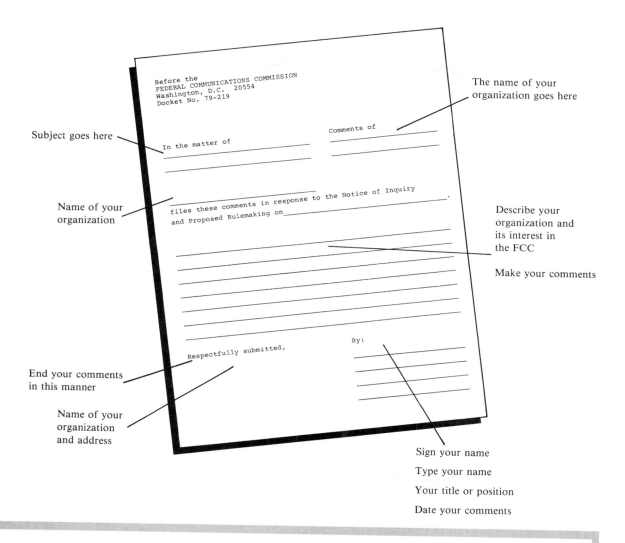

Before the
FEDERAL COMMUNICATIONS COMMISSION
Washington, D.C. 20554
Docket No. 79-219

The name of your organization goes here

Comments of _____

Subject goes here

In the matter of _____

_____

Name of your organization

files these comments in response to the Notice of Inquiry
and Proposed Rulemaking on_____.

Describe your organization and its interest in the FCC

Make your comments

Respectfully submitted,

By:

End your comments in this manner

Name of your organization and address

Sign your name

Type your name

Your title or position

Date your comments

vocal. Your message need not be highly technical or complex. It should simply be the honest and forthright opinion of a concerned citizen.

Write to the subcommittee or committee chairman, where relevant action is expected, so that your letter becomes part of the committee file or public opinion on the particular issue in question. And, it is always appropriate to send a copy of your letter to your own representatives. Letters to Congress should be addressed:

To Senators:

The Honorable NAME
U.S. Senate
Washington, DC 20510

To Congresspersons:

The Honorable NAME
U.S. House of Representatives
Washington, DC 20515

Capitol Communications

Your elected representatives can better represent your needs if you let them hear from you directly.

1. *Be specific.* Identify the issue that concerns you and *try to confine your discussion to that one area.* For example, don't write a paragraph about the problems with exposing children to advertising of sugared cereals and then devote another paragraph to another pet concern, such as energy conservation.

2. *Be brief.* State concisely and legibly your opinions, arguments and facts. Your position on the issue should be clear in the first paragraph, and you do not need to present every available argument on the subject to be persuasive.

3. *Include your expert knowledge.* Your letter can serve as a resource to the legislator, so include relevant facts and figures if they are available to you. Frequently, when defending their positions on an issue, legislators will use information received from constituents which has impressed them. It is particularly helpful in this instance if you cite any professional qualifications you may have: nutritionist, educator, etc. But again, do not feel that only professional credentials are relevant.

4. *Write as a member of an organization, where relevant.* If you are a member of a state, local, or national group which shares your position on the issue you are addressing, include that information. Where appropriate, you may use the letterhead of your organization, since this indicates a number of others share your point of view.

5. *Express your thanks.* Too often, legislators hear only from those who want something. It indicates real commitment to your issue when you take time to notice how the legislator has voted and then thank him/her for sharing your position. Conversely, it doesn't hurt to express disappointment for a vote cast against your position.

6. *Request an answer.* This shows you are truly concerned about the legislator's intentions on an issue. You may choose to respond to points made in that answer, but unless there are obvious errors or you feel very strongly about something the legislator has done, don't damage your credibility by responding to every communication.

7. *Keep copies of your letter and the response received.* It is helpful to know what you have said about an issue in the past and even more important to have specific evidence of a legislator's position on an issue.

Other Forms of Communication to Congress

If time is short, you may wish to call or use Western Union.

By Phone
The central number for the U.S. Capitol is 202-224-3121; ask for your representative or senator's office and you'll be connected. You may then either leave your brief message on the particular issue with the person answering the phone, or ask to speak to the legislative assistant handling that issue and discuss it with him/her.

Western Union
The following systems are in effect:

Public Opinion Messages: $4.25 for 20 words or less; $2.00 each additional set of 20 words or less. Same day delivery in Washington.

Mailgrams: $3.90 for 50 words or less, including name and address. Delivery with next day's mail.

Night letters: $5.90 for 15 words. $.18 each additional word. Next day delivery between 9 a.m. and 2 p.m.

Telegrams: $7.25 for 15 words or less; $.23 a word for additional words. Same day delivery.

Personal Visits

It's always impressive if you take the time to see a legislator in person about an issue. You need not come to Washington for that purpose (although, by all means, if you're here, take the time to stop in your representative's office to introduce yourself and express your position on a matter of concern). Most legislators have specific times for constituent visits *in their home districts.* You can also find out from the local district office when the representative will be in your area and then set up an appointment.

Here are some suggestions for such meetings:

1. *Be reasonably brief.* Legislators are usually very busy on their district visits, so use the time to your best advantage. Be on time, state your point early, outline your arguments succinctly, engage in some discussion, and conclude the meeting within a reasonable time. If the legislator wants to continue the discussion, he/she will ask you to stay or provide more information via mail, etc.

2. *Try to get a specific response.* A personal visit with your representative is your best chance to hear his/her position on an issue. Ask forthrightly to know where he/she stands. If you agree, indicate your appreciation. If you disagree, ask the legislator for his/her reasons and meet them with your arguments. If there is an effort to evade the question, push politely for a definitive answer and take the opportunity to make more arguments in favor of your position. Providing a written summary of your position is always helpful.

3. *Be polite.* No matter how much you disagree with the legislator's position, don't lose your temper. Don't necessarily give up, either. Time, new arguments, or persuasion by others may change the situation.

4. *It helps to show that you represent others.* You may wish to make your visit with a number of others from your community to illustrate the different kinds of people who share your concern: the medical profession, educators, parents, etc. This will also provide the legislator with a variety of arguments and insight on whom he/she can count on for support if he/she takes a position in your favor (or who will oppose that position in the case of disagreement). If you can't arrange a group meeting, you may want to take along a list of other groups or individuals who share your position.

5. *Follow up with thanks.* A brief thank you note after your visit will keep your name and meeting before the legislator and give you an opportunity to briefly restate your position.

local stations or the FCC. They can participate in FCC rule-making procedures. FCC policy is often initiated by the announcement that it is considering making a rule on a particular issue. The commission then asks for comments from interested parties. Citizen action groups have effectively used this rule-making procedure to let the commission, the broadcast industry, and the public know what they think about a particular issue and why changes need to be made.

Community action groups working to bring about reform have learned that it is absolutely essential not to act alone. The most effective citizen action campaigns and activities have taken place when diverse groups have banded together in a coalition to bring about change. More than anything else, local stations and government agencies are impressed by numbers. The groups that form the coalition may have very different private special interests. But they are all interested in making broadcasting better and in encouraging TV to serve the public interest.

If your group is concerned with bringing about change in the way television operates there are several suggestions we can make:

1. We repeat—don't act alone. Form a coalition with other groups in your community as well as with interested national organizations. You will benefit from the experience and advice of these other groups as well as gain much more attention for your cause.

2. Use the press. This is an extremely important point. Nothing will gain the attention of a broadcaster more quickly than adverse publicity. Also, the right story in the right place will help you enlist all kinds of support for your cause. A single newspaper column that mentioned Action for Children's Television and its address brought in over twenty-five thousand requests for ACT materials.

3. Research your subject thoroughly. It may be important for television reform groups to sponsor research, to provide themselves with facts to back their arguments. Research, especially research about television, isn't a weapon that can stand alone, and the findings of one research project can usually be disproved by another research project paid for by another or-ganization. Most research proves what the funder wants it to prove; the chocolate company Hershey has sponsored research that proves that cocoa is healthy for your teeth! Still it is vital that you have a thorough knowledge of your subject, and all the facts and figures to back up your argument.

4. Work toward bringing alternative messages to TV. Television can counteract the negative effects of programs and commercials with public service announcements that inform viewers about health services in their area—PSAs that emphasize the negative effects of smoking, that list inexpensive ways for viewers to spend family time together. Heroes on children's programs can encourage young viewers to help their parents around the house, to share with their friends, to spend their money wisely. These positive messages are extremely useful.

5. Study the performance of your local stations. Your group can look closely at a station's program listings in *TV Guide* or your local newspaper, and can make a detailed list of all the programs it has aired over a specific period of time. You can inspect the station's record of what it has broadcast, which, according to FCC rules, is available for public inspection. Do the programming promises that a station has made to the FCC match its performance? Is the station airing local programs that speak to the interests of the community it is licensed to serve? Are minority groups visible and are their particular concerns and needs addressed? It is very rare for the FCC on its own to challenge the performance claims made by individual stations. One of the most important services your group can render your community is to monitor a station's performance and call attention to discrepancies in the station's promises versus its performance.

Make Public Service Announcements

Although it is difficult to get over-the-air TV stations to open up the citizen input, it is possible. Elsewhere in this book, for example, we have mentioned public service announcements and have stated that they represent a way in which the public interest is served. It is possible for you and your organization to make your own public service announcements—carrying your message to thousands of viewers.

The Federal Communications Commission requires all television stations to provide free on-air time to nonprofit organizations offering a service or presenting an announcement "regarded as serving community interest." Whether your organization is offering a specific service, such as a hotline for young people with drug problems, or wishes to make a statement

Public service messages such as these can have an impact on viewers, especially when created by members of the community.

Produced by the Department of Health and Human Services and Distributed by the American Lung Association

PUBLIC HEALTH SERVICE
OFFICE ON SMOKING & HEALTH
ROCKVILLE, MD 20857

1. BROOKE: There's this guy who I thought was really terrific. I mean, well, self-assured.

2. And I really like that in a person. Anyway, one night I saw him at this party, and I got up the nerve to say, "hello."

3. And then, he takes out a cigarette! Blows my whole image of him.

4. I mean, I know I make some people nervous...but I thought he had it together.

5. VO: Smoking. It's a dead give-away.

6. BROOKE: I think people who smoke are real losers.

KEEP AMERICA BEAUTIFUL INC.
99 PARK AVE. N.Y. N.Y. 10016

American Cancer Society

about its programs in general, PSAs represent an effective way of getting your message across to a large number of people.

The fact that public service announcements are needed by local TV stations to satisfy their community service requirements works in your favor. On the other side of the coin, PSAs can be expensive to produce, and while the FCC requires local stations to air public service an-nouncements, it leaves it to the station to decide which PSAs will be broadcast. A high percentage of the public service announcements that make it to the air both locally and nationally are produced by the Advertising Council. The Council is committed to creating messages that serve the public interest, but it is made up of individuals who represent companies that spend a great deal of money advertising commercial products on local and national TV. The Coun-

Some Tips on Making a PSA

• Keep in mind the fact that while stations need PSAs to meet their community service requirements, your local station is still doing your group a favor. Be polite, and be as well prepared and professional as you can when dealing with station personnel.

• Make sure you know what size video tape your local station requires for airing PSAs. Will they accept 16 mm or 35 mm films? The least expensive form of PSA is that in which you present a slide with an announcer reading your message "over" it. Will your local stations accept a PSA in this form?

• Make sure you check out all the costs. The basic costs will include: film or video tape, the rental of editing equipment and editing time, the rental of camera crew or mobile equipment, payment to on-air talent, and reproduction costs for making copies of your PSA whether it be on film or video tape.

• When producing or writing a PSA for television, you have an added dimension: the visual. Remember to *use* it. Look at television advertisements, especially the most exciting or "successful" ones: you will notice that there is quite a lot of visual and audio information—scenes and angles change often, and audio information is varied. These are devices for making the advertisement lively, exciting and interesting.

• If you have a limited budget, you may want your PSA to be no more than a slide with an announcer reading copy over it. On the other hand, television PSAs can be canned on 16 mm and 35 mm film, or video-tape. Whichever you plan on using, be sure to check with the station first to see which kind of medium it prefers. *Most commercial stations do not have facilities for airing half-inch video-tape,* but *require two-inch tape or one-inch tape.* Recently it has become possible for commercial stations to transmit three-quarter-inch color cassette (the kind a "mini-cam" can produce). Not all stations can, however. Three-quarter-inch tape is usually used by stations for their news programs.

cil steers clear of controversial messages or those with a vested commercial interest.

Once your organization decides to produce a PSA it should contact the local TV station in your area. You need to find out such things as: does the station require announcements to be on 16-mm film or on videotape? What size videotape is required? Will an announcement done with 35-mm slides and live copy be accepted? What length announcements will be approved? What type of format does the station prefer? What are the reasonable chances of your message's being aired on the station? Will the station help in the production of the announcement? (Some stations will.)

Producing a PSA can be costly but there are ways to cut expenses and still come up with a professional-looking announcement that you will want to present to the station. You can investigate the possibility of receiving help from telecommunications students at a college or university in your area. Students planning careers in TV production are often eager to help produce the kind of material you need. And many of these students are both skilled and experienced. Since your message will provide a service to the community, you might also be able to enlist the free aid of professional TV technicians and on-air talent in your community. And perhaps you can get your local college or university to donate its equipment and studio facilities to you, which will cut your costs considerably.

In making your own public service announcements you have another outlet for participating directly in television, and you have the opportunity to bring to the air a much different kind of message from the commercial advertisements that dominate so much of the broadcast day.

Be Your Own Press Agent

Local newscasters need not be concerned solely with coverage of fires and scandals. Your organization can use TV to its own end by acting as its own press agent and arranging for coverage on the local news. If you're doing something important, don't be bashful. Let the news departments of your local TV (and radio) stations know about it. With the increased amount of time that stations are giving to newscasts, they're looking for material. Getting an interesting story about something important that a local organization is doing is good for them—and good for you.

Also, locally originated magazine-type programs have become increasingly popular. These shows offer you another opportunity to use TV for your own purposes. Call your local station and arrange for a meeting with the producers or one of the assistant producers of these programs. Like those who put on the newscasts, they're always on the lookout for stories of local or regional interest.

Your organization should also be aware of the editorials that are regularly presented on some local channels. It may well be that one or more of these editorials will deal with an issue with which your group is particularly concerned. You can ask for air time either to support or to challenge the station's position on a particular issue.

Cable and You

Of all the ways in which you can play a direct role in making television better for yourself and your children, none is more important than getting involved in the cabling process in your city or town. Some ten years ago, an FCC report stated that cable television carried with it the promise of an "economy of abundance" rather than an "economy of scarcity." By now it is clear that cable TV is far more than a sys-

The Name of the Game is Choice

Basic tier

Under Cablevision's proposed programming allocation, the following basic service will be available for $2 a month. Installation will be $25.

Channel

2—WGBH, Boston (Public Broadcasting System)
3—WLVI, Boston (Independent)
4—WBZ, Boston (NBC)
5—WCVB, Boston (ABC.)
6—WQTV, Boston (Ind.)
7—WNAC, Boston (CBS)
8—Boston City Channel: local origination programs
9—C-Span/Assembly Channel —US House, local public meetings
10—Cable News Network: all-day world news coverage
11—New York Stock Exchange
12—American Stock Exchange
13—Reuters news/readings for the blind
14—To be announced
15—To be announced
16—Entertainment and Sports Programming Network: 24-hours sports
17—UPI News and Sports wire: national, local sports
18—Racing results
19—USA Network/AP news: mostly sports
20—Boston Special Interest Programming: including Black Entertainment Television
21—Foreign Language Channel: multilingual programming
22—National Religion Channel
23—Boston Religion Channel
24—Senior Citizens Channel
25—WXNE, Boston (Ind.)
26—WGN, Chicago superstation with sports and old movies
27—WSMW, Worcester (Ind.)
28—WTBS, Atlanta superstation with sports and old movies
29—National and local health programming
30—National and local women's programming

31—National children's programs, including Nickelodeon
32—Local children's programming
33—American Educational Television Network: continuing accredited education
34—Campus Boston: local programming for post-secondary institutions
35—CBS Cable/Boston Arts: cultural programming
36—Telefrance/ARTS/The English Channel: arts and culture from US and Europe
37—The Music Channel: 24-hour videotaped music performances
38—WSBK, Boston (Ind.)
39—National, regional satellite weather
40—Regional radar weather
41—Time and alphanumeric weather reports
42—WPRI, Providence (ABC)
43—WJAR, Providence (NBC)
44—WGBX, Boston (PBS)
45—WSBE, Providence (PBS)
46—WVIA, Scranton, Pa. (PBS)
47—Municipal access channel for local government
48—Public access/Comparison shopping: compares local prices on grocery, pharmaceutical items
49—Access/Comparison shopping
50—Access/Swap 'n shop: classified ads free to subscribers
51—Access/Paid classified ads
52—Access/Local job listings
53—Directory Channel: channel-by-channel listings
54—Home Box Office: additional $7/month; movies and entertainment.

Omnibus tier

For $8 a month and a $55 installation charge, Cablevision will provide two-way capability and the following channels in addition to the basic tier:

Channel

55—Directory of premium programs
56—Modern Satellite Network: homemaker, consumer programs
57—Appalachian Satellite Network
58—Satellite Programming Network: public affairs, entertainment
59—Times-Mirror Shopping: two-way catalogue buying
60—WTEV, Providence (CBS)
61—WENH, Durham, N.H. (PBS)
62—WOR, New York superstation with sports
63—WPIX, New York (Ind.), with sports and classic movies
64—WUTV, Buffalo, N.Y. (Ind.)
65—WPHL, Philadelphia (Ind.)
66—WTAF, Philadelphia (Ind.)
67—WKBS, Philadelphia (Ind.)
68—74—To be announced

Premium programs

The following are optional premium programs offered by Cablevision and their monthly costs. Home Box Office is available on either tier but all other premiums are available only on the Omnibus tier.

Home Box Office: movies, entertainment, $7
Home Theatre Network: family entertainment, $4
Montage: foreign films, $4
Showtime: new movies, $8
The Movie Channel: current movies, $8
Boston Sports Channel: $8
Bravo!: arts, culture, $8
Escapade: adult films, $8
Cinemax: current movies, $8
Rockefeller Center TV: $8
Las Vegas Entertainment: $8
Galavision: Hispanic movies, entertainment, $8

By the middle of the decade, Boston, Massachusetts, will be hooked into a cable system with a capacity of 104 channels. Shown is the cable company's preliminary listing of programming and services that will be available.

tem to improve television reception. Cable also can be more than a mere provider of additional entertainment channels. Cable has the potential of allowing organizations (arts councils, mental health associations, labor unions, parent-teacher associations, schools, church groups, clubs, coalitions, and representatives of professions) to use television to serve them as they have never been served before. It can give a powerful voice to minorities, the elderly, and the disabled. It can become a vehicle through which children participate in the learning process. But none of this will happen unless the public gets involved.

You, as an individual or as a member of a community group, have the opportunity to see that the cable system that eventually gains the franchise in your city or town provides the maximum amount of service for the largest number of people. If your community has already awarded a franchise, you still have the chance to make sure that the cable company's license will not be renewed unless certain specific conditions are met.

Every week there are more municipalities in the United States that have franchising agreements with cable companies. In some cases, the process happens so fast the public doesn't know until it's all over. There are no federal laws and few state laws to ensure citizen participation in the cable franchising process. (New York and Minnesota are, thus far, the only exceptions). However, citizen participation is good business for cable companies in the long run since people are more likely to buy services for which they themselves have expressed a need. And munic-

ipal officials who involve citizens in the cabling process are practicing smart politics; citizens who get stuck with a cable system providing no public access channels or no funds for local programming are going to know whom to blame at City Hall.

In 1979 the Houston City Council debated for fifteen minutes before deciding to divide their city up between five groups of local entrepreneurs with no cable experience; none of the city's five franchises requires public access. Boston, on the other hand, took almost ten years to decide whether or not to allow cable into the city and whom to grant the franchise to. The contract that eventually emerged from this long process gives citizens fifty-two channels, including up to twenty public access channels, for only a $2.00 per month basic service, plus fifty-two more channels for additional fees and two institutional loops of fifty-two channels each.

Cable owners know how lucrative a cable franchise can be. Competition for franchises is intense and your community can use this to its advantage. If your city or town is in the process of selecting a cable company, it is in an excellent position to drive the hardest bargain possible. Above all else, don't take it for granted that your local officials (who will actually grant the franchise) are knowledgeable about television in general and the potential of cable TV in particular. They probably don't know a lot about television and you will want to seek the help of as many people who are familiar with cable operations as possible. Remember, you are awarding a contract that is going to make a lot of money for some company. And you are establishing a system that your community will have to live with for a good many years. Be careful and be demanding. Make sure that everything is in writing—the cost of equipment for access channels, all of the responsibilities of the cable company, the rights and the obligations of the community.

FCC rulings regarding cable TV have undergone many changes. In considering what to demand from a cable company, you will need to keep abreast of the current regulations and developments. (At the end of this chapter we have included a list of books and periodicals we think you'll find helpful.) For example, originally cable companies in major markets were required to provide either free or low-cost access channels. The Supreme Court then struck down that requirement. This means that you must make certain that your franchise agreement specifically provides for public access channels, perhaps the most important aspect of cable TV. Be sure to specify that these channels be free of commercials. Another important factor, which is always subject to change, is the maximum franchise-fee percentage that your community is allowed to charge a cable company. Since a cable franchise is so lucrative, your community has a vital interest in knowing the maximum amount it can collect from the franchise holder.

Some of the language that will be "thrown around" during the franchising process can be misleading. For example, an important aspect of cable TV is its ability to provide two-way communication. In some communities, subscribers are already able to take part in local government meetings, get immediate aid from police and fire departments, and benefit from a wide variety of other services. Any good franchise agreement provides for this capability. However, in some places local leaders have signed agreements that use the term "two-way capability" rather than "two-way operational system." There is a big difference. A two-way operational system comes complete with all the equipment needed to allow communication between two cable outlets. A cable system with "two-way capability" must, at a future date, have expensive equipment added to make it work.

Most important, you need to be aware of all the options available to your community through a cable system. Public access programming may well be the most exciting feature of cable TV. Yet public access is not the only kind of local programming available through cable. Your franchise must spell out in detail what your community requires in the way of local-origination programming; that is, channels that provide programs produced by the cable company, featuring local events such as high school athletic contests and school plays. It is vital that the concerned member of your community understand the differences between public access and local-origination programming.

Along with regular public access, which allows private citizens and groups to create and air their own programs free of charge, and locally sponsored programs, where local merchants get to advertise their goods and services at rates they can afford, it is important that your cable franchise include specific provisions for leased access. Leasing channels on a first-come, first-serve basis helps counter the monopoly nature of a cable franchise.

Your board of advisers and local officials should be aware of another feature of cable called an *institutional loop*. It can connect all the various units and branches of a particular institution with each other and with subscribers throughout the cable system. For example, all the libraries or all the hospitals or all the schools in a particular area could be "connected" and could share information with each other and with viewers at home. Your cable franchise should include specific provisions for the free wiring of cable (called a cable drop) in your community's public and parochial schools, colleges, libraries, museums, hospitals, clinics and health centers, churches and synagogues, and various agencies of your local government.

These are some examples of the types of things that you and other interested members of your community need to know in order to make the best cable franchising decisions possible. Again, the best way to prepare for cable is to read as much as you possibly can and contact as many experienced and knowledgeable people as you can before making any decisions. Following is a brief synopsis of the basic steps your community should take in its franchising deliberations.

Board of Advisers

The first step involves the naming of a board of advisers that will help local officials make decisions throughout the cable deliberations. This board, appointed by the mayor, the city council, or the selectmen, should include individuals representing a broad spectrum of the community interests.

Citizen Advisory Board

Along with the board of advisers, a separate citizen advisory board should be established, open to anyone in the community who is interested in how cable can serve the needs of individual groups and the community as a whole. It

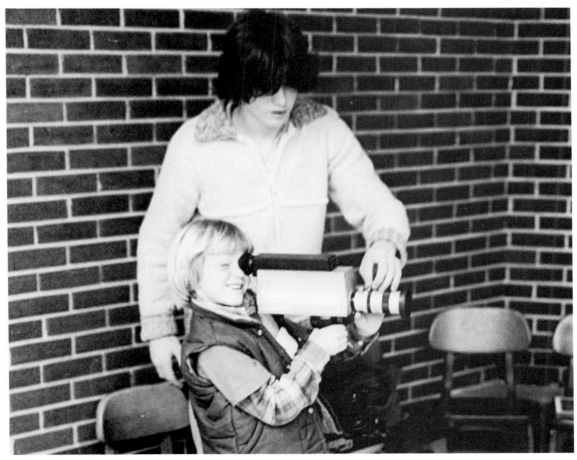

Paul Whiting/US Cable of Viking

should focus on specific issues. Those particularly concerned about the children of the community should concentrate on such questions as: how will the schools use cable? How will child-produced public access programming be funded? How can commercial-free children's programming be assured? Can the city ensure that cable services will reach children in lower income families?

The citizen advisory board should meet with and advise both local officials and the board of advisers before the writing of the city's request for proposals (RFP) from cable companies, and should continue to meet after the franchise is granted to make sure the terms of the agreement are carried out.

Assessing Community Needs

Before beginning to weigh the relative merits of various companies it is essential that the specific needs of your community be determined and set down in writing. The list of these needs should grow out of the work of the board of advisers, any consultants that have been hired to aid in the task, and, very important, public hearings which enable all citizens to voice their desires and concerns. This assessment phase should be carried out as thoroughly as possible. Every aspect of the cable operation should be considered, including how and where the cables will be put into place and what public sites (schools, libraries, hospitals, etc.) in the community should be linked into the system.

Request for Proposals

Once your board of advisers, consultants, and private citizens have ascertained the specific needs of your community, you are ready to issue a request for proposals. Your community's

Community cable in action.

Paul Whiting/US Cable of Viking

RFP should describe in writing every detail of the services it expects from a cable company. It should supply a deadline for the receipt of proposals and should provide for the payment of an application fee, which will pay for the cost the community has incurred in the franchising process. The RFP should detail every service the city or town requires from the competing cable companies. For example, if the community and local officials have specific requests for such things as public access channels reserved for minorities and the elderly, two-way capability in the library and the schools, or a media center to be established for community use, those requests must appear in the RFP.

The RFP should also spell out in writing such things as how the franchise agreement will be enforced and reviewed, and how public complaints and suggestions will be handled both during and after the franchise deliberations. It should also set forth specific dates for the completion of the various aspects of the cabling process.

You must make sure that the RFP calls for a variety of information from the competing cable companies, so that local officials have all the important information they need to make the best choice possible. Companies should be required to submit financial statements and projections of their expected costs in setting up operations in your community. Included in the information should be written statements about the methods the company will use to determine further rate increases. And the RFP should require all competing companies to submit in writing a detailed explanation of how they intend to protect subscriber privacy once the system is in operation.

Evaluating Proposals

The evaluation of the various proposals is the last phase before a franchise is awarded. One of the most important things officials can do during this phase is to check out how well each company has carried out its promises in other communities. Does the company's commitment to children in another municipality consist only of cartoon reruns? Has the company really been committed to local-origination programming? Has equipment in access centers been made available to all segments of the community? Is it lightweight enough for young people to handle? Has the cable company worked well with libraries, museums, art centers, and schools in other communities? Are promises to minority, foreign-language, disabled, and other specialized groups being carried out?

The evaluation of each company should be put in writing. These evaluations should be made available to all citizens in the community, and before a franchise is awarded a public hearing should be held in which applicants are given the opportunity to answer any remaining questions and citizens are allowed to voice their concerns and recommendations.

Community involvement in the cabling process should not stop once the franchise is awarded. There are many things that you can do to make sure that the interests of the community are being served by cable and that these services will not only be maintained but will grow throughout the years. Here are a few suggestions:

Stay in Touch

People who are dissatisfied with what their cable system is providing must make sure that the cable company knows it. Stay in touch with the manager of the local cable system. If citizens can convince cable operators, for example, that there is a ready-made local audience eager to subscribe to children's programming, that there are volunteers willing to work with children to help them produce their own cable programs, that there is a local business or foundation willing to underwrite the cost of production for a local children's show—*then* cable operators may act to improve their services to children. Smart cable operators know that the problem of unhappy subscribers will eventually be reflected in their profits.

Don't assume that local cable operators are full of great program ideas. Find out what is offered in other communities and pass on these suggestions in detail. Keep in mind, however, that what is possible in a large city may not be possible in a small town, and vice versa.

Barter with Rate Increases

It is not unusual for a cable company to request an increase in rates during the lifetime of its franchise. If the request is legitimate the rates probably should be increased, but you can use this request to your advantage.

Usually the city must hold a public hearing before it can vote on a request by the cable company to raise its rates. A strong citizen group can use the hearing to voice its request for better services. Be specific! Backed by citizens' demand, the city can often arrange a trade: a higher rate in return for more children's channels or better-equipped public access centers or more public access channels.

Use Franchise Renegotiations for Change

Cable franchises usually run ten to fifteen years. Often they are renewed automatically by city councils. But citizens and municipal officials can require cable companies to negotiate for their renewals, particularly if the community actively seeks a greater level of service. It is not enough to say, "Provide more local programming." Citizens who want changes should decide what improvements are most important to them and should encourage the city to bargain for them. If the city and cable company

are unable to renegotiate the franchise renewal successfully, the city has the option of revoking the franchise and asking for new bids.

Getting Access to the Screen

Throughout this book we have talked often about the need for more diversity in television and the fact that the new TV technologies represent a second chance for the realization of this diversity. If we were to pick the single most important way these new technologies present this second chance to the American public, it would be its potential to give viewers an opportunity to have a voice of their own on television. Despite the fact that the Supreme Court has clearly declared that "... It is the right of the viewers and listeners, not the right of broadcasters, which is paramount," there has not been any meaningful access to broadcasting for the majority of American viewers. And the fact that local stations are licensed to serve the needs and interests of their local communities has done very little in this regard. If the airwaves are ever to become the public resource they are supposed to be, the system must provide real opportunities for citizens from every walk of life to use these airwaves to communicate.

Public Access

Public access channels on cable TV make it possible for anyone, regardless of age or occupation, to become a television writer, director, producer, or cameraperson. They offer the first real opportunity for citizens and groups from every segment of the population to express their views and put forth their messages. Whether the issue is tenants' rights, prison reform, environmental concern, or neighborhood affairs, interested groups can create their own programming and join the ranks of broadcasters. Young

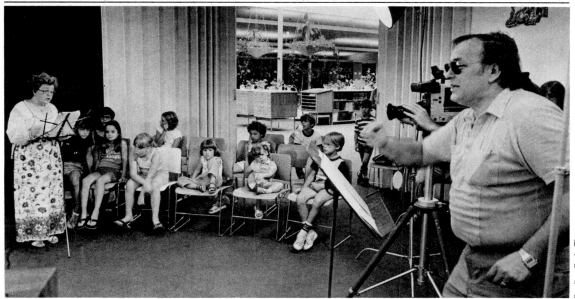

Reading Eagle Times

Andrew Skitko

Andrew Skitko

The public access system in Reading, Pennsylvania (BerksCable), represents the best example to date of ordinary citizens participating actively in TV. From youngsters to senior citizens, each Reading resident has the opportunity to be seen and heard on the local interactive cable system.

people can learn about their neighborhood and their community by interviewing residents and by investigating neighborhood issues. Effective analogies have been made between the telephone and access TV. Everyone can use the telephone for any purpose. It is the same with access TV. Instead of a small number of people producing all the programs for an entire nation, any citizen can create a show for an organization, a neighborhood, a community—or for himself or herself.

To make sure that public access becomes a smooth-running, effective component of the cable system in your community, you should work to see to it that a committee is appointed to set procedures for public access programming. Any effective franchise agreement must include the proviso that a comprehensive training program will be established to teach members of the community how to use public access facilities. Remember, the role of the cable operator, as far as public access is concerned, is not to produce programming but to make it possible for members of the community to produce it without censorship. Provisions in your franchise agreement should also anticipate the growth of public access participation. Some communities have negotiated the written stipulation that once the initial public access channel in the community reaches 80 percent of prime time programmming capacity, another public access channel will be made available. And don't forget, you will want to reserve at least one channel for interactive use when that capability becomes available in your community.

Early critics of public access programming point out that many of the programs that have been created to date have been amateurish and uninspiring. However, in places where citizens have taken a real interest in public access and have enlisted the support of cable operators, the resulting programming has more than mea-

sured up to the hopes of those who see in public access a chance for individuals to become part of the communications process. For example:

• In Dubuque, Iowa, public access programming includes a program produced by a local teacher that deals with solar energy and world peace. Another regular program is produced specifically for the handicapped. There is an educational series produced by young people seven through twelve years of age. (The series does have a thirteen-year-old engineer.) The League of Women Voters in Dubuque has made a voter registration and information tape, and a local play written and performed by local talent has been aired. Other programs in this one community include a regular show produced by a local church for congregation members who are house-bound, and programs on subjects ranging from local historical landmarks to the local housing shortage.

• In Lansing, Michigan, high school students wrote and produced a show called ''Bad News.'' This weekly series, which ran for three years, was designed to help viewers laugh at the news. For the past five years a program entitled ''Black Notes'' has been presented. It has attracted a regular audience with its discussions of the cultural efforts of the Black Notes Media Workshop. Public access channels on the Lansing Continental Cable System and the East Lansing National Cable System also include: ''WELM News,'' a formal newscast written and produced by Michigan State University telecommunications students; ''Tee Vee Trivia,'' a weekly parody of TV game shows featuring viewer telephone participation; ''Cable Talk,'' a nine-program series on the use of cable TV; and ''The Michigan State Majority Report,'' a weekly program produced by the state senate's Democratic office.

• In San Diego, California, a single community organization called the Community Video Center coordinates all the access programming that reaches the more than 150,000 homes that are wired for cable. This center produces programming for San Diego's large Mexican-American population, runs a weekly series that provides a free studio and camera crew to any citizen, and produces programming that includes telecasts of local events, poetry readings, concerts, and shows involving senior citizens in television production.

• In Reading, Pennsylvania, the Berks Cable Company offers the most sophisticated access programming in the nation. The system is interactive and has the ability to originate programming at sixty-four separate sites. Since January, 1976, a weekly program entitled "Inside City Hall" has afforded citizens throughout the city the opportunity to talk via two-way cable with their mayor and members of their city council. Citizens gather at various neighborhood centers and through the use of split screens and monitors get to talk face to face with their local officials. Those who are housebound follow what is happening on their home sets and have the opportunity to talk to the officials over the telephone.

The program has been so effective that similar procedures have been used to allow citizens to "attend" city budget meetings and to "sit in" on governmental deliberations of all kinds. The system is also used to deal with immediate problems in the community. For example, in 1981 a police raid on the local high school resulted in a great deal of tension in the community. Charges were hurled at the police for the way they handled the affair; many in the community questioned the way discipline was being handled in the school. Three days after the incident a two-hour interactive program was set up. Via two-way cable, officials from the police and school departments, student council members, and the public were all linked for a lengthy discussion of the incident and ways to avoid such a situation in the future.

Obviously access television in Reading has been effective, particularly in allowing citizens to participate in local issues. It has made people much more aware of how their government operates and has given them a way to let their voices be heard. Public officials are just as pleased with the system. Reading's mayor has stated, "The city has come to depend on [public access]. . . . we could [never] go back to the old way, being satisfied with one person's showing up for a public hearing."

In addition to its innovations in government-citizen relationships, access programming in Reading also includes programs that allow senior citizens and children to discuss various issues about the generation gap, and a series which enables doctors and lawyers to answer specific questions about neighborhood health and legal issues.

These are a few examples of how public access is changing the way people can use television. Public access itself is but one aspect of the changing nature of the television experience. Are Reading and Lansing the forerunners of communities across the nation that will seize the opportunity of a second chance at making TV the rewarding miracle it can be? Or do they merely represent outstanding exceptions to a new TV world more complicated but just as uninspiring as the television world we have known thus far? It's still too early to tell. But the answer will be determined by how much we involve ourselves in making TV an active, rewarding experience. As pioneer television broadcaster Fred Friendly has pointed out, the way in which we involve ourselves in seeing to it that the new technologies help TV serve the public and realize its enormous potential will, in the long run, "determine what kind of people we are."

9 Resources

Books

Brown, Les. *Keeping Your Eye on Television*. New York: The Pilgrim Press, 1979. A look at the achievements of citizen action groups, including the United Church of Christ, Action for Children's Television, the national PTA, and Accuracy in Media, with suggested guidelines for further action.

Draves, Pamela, ed. *Citizens Media Directory*. Washington, D.C.: National Citizens Committee for Broadcasting, 1977. Lists national and local media reform groups, public access centers, film and videotape producers and distributors, national trade associations, and much more.

Gordon, Robbie. *We Interrupt This Program . . . A Citizen's Guide to Using the Media for Social Change*. Amherst, Mass.: Citizen Involvement Training Project, University of Massachusetts, 1978. A manual for citizens and citizen groups that discusses how TV and cable TV work, and explains how people can use public access, video, and new technologies to get across their message.

Price, Monroe E., and Wicklein, John. *Cable Television: A Guide for Citizens Action*. Philadelphia, Penn.: Pilgrim Press, 1972. A helpful guide to taking an active role in creating good local cable service or improving an existing service.

Rivers, William L.; Thompson, Wallace; and Nyhan, Michael J., eds. *Aspen Handbook on the Media*. 1977–79 edition. New York: Praeger, 1977. A selective guide to research, organizations, and publications in communications, with nearly 700 listings and descriptions that can help media action groups find information and communicate with each other.

Stearns, Jennifer. *A Short Course in Cable*. 6th edition. New York: Office of Communications, United Church of Christ, 1981. An introductory guide to how cable works and how citizens can make cable work for them.

Periodicals

Community Television Review. National Federation of Local Cable Programmers, 3700 Far Hills Avenue, Kettering, Ohio 45429. Quarterly. Focuses on a different issue relevant to local cable in each issue; regular features include a calendar of upcoming events, reports on the activities of community access centers, and coverage of cable legislation affecting the local community.

Organizations

Action for Children's Television
46 Austin Street
Newtonville, Mass. 02160
617-527-7870
Consumer group that works to improve children's television viewing experiences by promoting diversity in programming and the elimination of commercial abuses. Initiates legal reform and promotes public awareness of issues relating to children's programming.

American Civil Liberties Union
132 West 43rd Street
New York, N.Y. 10036
212-944-9800
Works to preserve the civil liberties of Americans as set forth in the Bill of Rights. Defends the freedom of communication guaranteed by the First Amendment. Provides free legal aid in selected cases, conducts national educational campaigns on issues such as amnesty, lobbies on civil liberty issues, and publishes reports, handbooks, and books on such issues.

American Council for Better Broadcasters
120 E. Wilson Street
Madison, Wis. 53703
608-257-7712
A consumer group seeking to promote quality in broadcasting. Monitors programs and submits rating reports to sponsors, networks, broadcasters, congressional committees, and government agencies.

Cable Television Information Center
1800 N. Kent Street
Arlington, Va. 22209
703-528-6836
Publishes and distributes information about the economics, technology, and regulation of cable television.

Community Telecommunications Services
105 Madison Avenue
Suite 921
New York, N.Y. 10016
212-683-3834
A private, nonprofit consultation service. Provides legal, engineering, economic, and educational counsel on cable television at low cost to city governments and community organizations. Conducts workshops and other educational functions to teach community leaders about cable.

Consumer Federation of America
1314 14th Street NW
Washington, D.C. 20005
202-737-3732
A coalition of over 200 state and local consumer organizations, CEA lobbies Congress on communications issues.

Media Access Project
1609 Connecticut Avenue NW
Washington, D.C. 20009
202-232-4300
Specializes in the areas of public access, the Fairness Doctrine, and other First Amendment issues in communications. MAP represents diverse local and national organizations and individuals before the courts, the FCC, and the Federal Trade Commission.

National Association for Better Broadcasting
P.O. Box 43640
Los Angeles, Calif. 90043
213-474-3283
National consumer group concerned with promoting the public interest in broadcasting. Works to develop public awareness of its rights and responsibilities in broadcasting and to reduce violence on television by conducting surveys and monitoring studies and by participating in hearings before Congress and the FCC.

National Citizens Committee for Broadcasting
P.O. Box 12038
Washington, D.C. 20005
202-462-2520
Seeks to make media diverse and responsive to the public interest. Facilitates public participation in policy making and programming decisions, participates in litigation and FCC rule-makings and proceedings.

Public Communication, Inc.
c/o Communications Law Program
School of Law, UCLA
Los Angeles, Calif. 90024
213-825-6211
Specializes in First Amendment, access, and Fairness Doctrine questions, and other free-speech questions in the broadcast area; assists citizens in litigation; produces public service announcements for the print and broadcast media.

Appendix

Books

Brown, Les. *The New York Times Encyclopedia of Television.* New York: Times Books, 1977. An alphabetical listing of facts and short articles on a wide variety of television topics—programs, people, organizations, legal cases, technical terms, issues—well described and illustrated with photographs.

McNeil, Alex. *Total Television: A Comprehensive Guide to Programming from 1948 to 1980.* New York: Penguin Books, 1980. Information on more than 3,400 series, giving network or syndication affiliation, running date, entertaining descriptions of series (and of special programs), and casts. Great for trivia buffs.

Norback, Craig T., and Norback, Peter G., eds. *TV Guide Almanac.* New York: Ballantine Books, 1980. A handy directory and source of facts and information on TV topics ranging from audience research to becoming a contestant on game shows.

Steinberg, Cobbett S. *TV Facts.* New York: Facts on File, Inc., 1980. A useful collection of facts and figures on programs, views, ratings, advertisers, awards, polls and surveys, and the networks and stations.

Taishoff, Sol, ed. *Broadcasting Cable Yearbook.* Published annually. Washington, D.C.: Broadcasting Publications, Inc. The most comprehensive directory to the business of broadcasting. Covers broadcasting in general; television; radio; advertising and programming; engineering and equipment; professional services and associations—and cable, listing individuals, companies and stations.

25 Periodicals on Telecommunications

access. National Citizens Committee for Broadcasting, P.O. Box 12038, Washington, D.C. 20005. Biweekly. A newsletter on the issues, the agencies, and the people affecting media reform and citizen access to telecommunications.

Advertising Age. 740 Rush Street, Chicago, Ill. 60611. Weekly. Calls itself "the international newspaper of marketing." Covers advertising.

Broadcasting. Broadcasting Publications, Inc., 1735 DeSales Street, NW, Washington, D.C. 20036. Weekly. The Bible of the industry, *Broadcasting* discusses developments in network, local, and public television, and at the regulatory agencies. It features a calendar of major conferences and meetings and offers regular reports on FCC filings and actions.

CableAge. 1270 Avenue of the Americas, New York, N.Y. 10020. Biweekly. A sister publication to *Television/Radio Age* that covers new developments in technology, programming, and advertising for executives in the cable industry.

CableVision. Titsch Publishing, Inc., 2500 Curtis Street, Denver, Colo. 80205. Weekly. A newsmagazine on cable industry issues with regular coverage of programming, marketing, advertising, business, franchising, and government and law, *CableVision* also offers feature articles and commentary.

CHANNELS of Communications. Subscription Service Department, Box 2001, Mahopac, N.Y. 10541. Bimonthly. *CHANNELS* aims to "sort out and interpret the developments in the booming business of telecommunications with a view to the public's stake in them." Feature articles and commentary cover a wide range of issues of general interest.

COMM/ENT. 198 McAllister Street, San Francisco, Calif. 94102. Quarterly. This journal of communications and entertainment law is intended to be a research aid for lawyers.

Commmunity Television Review. National Federation of Local Cable Programmers, 3700 Far Hills Avenue, Kettering, Ohio 45429. Quarterly. A newsletter for people interested in local cable matters that focuses on a different topic in each issue. Regular features include a calendar of upcoming events, reports on the activities of community access centers, and coverage of cable legislation affecting the local community.

Home Video. United Business Publications, Inc., 475 Park Avenue South, New York, N.Y. 10016. Monthly. A magazine for the home video market, aimed at the consumer, that offers feature articles, previews, reviews, and test reports on new equipment.

Journal of Broadcasting. Broadcast Education Association, 1771 N Street, NW, Washington, D.C. 20036. Quarterly. A scholarly journal on the mass media that contains research articles and book reviews.

Journal of Communication. P.O. Box 13358, Philadelphia, Penn. 19101. Quarterly. This journal, published at the Annenberg School of Communications, is concerned with the study of communications theory, practice, and policy.

Journal of Popular Film and Television. Heldref Publications, 4000 Albemarle Street, NW, Washington, D.C. 20016. Quarterly. Articles on theory and criticism, interviews, filmographies and bibliographies that concentrate on commercial cinema and television.

Journalism Quarterly. School of Journalism, University of Kansas, Lawrence, Kansas 66045. Quarterly. Devoted to research in journalism and mass communications, with a lengthy book review section.

Media & Methods. American Society of Educators, 1511 Walnut Street, Philadelphia, Penn. 19102. Nine issues. A publication for teachers that covers all media, with ideas on how to use TV, radio and film in the classroom.

Media Report to Women. 3306 Ross Place, NW, Washington, DC 20008. Monthly. A feminist newsletter published by the Women's Institute for Freedom of the Press, subtitled "What Women Are Thinking and Doing to Change Communications Media."

Prime Time School Television. Suite 810, 120 S. LaSalle Street, Chicago, Ill. 60603. Monthly. A source of information for high school teachers about prime time programs and their uses as educational resources.

re:ACT: Action for Children's Television Newsmagazine. Action for Children's Television, 46 Austin Street, Newtonville, Mass. 02160. Semi-annual. Information, opinion, and news articles relating to issues and questions on children and television.

Teachers Guides to Television. 699 Madison Avenue, New York, N.Y. 10021. Semi-annual. Teacher's guides to upcoming TV specials and programs of interest, published in the spring and fall.

Television/Radio Age. 1270 Avenue of the Americas, New York, N.Y. 10020. Bi-weekly. A report on the industry for broadcast executives that covers programming, advertising, and business.

Television Quarterly. The National Academy of Television Arts and Sciences, 110 West 57th Street, New York, N.Y. 10019. Quarterly. Features articles on television theory and criticism intended for a general audience.

TV Guide. Box 900, Radnor, Penn. 19088. Weekly. Often overlooked as a source of information, *TV Guide* features articles on many issues and personalities in broadcasting as well as listing programs.

Variety. 154 West 46th Street, New York, N.Y. 10036. Weekly. A newspaper covering the international entertainment world, including pictures, music, and theater as well as radio and television.

Video Action. 21 West Elm Street, Chicago, Ill. 60610. Monthly. Covers tapes, discs, games, and cable from the consumer's point of view, with reviews of new releases and feature articles on equipment and new developments.

Videography. United Business Publications, 475 Park Avenue South, New York, N.Y. 10016. Monthly. A magazine for video producers that emphasizes marketing and production and examines technological developments and trends in programming.

Bibliography

Books

Aspen Institute on Communications and Society. *Television As a Social Force: New Approaches to TV Criticism.* New York: Praeger Publishers, 1975.

Baran, Stanley, J. *The Viewer's Television Book.* Cleveland, Ohio: Penrith, 1980.

Barnouw, Erik. *The Image Empire.* New York: Oxford University Press, 1970.

Barnouw, Erik. *The Sponsor: Notes on a Modern Potentate.* New York: Oxford University Press, 1978.

Brown, Les. *New York Times Encyclopedia of TV.* New York: Times Books, 1977.

Brown, Les. *Television: The Business behind the Box.* New York: Harcourt Brace Jovanovich, 1971.

Cantor, Muriel G. *Prime-Time Television: Content and Control.* Beverly Hills, Calif.: Sage Publications, 1980.

Carnegie Commission. *A Public Trust: The Report of the Carnegie Commission on the Future of Public Broadcasting.* New York: Bantam Books, 1979.

Clift, Charles III, and Greer, Archie, eds. *Broadcast Programming: The Current Perspective,* 6th ed. Washington, D.C.: University Press of America, 1980.

Comstock, George. *Television in America.* Beverly Hills, Calif.: Sage Publications, 1980.

Comstock, George, et al. *Television and Human Behavior.* New York: Columbia University Press, 1978.

Gerbner, George; Morgan, Michael; Signorelli, Nancy. *Programming Health Portrayals: What Viewers See, Say, and Do.* Philadelphia, Penn.: The Annenberg School of Communications, University of Pennsylvania, 1981.

Greenberg, Bradley S. *Life on Television: Content Analyses of U.S. TV Drama.* Norwood, N.J.: Ablex Publishing, 1980.

Greenfield, Jeff. *Television: The First Fifty Years.* New York: Harry N. Abrams, Inc., 1977.

Hadden, Jeffrey K., and Swann, Charles E. *Prime Time Preachers: The Rising Power of Televangelism.* Reading, Mass.: Addison-Wesley Publishing Company, 1981.

Head, Sydney W. *Broadcasting in America: A Survey of Television and Radio.* Boston: Houghton Mifflin, 1976.

Heighton, Elizabeth J., and Cunningham, Don R. *Advertising in the Broadcast Media.* Belmont, Calif.: Wadsworth Publishing Company, Inc., 1976.

Kaye, Evelyn. *The ACT Guide to Children's Television or How to Treat TV with TLC.* Boston: Beacon Press, 1979.

Leonard, John. *This Pen for Hire*. Garden City, N.Y.: Doubleday & Company, Inc., 1973.

Liston, Robert A. *The Right to Know: Censorship in America*. New York: Franklin Watts, Inc., 1973.

McLuhan, Marshall. *Understanding Media: The Extensions of Man*. New York: McGraw-Hill, 1964.

Murray, John P. *Television and Youth: 25 Years of Research and Controversy*. Omaha: Regal Printing for the Boys Town Center for the Study of Youth Development, 1980.

Newcomb, Horace, ed. *Television: The Critical View*. New York: Oxford University Press, 1976.

Norback, Craig T., and Norback, Peter G., eds. *TV Guide Almanac*. New York: Ballantine Books, 1980.

Price, Jonathan. *Video Visions: A Medium Discovers Itself*. New York: Plume, New American Library, 1977.

Real, Michael R. *Mass-Mediated Culture*. Englewood Cliffs, N.J.: Prentice-Hall, Inc., 1977.

Reel, A. Frank. *The Networks: How They Stole the Show*. New York: Charles Scribner's Sons, 1979.

Schrank, Jeffrey. *TV Action Book*. Evanston, Ill.: McDougall, Littell and Company, 1974.

Schwarz, Meg, ed. *TV and Teens*. Action for Children's Television. Reading, Mass.: Addison-Wesley Publishing Company, 1982.

Shanks, Bob. *The Cool Fire: How to Make It in Television*. New York: Vintage Books, 1976.

Shulman, Arthur, and Youman, Roger. *The Golden Age of Television: How Sweet It Was*. New York: Bonanza Books, 1979.

Smith, Robert Rutherford. *Beyond the Wasteland: The Criticism of Broadcasting*. Annandale, Va.: ERIC Clearinghouse on Reading and Communication Skills, 1980.

Steinberg, Corbett S. *TV Facts*. New York: Facts on File, Inc., 1980.

Window Dressing on the Set: Women and Minorities in Television. A Report of the United States Commission on Civil Rights. Washington, D.C., August, 1977.

World Almanac and Book of Facts 1981. New York: Newspaper Enterprise Association Inc., 1980.

Withey, Stephen B., ed. *Television and Social Behavior: Beyond Violence and Children*. Hillsdale, N.J.: Lawrence Erlbaum Associates, 1980.

Articles in Magazines and Newspapers

Boddewyn, J.J. "Advertising to Children: An International Survey," *Television and Children,* Winter 1981, vol. 4, no. 1.

Caldwell, Carol, "You haven't come a long way, baby." *New Times,* June 10, 1977, p. 58.

Cheng, Charles W., and Hirano-Nakanishi, Marsha. "Television's Asian Persuasion," *Re:ACT,* Action for Children's Television, pp. 16, 17.

Cohen, Dorothy. "Through a Glass Darkly: Television and the Perception of Reality." *The National Elementary,* vol. 56, no. 3, January/February 1977, p. 22.

Comer, James P. "Striking a Balance with the Boob Tube." *Parents,* October 1980.

Cronkite, Walter. "What's Wrong and What Isn't, with the Best Press Yet." *Broadcasting,* December 15, 1980, pp. 50–54.

Diamond, Edwin. "Is Television Unfair to Labor?" *American Film,* April 1980, pp. 15–16.

Diamond, Edwin. "The Network Gamble: Ratings or Prestige." *American Film,* November 1980, p. 64.

England, David. "Television and Politics/The Politics of Television." *Media and Methods,* October 1980, p. 17. An interview with David Halberstam.

Good, Paul. "Why You Can't Always Trust '60 Minutes' Reporting," *Panorama,* 1980, pp. 38–43 +.

Greenfield, Jeff. "How You Can Get Elected by Using Television." *Panorama,* June 1980, pp. 60–65.

Hickey, Neil. "Can the Networks Survive?" *TV Guide,* March 21, 1981, pp. 7–10.

"House Panel on Aging Tackles Ancient Ways of TV Commercials." *Variety,* February 1, 1978.

Knopf, Terry Ann. "Where Only the Men Are Super." *Boston Globe,* June 27, 1980.

Kowet, Don. "Try for the Impossible—But Carry a Rabbit's Foot." *TV Guide,* July 4, 1981.

Leonard, John. "Thank You, No: I'd Rather Read a Book." *Panorama,* August 1980, p. 80.

Levine, Richard M. "How the Gay Lobby Has Changed Television." *TV Guide,* May 30, 1981, pp. 3–6.

Loftus, Jack. "NBC's Day-Night Profits." *Variety,* May 14, 1980.

Martin, T.B. "Medical Video." *Video Action,* April 1981, pp. 6i–64.

O'Bryant, Shirley L., and Corder-Bolz, Charles. "Tackling 'The Tube' with Family Teamwork." *Children Today,* May-June 1978.

Rice, Berkeley. "The Unreality of Prime Time Crime." *Psychology Today,* vol. 14, August 1980, p. 26.

Salmans, Sandra. "Many Stars Are Playing Pitchmen." New York *Times,* May 3, 1981.

Simon, Roger. "Introducing Voodoo News." *Panorama,* March 1981, pp. 8-9.

Sklar, Robert. "A Question of Quality." *American Film,* November 1980, pp. 61-65.

"TV's 'Disastrous' Impact on Children: Interview with Neil Postman." *U.S. News & World Report,* January 19, 1981, pp. 43-45.

"What Do Call Letters Mean?" *P.D. Cue,* June 7, 1979, pp. 18-24, 22-26.

Winfrey, Carey. "Week without Television Tunes Several Families into Different Channels." New York *Times,* April 27, 1977.

Winslow, Ken. "Interactive TV: Programs That Respond to You." *Video,* February 1981, p. 24.

Speeches, Testimony, Polls, Conferences

Abel, Elie. "Looking Ahead from the Twentieth Century." Speech given at the Conference on Communications in the 21st Century. Richmond, Va., April 1-2, 1981.

ACT Speaker's Kit for Teachers, Parents, and Professionals, 1979, pp. 12-16.

Boorstin, Daniel. "Broadcasting Books to Young Audiences." Speech at Library of Congress, Washington, D.C., March 7, 1980.

Gallup. "Study of Attitudes toward Advertising." National Advertising Review Board.

Harris, Louis. "Americans Express Some Skepticism about TV Advertising." Survey released March 16, 1979.

"House Committee Hears Testimony on Portrayals of Older People on TV." News Bureau, Philadelphia, Pa., April 26, 1980.

Hufstedler, Shirley M. University of Pennsylvania, Remarks Made to ACT 8th National Symposium. Washington, D.C., March 20, 1980.

Johnson, Robert L., Head of Black Entertainment Network. Remarks to ACT 8th National Symposium. Washington, D.C., March 20, 1980.

Katz, Elihu; Dayan, Daniel; and Motyl, Pierre. "In Defense of Media Events." Paper prepared for the Conference on Communications in the 21st Century. Richmond Va., April 1–2, 1981.

Lear, Norman. Speech at ACT 8th National Symposium. Washington, D.C., March 20, 1980.

Lull, James. "Social Uses of Television in Family Settings and a Critique of Receivership Skills." In *Education for the Television Age,* edited by Milton E. Ploghoft and James A. Anderson. Athens, Ohio: Ohio U.: 1981. From the National Conference on Children and TV, Philadelphia, Pa., November 4–7, 1979.

O'Bryan, Kenneth G. Remarks made as witness on behalf of the Federal Trade Commission, January 17, 1979.

Index

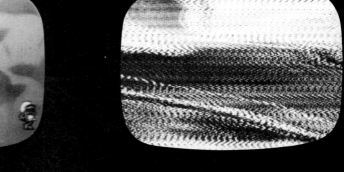

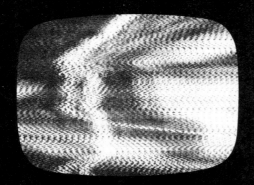

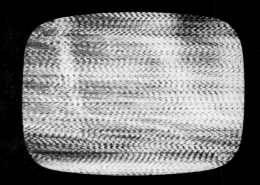